Medjugorje

Facts, Documents, Theology

Medjugorje

Facts, Documents, Theology

Michael O'Carroll, CSSp

VERITAS

First published 1986 by
Veritas Publications
7-8 Lower Abbey Street
Dublin 1

Second edition published 1987
Third edition published 1988
This edition published 1989

ISBN 1 85390 073 7

Cover design by Eddie McManus
Typesetting by Printset & Design Ltd
Printed in the Republic of Ireland by
Mount Salus Press Ltd

Dedication

To the United Sacred Hearts of Jesus and Mary

Contents

Introduction

Medjugorje presents a challenge to anyone who has given time to the study of Marian theology and to the Marian experience of the Church — through the liturgy, devotions, apparitions and genuine mystical phenomena. This book is my answer to the challenge.

I had known vaguely about Medjugorje since 1983 when, while working with Legionaries of Mary in the Naples area, I met an Italian Jesuit who was already involved in the movement around it. In the spring of the following year I had an opportunity to discuss the events with friends who had been there, to study video cassettes and to read the literature.

In October of that year I went for the first time to Medjugorje and spent a week there, from 28 October to 4 November. I was fortunate to meet there Fr René Laurentin, about whom there is much in this book, with whom I have worked occasionally over the years and whose writings are well known to me. (I had read his work, *La Vierge apparaît-elle à Medjugorje?*) The Pontifical Marian Academy and the French Society of Marian Studies, of which we are both members, have given me many opportunities to observe and appreciate his remarkable qualities.

I was very impressed by the fact that when I met him at Medjugorje he had reached complete conviction on the authenticity of the apparitions; in the book he inclines to that view but as a scientist he states the case objectively. He had by now ceased entirely to see any force in the arguments against authenticity.

I returned to Medjugorje again in May 1985 and was able to study with keener interest the pattern of events, by now fixed: the evening liturgical celebration with the other prayers, principally the Rosary and the seven Our Fathers, Aves and Glorias, the arrival of the visionaries in the room off the sanctuary, their visions and the edifying way in which they led the whole church in prayer. I was present during the visions, as on my previous visit and as I would be on my third in February/March 1986. To say I was impressed by this utterly unique manifestation of the Catholic faith is to under-state. It is not only the crowds of people from all over the world, whose numbers have been known to reach over 100,000; it is also the unselfaware quality of the prayer and the evident commitment of the parishioners.

The parish of Medjugorje is the first patent miracle of Our Lady, Queen of Peace. The parishioners are a case history. Their dissensions, at one time acute, have vanished. Their prayer is of a kind seen nowhere in the world. If all that we have been told by Church leaders, spiritual guides and ardent apostles over the years is true, if the exhortation of the Master himself is paramount, here, before our eyes, is a whole-hearted response. If prayer and primarily prayer can save the world, here salvation has begun.

It is the impact of this corporate faith and fervour which accounts for two things: rarely does anyone who has been to Medjugorje express doubt on the authenticity of what is alleged to happen there, the apparitions that is; and those who have been there feel a powerful desire to return. Medjugorje has too a lesson for students of history who may doubt the truthfulness of glowing accounts which record the corporate faith and fervour of ages such as that of the monastic movement in Ireland from the sixth to the eighth century, or of Europe in the twelfth and thirteenth centuries. Is human nature capable of such things? I would have asked 'Is any place in our time, with its burden of materialism and despair, capable of such things?'. I now know the answer.

On my third visit to Medjugorje I discussed this book with the Franciscans who so admirably minister to this unique parish, especially Fr Svetozar Kraljevic, Fr Yanko Bubalo and Fr Rupcic — each of whom allowed me to use and quote the material they had published or prepared for private distribution — Fr Tomislav Pervan and Fr Ivan Dugandjic; the latter is a member of the episcopal commission established by the Bishop of Mostar and he was most generous with his time and with his files. I am most grateful to these over-worked, dedicated priests for the help they gave me. I also wish to thank Fr Barnaba Hechich, OFM, a

Croatian in the Antonianum, Rome, for sending me valuable documents. I thank Peter Batty whose *Mirecorder* I used to advantage.

I made it clear to one of the Franciscans in Medjugorje that I intended to publish the integral text of the episcopal memorandum sent out as a letter to the world's press in December 1984. I have dealt likewise with every text emanating from the Bishop. This I consider fair and ultimately conducive to the triumph of truth. It is clear from my book that I cannot accept the Bishop's opinions; nor do I now feel obliged to do so. My hope is that he will change his outlook and his assessment of the mighty events that have occurred within his diocese.

I have not interviewed the visionaries. Apart from a few words with Marija every evening in the sacristy and a fleeting encounter with Jakov in his uncle's home, I have not had personal contact with them. I have not the heart to add to their fatigue, besieged as they are by all and sundry, especially sundry. Their views and their stories have been reliably collected by competent reporters: Vicka has contributed to a whole book through such interviews and Marija gave an important interview to the Canadian review, *L'Informateur*, a copy of which was made available to me by Fr Ivan.

I offer one general reflection to the reader of my book. To argue for the authenticity of an apparition is not to canonise visionaries, nor to treat them as angels removed from the human condition. This means that they may occasionally err or lapse. I report an instance in which one of the visionaries, Ivan, did lapse under pressure — I record it with something short of disgust at the pressure put upon the boy.

Popes have made mistakes; so have Doctors of the Church and everyone in the hierarchy of government and of doctrine descending from both. Pius IX was unfair to Newman, who may one day be a saint and Doctor of the Church: at least that forecast was the opinion of another Pope, Pius XII. The saintly Pius X did not like Cardinal Ferrari of Milan, who may also be canonised. And what are we to think of the victims of the Modernist witch-hunt? Men like Fr Hugh Pope, whose books would now be dismissed as unreadably conservative? We accept the condemnation of Modernism itself.

So we must not expect too much from visionaries. I make it

clear in the first chapter of my book what we must expect from them. In my opinion the visionaries of Medjugorje meet the test magnificently. I admire bishops who 'hold the rampart' as did the great Cardinal Wyszynski, whom I knew personally. I have something less than admiration for those whose thunderbolts are launched at helpless old women or young girls.

Rare? I do sincerely hope so. There is still a place in our religion for chivalry; it imperatively commands respect for the human person.

For the third edition the monthly messages are brought up to date and Appendices VI to IX have been added.

Michael O'Carroll, CSSp
Blackrock College

Feast of the Annunciation, 25 March 1988

1

APPARITIONS OF OUR LADY

(i)

Apparitions of Our Lady are mostly thought of as having occurred recently, within the last century and a half; it is supposed that they began with the Miraculous Medal in 1830 and they come down to this very year. This summary approach is understandable when the subject is public apparitions, those which take place out of doors, are sometimes seen by more than one person, or are revealed by one visionary to the world. It would be a lengthy undertaking to study all the apparitions recorded in the lives of the saints which were private at the time of their occurrence, though they may have been discovered and narrated later.

Early in the history of the Church, in the life of a third century eastern saint, Gregory the Wonderworker, we meet the theme or problem: another Gregory, of Nyssa, a famous theologian of the next century, tells the story. Mary appeared to Gregory during the night, with St John the Apostle. She was surrounded with light and she told John 'to make known to the young man (Gregory) the mystery of piety'. John 'said he was ready to do this for the Mother of the Lord, because this was her wish.'[1] There was no movement of public piety following the incident.

The first apparition in modern times with a wide, continuing impact occurred in the Alsatian Vosges on 3 May 1491. Our Lady appeared to a group of men and spoke words of dire warning. God's wrath, she said, was ready to come down like a hailstorm. Many of the good things achieved by Christianity would soon be destroyed. The warning fell on deaf ears, not least on those of Pope Alexander VI, who, within a few years, however, had issued a Bull declaring the vision authentic, making the spot 'resplendent with portents and miracles', a place of pilgrimage. So it remains, *The Three Ears of Corn*.

Something more fruitful and of immensely greater effect, was reported from the hill of Tepeyac outside Mexico city in 1531, at a spot later named from a previously existing Spanish town, Guadalupe. An Indian peasant, Juan Diego, was stopped as he crossed the hillside by a beautiful Lady, who identified herself as the 'eternal Virgin, holy Mother of the true God' and 'merciful Mother' of men; she told him to go to the Bishop of Mexico, Fray Juan de Zumarraga, and say that she wished to have a church built at the place of their encounter.

The Bishop asked for a sign and he received this quickly: roses gathered in winter time. The Mexican was to hold these tightly in his cloak or *tilma*, until he was in the Bishop's presence. He obeyed the order, was given entry to the episcopal room and opened his cloak to show the roses. The image of Our Lady was stamped upon it.

The fabric of the cloak is woven grass, which has a life span of about thirty years. It was enshrined and survives to the present time untouched by any human artifice. On 14 November 1921 it survived a gelignite attack from within eight feet; the bomb had been hidden in a bouquet of flowers. The image and its glass shield were unscathed though the huge crucifix and the candlesticks were twisted, the marble altar pulverised and every window in the building shattered.

Guadalupe is probably the most frequented shrine in the world. Some ten million people from every walk of life, believers and non-believers, go there annually. It was visited by President Kennedy and President de Gaulle. The piece of cloth has been scrutinised by historians and artistic experts and by scientists from the Massachusetts Institute of Technology; its status remains unaltered, honoured by none more enthusiastically than Popes down to the present day.

Our Lady appears alone. She asks for a sign of honour to be given to her. Luckily for the Mexicans her request was granted, because her immense power was to be evident in their history. The conversion of the country begins from that moment on the hillside and from the courage of the Franciscan bishop. Within two generations millions of converts had been made and the influence throughout all the Americas has been incalculable. This was the resurrection of a native people, liberation in the fullest sense, led by Our Lady.

We move forward to the seventeenth century to consider a phenomenon which cannot be classed as an apparition, but which is not altogether unrelated. In 1655 Walter Lynch, Bishop of Clonfert, fleeing from the Cromwellian persecution, reached the continent of Europe and finally settled in Györ, a town in western Hungary. He was made auxiliary to the local bishop, was much respected, and was buried in the cathedral. A picture of Our Lady which he donated to the bishop was enshrined and honoured. On 17 March 1697, it was the object of an unusual happening: tears of blood were seen to flow from it, for a long time, by very many people. Testimony to the fact was given by disinterested people, state officials and heads of non-Catholic religious bodies. The picture was henceforth venerated, a centre of special prayer. The year of the miracle was the darkest and most terrible for Irish Catholics. Another dark moment marked the two hundredth and fiftieth anniversary, in 1947, and the principal ceremony in honour of the Irish Madonna was the occasion of one of the last great sermons of Cardinal Mindszenty, before his imprisonment and torture.

As in Guadalupe, the emphasis in the next important apparition, the Miraculous Medal (1830) is on Our Lady's personality. She is there in the centre of the emblem. The prayer is to her. On the reverse side are the two hearts, the Marian monogram, and the twelve stars. The medal caught on. Before St Catherine Labouré died in 1876 one thousand million medals had been distributed throughout the world. The saint, so the conventional story runs, was not known: she did nothing to reveal her identity, but apparently it was guessed.

Here we meet something that recurs again and again in the subsequent narratives of such things: the element of secrecy. It was the visionary's own identity that was to be kept secret in this case. In the next Marian apparation, at La Salette, in the French Alps above Grenoble in 1847, the theme varies. This time, as previously, Our Lady was seen by people of lowly origin, Mélanie and Maximin. She spoke to them, telling of the hardship to come, shedding tears; and to each she entrusted a secret. They divulged it to Pope Pius IX. There was one apparition only, on 19 September 1847. Four years later, to the day, the bishop recognised it as authentic. It is known that the children were of somewhat irregular conduct in their later years. Their testimony had been accepted and officially nothing changed.

At this stage it may be well to state that the recipients of such heavenly favours are not automatically guaranteed personal sanctity. Only two have been canonised so far, Catherine Labouré and Bernadette.

These favours are in the category known by theologians as *gratiae gratis datae*; they are given by God of his choice, without any direct link with the spiritual state, the merit therefore, of the recipient. This depends intrinsically on *gratia gratum faciens*, sanctifying grace, which is the principle of perfection. A person far advanced in grace may not receive any noticeable gift from God. Such gifts are generally granted for the benefit of others. They may be given to those already advanced in grace with God, or those who receive them may also receive a notable increase in interior, sanctifying grace. The distinction does not imply mutual exclusion.

Bernadette's legend has a universal appeal. Her honesty, almost disconcerting, her refusal to play the little saint, her wit — sometimes bordering on the caustic — her courage and stamina went with an intuition of wholly admirable spiritual reality. She knew that Our Lady chose Bernadette not because of who Bernadette was, but because of who Our Lady was. Many would say that or even think it, on the surface of their minds. She lived it; it was a conviction that was totally part of her. She was Pyrenean granite, granite shining in the sun.

Bernadette too saw only Our Lady. The message came from Our Lady and with it three secrets. These she never disclosed; she said that if the Pope himself asked her to do so she would refuse. Conjecture about the secrets has been published. The exercise is futile.

The saint suffered much from those around her, from those with authority over her. With her a new phase of Church life opens. Henceforth there will be rigorous scrutiny, interrogation, cross-examination of those who claim to have had a supernatural vision, especially if it is one giving a message of universal importance.

Any inquiry into an alleged supernatural event or revelation which will have an effect on the life of the Church must be conducted according to strict rules, which will be considered briefly later. But visionaries, true or false, have the same personal dignity, the same personal rights, the same claim on our respect as all other human beings. Respect for the person is a key concept in social philosophy, fully endorsed by popes and the Second Vatican Council.

Bernadette also exemplifies another constant in the history of apparitions. It is always the laity that are favoured. Generally children or young people like Bernadette, not priests. We are dealing with *public* apparitions; the lives of saintly priests (whether canonised or not) down to quite recent times record apparitions. Père Lamy who died in 1931 is a well-known case.[3]

The fact remains. Those who have had an essential role in the great apparitions taken into the life of the Church have been lay people. The female sex predominates. When there are groups of visionaries, women or girls are generally more numerous than boys or men. The fifteenth century apparition in the Vosges, as we have seen, was granted to men. Though single visionaries are mostly female, this is not a general rule. If it were, Juan Diego would be an exception, as would Bruno Cornacchiola, witness to the event at Tre Fontane in Rome on 12 April 1947, and the Moslem who first saw Our Lady at Zeitoun near Cairo in 1968 — his finger, severely injured, was instantly healed.

Pontmain in France, on the borders of Mayenne and Brittany is next in chronological order: on 17 January 1871, during the Franco-Prussian war, Our Lady appeared to four children. Although she did not speak to them, they deciphered a message in writing, an exhortation to prayer and a promise that it would be heard. Hostilities ended soon afterwards.

The event at Knock took place over eight years later on 21 August 1879. John Paul II visited the shrine in the centenary year, raised the church to the status of a basilica and gave the Golden Rose as a sign of papal blessing and encouragement. There is much scope for theological analysis of the apparition. The Lamb was seen; he was on the altar beside the Virgin crowned, with St Joseph and St John and, in the background, angels hovering. This is the only apparition of the Lamb in history, the powerful symbol linking the Old and New Covenants. The heavenly tableau was seen by all present rather than being reserved to a few, or a solitary witness, as was usually the case elsewhere. No word was spoken, no message given.

Students of the Knock apparition will find Mary O'Connell,

née Beirne, an admirable witness. Her testimony was given to two commissions set up by the Bishops of the diocese — in 1879 soon after the apparition and in 1936, shortly before she died. She did not waver in clarity or firmness. On the second occasion when her testimony was read out to her she added: 'I make this statement knowing that I am going before my God.'

Fatima, which comes next in the series, has touched the Church at the level of the Papacy more than any other event of its kind: Pius XII, without any overt allusion to the request from Fatima (though he was addressing those at the shrine), did something that was asked by Our Lady. He consecrated the world to her Immaculate Heart on the occasion of the Silver Jubilee in 1942. She had specified the request for Russia. The Pope had alluded to that country without naming it in 1942. Ten years later, in the Encyclical, *Sacro Vergente Anno*, he was explicit. Paul VI made the pilgrimage for the fiftieth anniversary in 1967; he issued an Apostolic Exhortation, *Signum Magnum,* on Our Lady for the occasion and presented the Golden Rose to the shrine.

John Paul II went to Fatima in 1982 in thanksgiving for his escape from an attempt on his life the previous year. As Paul VI had done at the conclusion of the third session of the Council in 1964, he repeated at Fatima the act of consecration of mankind to the Immaculate Heart of Mary. He did so again, in Rome during an episcopal synod meeting.

Here we meet two different factors at work. The world knew for some time that apparitions had taken place in Fatima in 1917, the visionaries being three young children. That is one factor. The other is the survival until the present time of one of the trio and the visions granted to her in the intervening years. It must also be noted that apparitions took place in Fatima in 1916. In the visions which she received in 1925 and 1929 Sister Lucie was informed about devotion to the Immaculate Heart of Mary, about one form it should take, the five first Saturdays, and what God wished in regard to the consecration of mankind. It was to be done by the Pope collegially, that is with the active participation of all the bishops.

Would all the bishops participate? Scarcely if one is to go by what some of them said about Our Lady during the Second Vatican Council. This is sad. But to ascertain and assess every aspect of the Fatima story, before, during and after, we await the multi-volume work of the specialist in the subject, Fr Joaquin Maria Alonso, CMF. He had already published the different memoranda of Lucie, disclosing another complicating factor: we had not been told everything that happened in 1917.

(ii)

Since the 1920s alleged apparitions have increased considerably in number. C.M. Staehlin, in his book, *Apariciones*, mentions the figure of thirty series of apparitions of Our Lady investigated in Western Europe between 1930 and 1950 and about 300 cases of individual apparitions to children. Dom Bernard Billet, OSB, a specialist, gave the exact numbers some years ago for one period: 210 between 1928 and 1971. Of these only two had received ecclesiastical approval, Beauraing and Banneux, both in Belgium. There was one witness at Banneux, Mariette Beco, who is still alive at the time of writing — she saw the Pope personally when he went to Banneux. Of the five witnesses at Beauraing, three were living in 1981.

Are we to conclude that the 208 alleged apparitions which have not been approved are bogus? The statistic is sometimes brandished to show that the Church rejects so much arbitrary excrescence. The assumption is that each case has been properly investigated and assessed, an assumption that is unwarranted.

Leaving out a certain number which would be rejected by common sense allied with sound Christian faith, we have no right to go beyond an empirical generalisation: a number of alleged apparitions have not been approved. There are such things as clerical prejudice, lack of nerve in face of public mockery and cynicism, and a pervading atmosphere of scepticism. The Patriarch of the Coptic church in Egypt had no such fear. Within five months of the apparition at Zeitoun on 2 April 1968, he pronounced it genuine.

There are two questions of general import that should be answered. How is the objective, the real character of an apparition, established? What should one's personal attitude to any apparition be?

The general theological position may be taken for granted in regard to the possibility of apparitions. Those in glory invisible to us on earth can be made visible by the power of God. According to Fr Karl Rahner:

> The possibility of private revelation through visions and associated auditory experiences is evident in principle for a Christian. God as a free personal being can make himself perceptible to the created spirit, not only through his works but also by his free, personal word. And he can do it in such a manner that this communication of God is not simply himself in the direct vision of the Godhead, or in the dimension of a blessed intellect emptied of all that is finite, but also, and for a Christian who believes in God's Incarnation this is essential, in such a way that his communication is bound up with a particular place and time, with a concrete word or command, with a finite reality or truth, and so that it occurs with, or is connected with, the 'apparition' of an object presented to the internal or external senses, which object represents and manifests God, his will, or the like.[6]

Rahner concludes that:

> The history of Christianity would be unthinkable without prophetic and visionary elements (in the broadest sense). To try to explain all these things by natural or even abnormal human causes, would be logically to deny that any historical activity of the personal God revealing himself in the Word was possible at all. But this would be to repudiate the character of Christianity as an historical, supernatural, revealed religion.[7]

> Therefore, anyone who absolutely rejects the possibility of special revelations offends against faith; and anyone who denies that they may occur even since the apostolic age offends against a doctrine which is theologically certain.[8]

Since we are dealing with private revelations related to Our Lady, we do well to insist that everything depends on divine power, a divine initiative. No one need fear that Our Lady is taking over the Church independently of God. As God's creature she depends absolutely on him and, in her knowledge, plenary in theory and practice, of that dependence, lies her excellence.

(iii)

With these ideas rightly assumed we still face many problems which can only be touched on here. What is the value of a Church pronouncement? How are we bound to assent to it? In the sixteenth century the Fifth Lateran Council and the Council of Trent, in the face of many abuses, laid a heavy responsibility on bishops to conduct rigorous inquiries and for any important, novel subject asserted the rights of the Pope. Benedict XIV, a great Church lawyer and, before his election as Pope, author of the classic treatise on the investigation proper to the Beatification of Servants of God, wrote thus:

'It should be known that the approval given by the Church to a private revelation is nothing but permission granted, after an attentive inquiry, to make known this revelation for the enlightenment and good of the faithful. Even when these revelations are approved by the Church they should not be given the assent of Catholic faith. Nevertheless they should be given an assent of human faith, following the rules of prudence, by which such revelations are probable or believable for pious reasons.' He added that such decisions were not absolutely binding: 'Without prejudice to the integrity of Catholic faith a person may withold his assent to such revelations and withdraw from them provided he does so with due modesty, not without reason and without contempt.'[9]

Official teaching continued on this line and this principle was formulated by the Congregation of Rites in 1877:

The Apostolic See has neither approved nor condemned such apparitions or revelations but merely permits Catholics to believe in them — where they have the support of credible witness and documents — with a purely human faith.[10]

In 1907 a feast of the apparitions of Our Lady of Lourdes was introduced and this could have led to some speculation on a change in official attitudes to apparitions. St Pius X in the Encyclical *Pascendi dominici gregis*, 8 September 1907, repeated the ruling of 1877 adding:

> The authority of the Church does not guarantee, even in this case, the truth of the fact. It simply does not prevent belief in things for which motives of human faith are not lacking.[11]

The 1877 principle was also quoted by the Provincial Council of Malines in 1937 in regard to Beauraing and Banneux.[12]

This was how things stood until the International Mariological Congress held in Lourdes in 1958. The president of the Pontifical Marian Academy, Fr Karl Balic, OFM (a Croat), submitted two questions to an open debate: Is the assent given to apparitions and private revelations one of divine faith? Does not the official approval of Lourdes and Fatima go beyond simple permission and involve infallibility? One particular reply to the questions, by Dom F. Roy, OSB and opinions expressed at the International Mariological Congress held at Fatima in 1967 likened the approval given to apparitions to the canonisation of saints; it was more than simple tolerance, an approval that called for theological faith.[13]

Investigations of apparitions deal with testimony. If the testimony is to something incompatible with the tenets of the faith or with scientifically established truth, it can be discarded at once; the matter is settled and no further inquiry need be made.

But such a value judgement calls for precision. It is not sufficient to say that an alleged apparition is undignified. Standards of dignity can vary considerably and betray very subjective, basically false ideas.

Determining what is or is not compatible with divinely revealed truth demands, in the first instance, a thorough grasp of theology, not a hastily assembled batch of half-truths or fashionable slogans. If, in the seventeenth century, a visionary reported Our Lady as saying that she was the Immaculate Conception, some theologians would have dismissed the claim out of hand. That was the time when Hippolyto Marracci, probably the most prolific Marian theologian of all time, was ordered not to leave his community — a kind of house arrest — for publishing books on Our Lady's Immaculate Conception. He had not used his own name, but the powerful men of the Inquisition, who disagreed with the doctrine and wished to repress it, tracked him down.

Assuming that doctrine is not offended what criteria are to be used in judging the word of a witness, i.e. testimony? Principally three: Is the witness (a) a competent observer, (b) an accurate reporter, (c) truthful?

Much of the inquiry hinges on competence to observe. Fr Rahner warns against reliance on piety or personal honesty, even personal integrity. He contends that along with these there is a possibility of factors studied by parapsychology. 'If genuine (natural) telepathy, telaesthesia, cryptaesthesia, and even physical mediumistic powers exist (and such possibilities must at least be seriously reckoned with), then we must disregard many phenomena formerly, perhaps, accepted as decisive proofs of the supernatural origins of visions.'[14] But he also says that God may use these very powers to his own ends. It is evident that professional expertise is needed.

The witness must narrate exactly what has been observed. His mentality, the stock of ideas with which he sees and interprets day-to-day events, may affect the narrative of what has been observed. Mental development over a period of time may also colour a story once told barely. All authorities admit that the recipient of a genuine apparition may still be mistaken in particulars.

Finally there is truthfulness. But people do not lie about sacred things! The iron law of history is that people will, that is can, lie about anything. The tests here are those which we apply to all testimony, to historical documents, evidence tendered in courts of law.

(iv)

There is the other question, one of spirituality. It is first of all important to retain the clear perspective of the Christian religion.

It is founded on a public revelation in Christ, completed before the death of the Apostles, transmitted through an institution which he founded. Any other divine intervention is necessarily related, and subservient to, this public message from God to man in Christ.

On the human side, of the subject that is, the essential response to God's self-communication is faith. 'The assurance of things to be hoped for, the conviction of things unseen' (*Heb 11:1*). Apparitions cannot replace faith; faith is needed to judge them. They are secondary to faith and they must serve it.

Faith is permanent; apparitions are transitory; faith is not localised, caught in the web of space and time, to the same degree that they are. Faith is an interior conviction springing from God's intimate testimony; apparitions are particular facts, discerned through complex situations.

Each person has, with spiritual advice if necessary, to choose freely in these matters. Individuals vary in their attitude to God and in the way God leads them. They vary also in different phases of their lives, needing certain helps at one time, dispensing with them at another. Pluralism here is as vast as the number of persons striving to love God; and this pluralism enjoins, along with the exercise of one's own freedom, respect for the free choice of others.

Those who derive spiritual benefit from involvement in the phenomenon of Medjugorje will quickly recognise that it has many distinctive features.

Medjugorje has come to public notice at a time when very many apparitions of Our Lady are reported. Kibeho in Rwanda is well known, but is not alone. Stories have come from Hungary, Italy, Japan, Holland, Nicaragua and from Egypt again. Last summer Ireland had not only the phenomenon of the moving statues; there were also Marian apparitions at a spot near the famous Cistercian Abbey of Mount Melleray. Yet Medjugorje is dominant, in some ways, and is so within the long chain of such happenings.

The apparitions have lasted longer, on consecutive days, than any previously recorded, from 24 June 1981 to date. At San Damiano, Mama Rosa claimed to see Our Lady every *Friday* for nineteen years; not every day.

They have drawn an immediate and wholly unparalleled

worldwide participation. This is evident in the crowds travelling to Medjugorje from so many different countries;[15] it is also manifest in the very many centres organised throughout the world to spread knowledge about Medjugorje and foster interest in it. The best known is the Boston Center for Peace.

Another aspect of this international movement is the number of people who freely admit that their lives have been altered by the message reaching them from this spot, returning to practice of the Catholic faith in some cases, while in others there has been more intense commitment to the faith as demanded by the programme outlined in the apparitions.

The apparitions have sparked off a spiritual revolution in the parish of Medjugorje. Again, never has a whole community been so affected and transformed and brought to such a pitch of fervour.

It is distinctive too in the history of apparitions to find the visionaries in such a close relationship with religious, with the sisters of the local convent and the fathers of the Franciscan community.

In no previous apparition or series of apparitions has a theological expert of the quality of Fr René Laurentin been present from an early stage. He is scarcely rivalled in knowledge and critical judgement in the entire history of apparitions.

Likewise, the medical experts who have studied the phenomena of Medjugorje have made history. The specialists from Milan and Montpelier universities rank higher than those who have been consulted in previous cases and the most modern techniques have been used.

We have seen that secrets enter into the story of many Marian apparitions. The number revealed at Medjugorje is the highest on record, ten in all. They are to be delivered to each of the visionaries gradually. Two have already heard them all.

There are other unusual features in the story, which will become evident as it unfolds. It may appear premature to attempt an opinion on the general effect of Medjugorje on the whole Church. The development so far raises a theological question which we shall have to consider: the value and effect of the *sensus fidelium*, the sentiment of the faithful.

Due possibly, but certainly not altogether, to the rapidity of modern communications, the impact on the Church as a whole has certainly been greater than that of Lourdes or Fatima over an equivalent period, five years. The abundant literature, the pastoral dimension away beyond the place itself, the characteristic spirituality, the example of parochial spiritual pedagogy all warrant high expectation. This is heightened by the character and history of the people, as by the regime.

1. *Vita Gregorii Thaumaturgi*, attributed to St Gregory of Nyssa, despite objection by one patristic scholar, Mgr. G. Jouassard, pp 46, 912; in ancient times apparitions are also reported in the lives of Theophilus (7th century), St Mary the Egyptian (6th century), St John of Damascus (8th century).

2. All previous works on St Catherine Labouré and the Miraculous Medal are superseded by R. Laurentin, *Catherine Labouré, Documents*, 2 vols, Paris, 1976, 1978; *Vie de Catherine Labouré*, Paris, 1980; 2 vols; English translation, London.

3. Cf. Count Paul Biver, *Père Lamy*, London, 1951.

4. For Pontmain cf. R. Laurentin, *Pontmain*, Paris, 1971, 3 vols; for Knock, W.D. Coyne, *Cnoc Mhuire in Picture and Story*, 6th ed., Dublin 1957; T. Neary, *I Comforted them in Sorrow*, Knock, 1979; M. Walsh, *The Apparition at Knock*, Tuam 1955; id. *Knock, The Shrine of the Pilgrim People of God*, Tuam, 1973; C. Rynne, *Knock, 1879-1979*, Dublin, 1979; *Knock Shrine Annual*, ed. J.C. Coyne, 1938 to 1986. . .; for Fatima, cf. article 'Fatima' in *Theotokos* by M. O'Carroll, bibliography, 148; in English, *Fatima in Lucia's own Words*, ed. L. Kondor, preface J.A. Alonso, CMF, the expert who, before his death in 1981, had 17 volumes prepared on the subject — the book carries the *Imprimatur* of the Bishop of Leiria.

5. C.M. Staehlin, *Aparicones*, Madrid, 1954; for Beauraing, cf. Mgr. Toussaint, C. Josef, SJ, *Beauraing, Les apparitions*, Paris, 1981; for Banneux, cf. the definitive work R. Rutten, SJ, *Histoire critique des apparitions de Banneux*, 616 pp., Namur, 1985; for Dom Billet's analysis with tables of apparitions, 1928-1971, cf. *Vraies et fausses apparitions*, symposium, annual session of the French Society for Marian Studies, Paris, 1973, 9-20.

6. *Visions and Prophecies* (English translation of *Visionen und Prophezeheiungen*) London, 1963, 13.

7. *Ibid.*, 15.

8. *Ibid.*, 16.

9. *De servorum Dei beatificatione*, Bk II, ch. 32, no. 11; cf. Bk III, ch. 53, no. 15; *apud* R. Laurentin, *Année Sainte*, Paris, 1983, 130.

10. *Decreta authentica Congregationis rituum*, III, 1900, 79; ASS XI, 509ff.

11. *Actes de St Pie X*, Paris, Bonne Presse, III, 175.

12. *Acta et decreta Concilii Provincialis Mechlinensis quinti*, Malines, 1938, VIII, 5ff.

13. Papers in the Acts of the Lourdes Congress, *Maria et Ecclesia*, Rome 1962, 2-56; the point was taken up at the International Mariological Congress in Fatima in 1967; cf. Acts of the Congress *De primordiis cultus marianin*, VI, 3-12; cf. also. C. Balic, OFM, *De auctoritate Ecclesiae circa apparitiones seu revelationes*, *Divinitas* 2(1958), 85-103.

14. *Op.cit.*, 77, 78; in the present work the role of the *sensus fidelium* now accepted as a factor in the transmission of divine revelation will be considered in the final chapter.

15. For the fifth anniversary, 24 June 1986, 100,000 people from the five continents were present; there were 200 priests, of whom 120 concelebrated.

2

BACKGROUND

(i)

Yugoslavia came into existence after the First World War, a composite of different nationalities, creeds and languages. Despite tensions, differing memories and aspirations it held together under a monarchy until the Second World War. Invaded and quickly overrun by the Germans and Italians in 1941, it was dismembered. There was one significant novelty. On 10 April, when German troops entered Zagreb, capital of Croatia, a general, one-time officer in the Austrian army, Slavko Kvaternik declared the 'Independent State of Croatia' in the name of Ante Pavelic, co-founder with him of the *Ustase*, an organisation whose members vowed to oppose the Yugoslav state and attain what the Germans now granted them.

Pavelic had lived for some time in Italy, the protegé of Mussolini, who had given him facilities of different kinds to enlarge and strengthen his clandestine organisation. It was a Macedonian member of the movement who, on 6 October 1934 killed King Alexander, dictator of Yugoslavia, as he was being received by the French President, Barthou, at Marseilles; Barthou also died in the act of terrorism.

Pavelic reached Zagreb on 16 April with the title Poglavnik (an equivalent term for Führer or Duce) and it seemed that Croatian nationalism, one of the strongest forces of its kind in history, was to have the fulfilment of hope sustained through centuries. Croatian identity had survived prolonged bitter discrimination in the days of the Yugoslav monarchy, as through centuries of Moslem rule.

The identity is intimately linked with the Catholic faith, the religion of the Croats for thirteen centuries; the similarity with Ireland and Poland is manifest. It was an element in the opposition to the Serb Orthodox which, under the Pavelic regime,

16

degenerated into religious war. Pavelic sought every means to identify with the Catholic Church, whose authorities in the country, at the outset, hoped for much from him. A monarchy was expected in Croatia with a member of the house of Savoy, the Duke of Spoleto, enthroned.

The Vatican was placed in a delicate position by the new turn of events. Diplomatic relations had existed with the previous monarchical regime and there was no international treaty ratifying the change. When Pavelic came to Rome in 1941 and his Italian allies put pressure on the Pope to receive him as head of the new Croatian state, Pius XII followed established Vatican procedure. Nothing in the way of political recognition could be given while war continued and new arrangements were not agreed to by treaty.

The Pope was faced with protest by the Yugoslav Legation at the Vatican which remained there despite the collapse of the state. His solution to a vexed question was to receive Pavelic as a private individual, as a Catholic; his official suite were not allowed to assist at the audience. The Secretary of State, Cardinal Maglione, sent a circular to the Vatican representatives stating that the audience had no political significance. The Yugoslav Minister was also reassured by the Secretary of State.[1]

Meanwhile, within the country, relations between the regime and the Church deteriorated. Pavelic went back, furious that he had been denied the official backing of the Papacy. It was made clear that Abbot Joseph Ramirus Marcone, Legate of the Holy See in Croatia, was, in diplomatic rank, merely an Observer.

The vicious programme enforced against the Orthodox and Pavelic's active support of the Nazi anti-semitic policy were most disturbing to any expected harmony between Church and State. Crises produce or enlarge personalities and the one which emerged now was the Catholic Archbishop of Zagreb, Aloysius Stepinac. After the war, when the heads of Catholic hierarchies in eastern Europe, delivered to Stalin by the 'Treaty' of Yalta, became, in one country after another, the principal targets of persecution and the prime victims of show trials, he was the Yugoslav representative in the malevolent campaign.

He cannot be impugned for involvement in the massacres of Serb Orthodox — nor can any other bishops of the time — nor for failure to oppose the anti-Jewish policies; he constantly opposed such evils. In May 1943 he submitted to the Vatican Secretary of State, Cardinal Maglione, an itemised list of thirty-four occasions when, in one way or another, at every level, he had defended human rights. He had, on two notable occasions, the Feast of Christ the King in October 1942, and the commemoration ceremony for the coronation of Pius XII in March 1943, publicly condemned racist theories and the violence committed in consequence of them or of extreme nationalism; he had defended the inalienable rights of the human person and the rights of minorities. Maglione, in an official comment on the Archbishop's memorandum, admits that though persecution of the Orthodox may have been exaggerated, it was undeniable.[2]

(ii)

That phase of Croatian history ended with the defeat of the axis powers, Pavelic's sponsors and backers in 1945. Is it all to be consigned to oblivion, 'water under the bridge'? There is no such thing as 'water under the bridge'; there is history, which is fed by corporate memory. No more powerful example of corporate memory exists than nationalism intertwined with the Catholic faith.

This corporate memory was to take in a new stock of ideas and experience. After a bitter internal struggle Tito was the unchallenged master of the country in 1945. He installed a marxist regime and it showed the same ugly features as did the others in the Russian orbit at the time. Allied responsibility for the establishment of Tito's dictatorship with all that followed is a matter for historians. His complete control was manifest in the first 'elections', in which *over* 99 per cent voted for him and his republic.

Tito's rule extended to six republics which are federally joined: we will be concerned with one, Bosnia-Hercegovina, which has about 600,000 Croats within its borders, most of them Catholics. To add to the complexities there are five officially recognised nationalities: Serbs, Croats, Slovenes, Macedonians and Montenegrans, to which may be added Moslem Croats, granted national status in 1960 and eighteen ethnic minorities, the largest of which are the Albanians and Hungarians. There are fourteen languages, four of them official — Croatian, Macedonian, Serbian and Slovenian. Two alphabets are used, Roman and Cyrillic.

The religious statistical picture is also variegated: Orthodox, 13,700,000; Catholics, 7,715,000; Moslems, 2,319,000; Protestants 220,000; Jews, 7,800; other faiths, 2,000; no religious beliefs, 1,900,000; atheists, 1,343,000.

To that amazing ethnic, political, religious and therefore cultural mosaic the post-war government turned the fury of its ideological drive. If the Poles presented the marxists with a problem because they are a homogeneous religious entity and you cannot put the whole town in jail, the Yugoslavs had a possible advantage in such amazing diversity, which is not fragmentation. But the first years of Tito's rule were fairly horrendous, on the customary pattern.

The Constitutions of the Yugoslav State and the Constituent Republics contained phrases guaranteeing 'liberty of conscience and of worship'; there are also demands for 'the separation of Church and State', prohibition of 'the abuse of the Church and of religion for political ends', and of 'political organisations with religious backgrounds'. Religious communities 'whose teachings are not opposed to the Constitution are allowed to exercise their religious functions and celebrate their religious rites.'

These phrases have a different interpretation in a marxist state from that they would receive in western democracies. Separation of Church and State does not mean respectful coexistence; it means separation from the Church of the people who make up the State, and war on the former.

The war was soon on. The media, under rigid state control took to vilification and innuendo. Discrimination against practising Catholics was widespread. The Catholic press and Catholic associations were suppressed. Education, as is routine in such situations, was victimised: all Catholic schools, save a few minor seminaries, were shut down. Prelates were put on trial and priests and bishops interned.[3]

Two cases of judicial persecution were widely reported. In September 1946 Archbishop Stepinac was arrested. Attempts had been made on his life by hired gunmen. Tito had asked a papal visitor to Yugoslavia to remove the Archbishop from the country. Stepinac had written courageous letters protesting against the violence of communists (24 March and 20 September 1945, 27 August 1946) and this sealed his fate.

The charges against the Archbishop were political. Witnesses were called for the prosecution and practically none for the defence; all those who might have given evidence in his favour had been arrested. He rebutted every charge made against him, but on 13 October 1946, he was condemned to sixteen years forced labour and to the loss of his political and civic rights for a further five years.[4]

A second trial took place in 1948. Bishop Peter Cule of Mostar was arrested on 22 April and brought before the People's Court on the charge of collaboration with the Ustase regime. No worthwhile evidence was offered. Bishop Cule rightly declared that the only reason he was in the dock was that he had defended the rights of the Church and of religion. He reminded his judges that this was a right guaranteed by the Constitution. He was condemned to eleven years in prison. His secretary, Fr Mate Nuic, was condemned to eight years in prison because he had not given evidence against his bishop. While being transferred to forced labour, Bishop Cule was injured in a railway accident.

The other religious communions suffered likewise. The Orthodox Metropolitans of Sarajevo and Montenegro were given sentences of eleven years and Moslem notabilities were also punished.

(iii)

The year 1948 was sensational. Tito broke with the Kremlin — Stalin was still living. Henceforth he would look for friends outside the Russian orbit, eventually making common cause with the non-aligned; he would have to measure carefully policies and activities which would tarnish his image in countries of the West where the Catholic Church is respected.

This did not mean immediate change. Gradually, however, the attitude towards the Catholic Church softened with sporadic instances of the hardline. Archbishop Stepinac was released in 1951, after serving six years; he was to remain, under police surveillance, in his native village, Krasic. Two years later Pius XII created him Cardinal.

In 1956 the Vatican was allowed to appoint new bishops. 'Charges' against the clergy were suspended. Some religious presses were allowed to operate. Seminaries were reopened and Catholic faculties came into existence. All Yugoslav bishops attended Vatican II.

Economically Yugoslavia was determined to take its share of the tourist boom in the sixties and seventies. Commercial links with the west grew strong. In some ways, the country was attaining western standards of living and communication with the outside world was normal.

The Church of Vatican II has not been under pressure from the Yugoslav government. A native of the country, Cardinal Sepir, was appointed to a prestigious post inside the Roman Curia, head of the Congregation for the Doctrine of the Faith. One of the greatest authorities on Marian theology in our time, the Croat Fr Karl Balic, OFM, founder and president of the International Marian Academy, given pontifical status by John XXIII, was involved in a symbolic episode in the new order of things. After an absence of thirty years from his native land he returned to organise and conduct the first great international Catholic gathering held in Yugoslavia in modern times, the International Mariological and Marian Congresses of 1971.[7]

The happenings at Medjugorje, with which this book is concerned, continue great Marian traditions among the Croatians, with which that Congress was partly occupied. Medjugorje is a centre of Croatian piety outside Croatia. The history of the Catholic Church in the republic of Bosnia-Hercegovina, where it is situated, is tortuous. Between 1684 and 1878 the area was under Turkish, i.e. Moslem, domination. In 1735 the Franciscans who had ministered heroically to the people were given official responsibility for them with a Vicar Apostolic. When the Turks withdrew in 1878 Austrian troops moved in and the territory was annexed by Austria in 1908. Pope Leo XIII had established a regular hierarchy in 1881 with an Archbishop at Sarajevo and bishoprics at Banjaluka and Mostar. The Pope hoped that, in time, the secular clergy would take over ecclesiastical administration.

Thereon hangs much of the story of the Church in Hercegovina. The faithful had become deeply attached to the Franciscans and found the change difficult; in places they did not accept it. There have been incidents in which Franciscans have clashed with diocesan authorities over the assignment of personnel.

The parish of Medjugorje, as so many pilgrims know, is in the care of Franciscans, and this fact has been important in the development of events. It has a population of about three and a half thousand people, living in the villages of Bijakovici, Miletina, Vionica and Surmanci. It is situated in the mountainous region inland from the Adriatic above Split on the one hand and Dubrovnik on the other. Tobacco and grapes are the source of livelihood, although some wheat is also grown. Local economics are changing, with the new and unexpected influx of foreign currency.

(iv)

What is the present state of religion, religious practice especially, in Yugoslavia? We do not have to guess. The media throughout the world picked up the results of a social survey made early in 1985 by the Faculty of Sociology in the University of Belgrade. The theme was 'Religion and Society' and the findings were published and assessed by Danica Manojlovic in the monthly magazine, *Nada*.[7] The survey admits honestly that young people are coming to church, unafraid of what people will think; young people are increasingly seeking marriage in church; the number of baptisms is likewise on the increase and the surprising thing here is that adults ask to receive the sacrament.

Analysis of these and similar trends leads to an examination of the marxist ideology at work. One theorist contends that marxism has been perverted by an atheistic orientation. Marx did not preach the struggle against God, but the struggle for man. Young people are no longer satisfied with materialistic values; they realise that we need spiritual fulfilment. And they are prepared to view objectively and with admiration the multiple services rendered by priests to those of every age and condition, especially those in need.

'If we continue in this way, if we do not turn to youth, to their parents, to young people and old, and if in time we do not meet their aspirations, they will become the source of new members for the Church. Religion amongst us is growing strong, because the (marxist) revolution is halted. Without radical changes in the stalemate conditions of our society, we can do nothing to hold back the strengthening of the religious outlook on life.' At Medjugorje Our Lady said that in Russia in the future God will be glorified more than elsewhere; are we seeing the beginning in the spiritual revival within a country which could well influence Russia?

1. The eposode of Pavelic's visit is fully documented in the Vatican War Documents. Cf. *Actes et Documents du Saint Siège relatifs a la seconde guerre mondiale* IV, Rome, 1967, 44-47, with the references to the official documents throughout the volume; the section on Croatia, 259ff. in Carlo Franconi's *The Silence of Pius XII* has to be read with great caution because of this author's anti-Catholic bias and his obsessional antipathy to Pius XII.

2. In *Actes et Documents du Saint Siège relatifs à la seconde guerre mondiale*, IX, Rome, 1975, *Le Saint Siège et les victimes de la guerre janvier-decembre*, 1943, 34 separate items from the first days of the Croatian regime, through 1941, 1942, 1943, until the preparation of the volume, pp.224-229; previous documents sent to the Secretariat of State give details of the attempts made to save the Orthodox from the fury of uncontrolled Ustase members, and the Jews in the country from the anti-semites. Chapter and verse is offered; Falconi could not perhaps have known these facts, as he wrote his book before the appearance of the relevant volumes of the War Documents.

3. For the measures taken against the Church in Yugoslavia cf. Albert Galter, *The Red Book of the Persecuted Church*, Dublin, 404-451.

4. On Cardinal Stepinac, cf. op.cit., 428-29.

5. Cf. Xavier Rynne, *Letters from Vatican City*, London, 1963, 129.

6. *Acta Congressus Mariologici Mariani in Croatia*, Rome, 1971.

7. *Nada*, No. 232, 233, 234, January, February, March 1985.

3

HOW IT BEGAN

(i)

Many accounts of the beginnings of the Medjugorje phenomenon have been published. Now we have an exact narrative given by a highly articulate member of the group: Vicka Ivankovic, twenty-one years of age, gravely ill for some time and at the moment of the statement, mentally alert. The occasion was a long question and answer session between Vicka and the Croat Franciscan, Yanko Bubalo, a well-known poet; it took place in December, 1983. The questions are transcribed with what she said of relevance.[1]

Bubalo: How did the first apparition take place?

Vicka: It was the feast of St John, 24 June 1981. . . about five in the afternoon. . . That was a feast-day. But I did not go to Mass, because I had to go to Mostar for the additional class in mathematics. I had failed my end of school examination, and the school had organised repeat classes. . . I had returned home about midday. The coach was packed and it was very hot. Mirjana and Ivanka called to see me. We had decided in the morning to take a walk in the late afternoon; we were always together. But when I came home, I went to have a sleep. . . It was my sister Zdenka who awakened me: 'Get up quickly, you're late for school.' It was a joke. I got up and dressed. And I went off to look for Mirjana and Ivanka. (I went) first to Jakov's mother (She is Mirjana's aunt). . . They had called and had told Mirjana's aunt that they were taking a walk on the road going to the village of Cilici. . . I could catch up with them there. I set out. I found Mirjana and Ivanka; with little Milka

24

Pavlevic, daughter of Philip. All three were staring at something. They seemed frightened. They beckoned to me to come over. I hurried. Strange! What are they staring at with such attention? They shouted, 'Vicka, look at the Virgin!' But what is wrong with all of them? What Virgin? Perhaps it's a snake they've seen, or else it's a joke. I took off my shoes and, barefoot, I fled like one who is mad. . . . Why, I ran to the village here. Where else would I go?. . . Wait, I haven't finished. When I reached the village I burst into sobs. It was overwhelming. Why were they having fun with Our Lady? I didn't know what to do or where to go. . . While I was still there, the two Ivans arrived: Ivan Dragicevic, Stanko's son, and Ivan Ivankovic, son of the late Jozo. They had apples in a plastic bag. . . But it wasn't apples that I wanted. There was only one idea in my head, this exclamation, 'Look at the Virgin!' Still sobbing, I asked Ivan (Stanko's son), to accompany me to the three girls who said they were seeing the Virgin. He agreed and we went off there. On the way I said to him: 'I don't want to see her. I just want to be there!'. . .

Then we too saw her. Ivan fled straightaway, climbing over a fence. He left the apples and everything he had. . . I remained and I looked. It was the outline of a marvellous young girl. She held a child in her arms. She was looking after him. She would cover him and then show him to us. Several times she beckoned to us with her hands. . . We were too frightened to come near her. . . I don't know how long she stayed, five or six minutes perhaps. Then I ran away again, home, of course. I was happy and at the same time frightened. I was afraid, but satisfied. I threw myself on the sofa and I could not stop crying, crying. . . Now I'll go back to the beginning. While Mirjana and Ivanka were out walking suddenly Ivanka sees the Virgin, she says so to Mirjana who answers: 'No, it's not the Virgin. Why would she appear to us?'

Bubalo: Then Mirjana did not see her, that time?

Vicka: No. No. They came down to the village and met little Milka; who asked them to help her to let out the sheep.

Bubalo: Who was the shepherd of these sheep?

Vicka: Milka. Mirjana and Ivanka had nothing to do with them. Milka let out the sheep, and they all came back to the village. And while they were returning Ivanka saw our Lady in the same place. She said so to the others. They also saw her. No doubt about it. It was the Blessed Virgin. It was then that I came up with them.

Bubalo: But how was Ivan Ivankovic there?

Vicka: He was with Ivan Dragicevic. And when we went up the mountain he met us.

Bubalo: Did he also see?

Vicka: Yes, but not as clearly as we did.

Bubalo: Did Our Lady speak to you?

Vicka: No, no one heard anything. She beckoned to us with her hand, and she showed us the child.

Bubalo: But did you all see her in the same way?

Vicka: I don't know. She was at a distance. Then she left. I came home. Mirjana and Ivanka followed us. At home we told everything.

Bubalo: What did the others say?

Vicka: It depends. Some believed. Others were astonished. Some explained the event in one way, others in another. It was a flying saucer. . . They said anything at all.

Bubalo: Afterwards you went off to bed?

Vicka: What else could one do? Next day we had to be up at dawn, to gather the tobacco, watch the flock, the daily round.

Bubalo: But why did Ivanka say at once: it's the Blessed Virgin? Why did she not think of something else?

Vicka: I don't know. But who else could she have thought of? A wonderful young mother with a child and a crown on her head. It was clear.

(End of the first session)

Bubalo: We are now at 25 June 1981. You had resumed your activity, each in her own way. Had you forgotten already what had happened the evening before?

Vicka: Not at all. We were speaking of it, dreaming of it.

Bubalo: Had you come to a decision? Let's leave that. Let us take a new page.

Vicka: It was strange. We did not want to give up, the three of us. . . Ivanka, I and Mirjana. We agreed to go, at the same time, where we had seen Our Lady on the previous day. If it was really Our Lady perhaps she would come back. . . At about the same time then we took the pathway up on the look-out where she had appeared the first time. . . .Was there nothing? Suddenly light shone out, Our Lady was there. . . This time there was no child. . . It was again Ivanka who saw her first, afterwards Mirjana and I. . . Wait now. Before leaving the village, I had promised Marija and little Jakov that I would call them if we were seeing something. Then when we saw Our Lady, I asked Ivanka and Mirjana to wait a while. I called the others and they came at once running. . . Our Lady, with a sign of her hand, invited us to approach her, and we began to run as if we had wings. . . Marija and Jakov did not see her at once but they followed us. . . .By what path? There isn't a path. We went up straight through the brambles. We ran as if we were borne along. We felt neither stones nor brambles. . . Nothing. As if the ground were covered with sponge or rubber. Impossible to explain! No one could have passed us out. . .

Bubalo: And during this race, did you see Our Lady?

Vicka: Certainly. Otherwise we would not have known where to run. But Marija and Jakov saw nothing, they followed us.

Bubalo: But when they got to the top they also saw her?

Vicka: Yes. At the outset their vision was not clear, but little by little it became clear. . .

Bubalo: Vicka, you told me just now that you scaled the hill quite easily. Yet you told me one day that Mirjana and Ivanka had fainted.

Vicka: Yes, but it didn't last long.

Bubalo: What did you do when you reached the top?

Vicka: I couldn't say. We were overwhelmed. We were afraid too. It is not easy to behave before Our Lady. However, we fell on our knees and we began to pray.

Bubalo: What prayer did you recite?

Vicka: I don't remember. Doubtless the *Our Father*, the *Hail Mary* and the *Gloria*. Nothing else.

Bubalo: You told me that little Jakov fell.

Vicka: Yes, he was so moved that he fell into the brambles. I thought 'Eh, my little Jakov! You won't get out of it alive.' But he got out. And quickly. After he kept on repeating, 'Well, now that I have seen Our Lady, I shall not be sorry to die.' Imagine, he had no sign of the fall into the brambles. Our Lady protected him.

Bubalo: What was Our Lady like that day?

Vicka: She was wonderful! Smiling, gay. . . There are no words to describe her.

Bubalo: And that day did she talk to you?

Vicka: Yes, she prayed with us.

Bubalo: Did you ask for anything?

Vicka: I didn't. Ivanka did. She asked about her mother who had died in hospital, shortly before. And Our Lady had answered: '*Your mother is well. She is with me.*'

Bubalo: Did you hear Ivanka's question?

Vicka: Yes, of course.

Bubalo: And did you hear Our Lady's answer?

Vicka: Yes, but not Marija and Jakov.

Bubalo: Why not Marija?

Vicka: Who knows. It's like that. That's all.

Bubalo: Was Marija sad over it?

Vicka: Probably.

Bubalo: You haven't told me if Ivan was with you?

Vicka: He was there. He saw as we did.

Bubalo: How did he come to be there?

Vicka: He is shy, but he did as we did. He followed.

Bubalo: Then everything went well?

Vicka: Wonderfully! There are no words to tell it. It was as if we were not on earth. Nothing bothered us, heat or brambles. Our Lady was there, we forgot everything else.

Bubalo: Did you that day make other requests?

Vicka: Mirjana asked Our Lady to leave us a sign so that people would not spread stories about us. . . And the hands of Mirjana's watch turned.

Bubalo: Difficult to check. Did you ask anything else?

Vicka: Yes, would she come back. She nodded yes with her head.

Bubalo: It was in the brambles that you saw her, I think?

Vicka: Yes, through the brambles, she seemed to stand in a little clearing, between three clumps of brushwood. It's not important.

Bubalo: And you sprinkled Our Lady with holy water, didn't you?

Vicka: No. No. That happened the third day.

Bubalo: How long did you remain with Our Lady that day?

Vicka: Until she left us, saying, *Goodbye, my angels.*

Bubalo: You were how many?

Vicka: Six, myself, Ivanka, Mirjana, then Ivan, Marija and Jakov.

Bubalo: Were there people with you?

Vicka: At least some fifteen. More! Mario, Ivan, Marinko were there. . . I don't remember anymore all who were there.

Bubalo: Adults?

Vicka: Yes, Ivan Ivankovic, Mate Sego and others. They were persuaded that something was happening. The speed with which we had scaled the hill had impressed them. And then certain of them had also seen the light at the moment Our Lady arrived, and so on.

Bubalo: Were Milka and Ivan Ivankovic, who had come the first day, present with you that day?

Vicka: No. Milka had been retained by her mother, to help
her. And it was Marija who came. As for Ivan, older
than us, he didn't want to come back with these
youngsters. That's it. . . It's true (that Ivanka wept
on the way back). Almost all of us wept, Ivanka more
than us others, . . . because Our Lady had spoken
to her about her mother who is now with her.

(End of the second session)

Bubalo: We are now at the morning of the third day. Were
you hesitant about going there?

Vicka: Oh no! We were awaiting six in the evening
impatiently. We were hurrying in our daily tasks to
be able to go there. (So we set out.) We were a little
frightened, but Our Lady was drawing us. From the
moment we set out we were looking on every side in
the hope of getting a glimpse of her.

Bubalo: Who was with you that day?

Vicka: Well the six of us and many people. We were on the
look-out as we went up. . . . A light shot forth, three
times. . .

Bubalo: What use was this light? It was one of the longest days
of the year. At six o'clock the sun was still very high!

Vicka: Yes, but Our Lady sent us this light to show us the
place where she would be standing. . . Many saw it.
I don't know how many. The important thing is that
we, the seers, saw it. . . The light and Our Lady. . .
Higher up than (the evening before). At least 300 or
400 metres higher.

Bubalo: Why?

Vicka: Ask Our Lady!

Bubalo: Marinko, who was there, has told me that it happened
in front of a rock where you can see an old wooden
cross. It's probably an old tomb.

Vicka: I don't know anything about it. I never went there
before or after.

Bubalo: And what did you do when you saw Our Lady?

Vicka: We ran as if we had wings. Over there there is nothing but brambles, stones. . . The slope is quite steep. But we flew like birds. Everyone ran, we and the crowd. They say that there were more than a thousand persons. Yes, surely, much more. But no one counted them. . . I believe it was Ivan who (was first to Our Lady). . . .We were a little embarrassed for Ivanka and Mirjana were upset again. We looked after them for a while, but it quickly passed.

Bubalo: And what was Our Lady doing during this time?

Vicka: She had disappeared. We began to pray and she returned. (She was) as the previous day, only still more joyous, wonderful, smiling. . .

Bubalo: That was the day you sprinkled her?

Vicka: Yes, yes. (Why?) Everyone commented on the events in their own way.

Bubalo: Then someone recalled that Satan dreads holy water?

Vicka: Yes. How often have I heard my grand-mother say about someone: 'He is afraid, like the devil, of holy water'. The elderly women had told us to sprinkle the apparition with holy water.

Bubalo: Where did you find the water?

Vicka: But in each of our Christian families there is salt and holy water.

Bubalo: Who had made this holy water?

Vicka: My mother made it (How?). As if you did not know. She put the blessed salt in the water and shook the mixture. We all recite a *Credo*. That was it. . . Marinko brought it. It was I who sprinkled the apparition, and I said in a loud voice: *If you are Our Lady, stay with us; if you are not her, leave us.* She smiled. I think she was pleased.

Bubalo: But she said nothing.

Vicka: No, nothing.

Bubalo: Did one drop of water at least reach her?

Vicka: Certainly. I went quite near her and I did not spare the water.

Bubalo: In your home, have you the custom of sprinkling the
house outside and inside and outside, as was done
when I was a child?

Vicka: We are Christians.

(ii)

This is how Vicka remembered the first momentous happenings.
She gave Fr Yanko further details of this third day. Ivanka had
asked Our Lady if her mother had a message for her. 'Your
mother asks you to be kind to your grandmother, who is aged.'

All heard Ivanka's question, but only the visionaries heard
Our Lady's answer. Mirjana asked Our Lady her name. She
answered in a loud voice: "I am the Blessed Virgin Mary." This
comforted the visionaries but they were not entirely at ease.
Hundreds of questions were running through their heads — How
did Our Lady happen to be there? What did she want them to
do? How would it all end? And so on. Our Lady bade them
farewell and departed.

On the way down one of the visionaries, Marija, who had
gone on ahead of the others, suddenly felt herself being pushed
to the left side of the road at a particular spot. There the Blessed
Virgin appeared to her alone. There was a great cross behind
her. She was very sad and wept as she spoke to Marija, who
was overcome almost to the point of physical collapse. The others
arrived on the scene and comforted her somewhat. Then they
had to endure a long session of questioning from the crowd who
besieged them and stayed long into the night.

So far all was bliss, idyllic almost. Whatever tension there was
came from the very nature of the events, which also brought
their own inestimable compensation. It all reads like a spiritual
fairy tale. On the afternoon of the fourth day hard reality intruded
when officers from the Ministry of the Interior took the children
to the nearby town of Citluk. A doctor was on hand to examine
them, though as Vicka said 'they knew that we were healthier
than they themselves were.' Another doctor refused to do the
work, as 'she was an intelligent woman'. Ivan was subjected to
an hour's interview, mostly a monologue by the doctor — Ivan
is quiet and gentle.

Vicka is not so. She entered the room before she was summoned — Mirjana had been summoned, but Vicka was impatient. 'Is it over?' she asked the doctor. 'It's not your turn, but you can take a seat' he replied, to which she countered 'I am, thank God, young and healthy. I can remain standing. When I need a medical consultation, I shall come of my own accord. Now is it finished?'

The doctor, plainly embarrassed, asked her to hold out her hand. She did so, saying: 'Look these are my two hands with ten fingers. If you don't believe me, count them yourself!' Then she left.

Now the anxiety was to get to the mountain to meet the Blessed Virgin. It was nearly six o'clock, so they all took a taxi, except Ivan who travelled with a relative. A hasty drink at home to quench their thirst and then they were on their way: 'We would have gone there, even if we had been told that we would be shot. But one thing was puzzling us: we did not know where to go, where Our Lady would appear.'

The group of children split up, agreeing that whoever saw Our Lady first would alert the others. But each group saw a light, the signal of Our Lady's presence and they were all quickly there together. The children were overwhelmed by an immense crowd and then there was a curious incident. Pressing around the visionaries, some of the crowd actually walked on Our Lady's veil, which of course they did not see. Was she vexed? 'Look' said Vicka, 'Our Lady cannot be vexed. She is not like us. She had no problem. It was around us that the people crushed each other.'

Our Lady disappeared momentarily. Why, asked Fr Yanko, did she have such a long veil? 'How should I know?' replied Vicka. She was equally terse in her explanation as to why Our Lady appeared three times that day: 'I don't know. Ask her. It's true that people were very annoying.'

On this fourth day the children began to put questions to Our Lady. Jakov asked her: 'What do you want from the Franciscans?' He had probably been prompted by them to ask this. Our Lady answered that the Franciscans should persevere in the faith and protect the faith of others. Jakov and Mirjana asked Our Lady for a sign, since people were treating them as liars or as if they were drugged. 'My angels, injustice has always existed. But have no fear.' She also let them know that she would come again. Ivan had not been with them, as his parents had told him not to go. Our Lady appeared to him as he prayed alone a little above his home. She also appeared to the others as they were on the way home. She greeted them and bade them good-bye: 'Goodbye, my angels. Go in the peace of God.'

(iii)

We, who study these events now, who may have been at Medjugorje and seen the day-by-day evolution of events, may need an effort of imagination to go back to these early days when surprise and emotion were compounded by popular commotion. The fifth day was a Sunday. In the morning after Mass the children went through a wearying interrogation by the parish priest, Fr Jozo.

In the afternoon they succeeded in making their way to Podbrdo where they were given some space. The crowd was estimated at 15,000 persons. Without delay, while the children prayed, Our Lady appeared. Immediately, a striking feature of the whole dialogue between heaven and earth became apparent. The children questioned Our Lady. Vicka can remember asking her what she expected of the people present: '*Let* the people pray and persevere in the faith,' was Our Lady's reply. What did she expect of our priests: '*Let* the priests be strong in faith and help you.' The second part of that directive would certainly be meaningful in the days and years ahead.

Why did Our Lady not appear in the church where all could see her? 'Blessed are they who believe without having seen' was the comforting reply. Asked would she return, Our Lady replied: 'Yes, in the same place.' Did she prefer prayer or songs? She liked both. Vicka asked her again what she expected from all those present. There was no reply but since she disappeared without a word they thought she would return. When she did so Vicka asked the same question three times. Once again, but more fully this time, Our Lady called for faith: those who do not see must believe as do those who do. She made no reply to Vicka's request for a sign so that the visionaries would not be taken for liars or play-actors.

(iv)

Apparitions have occasionally provoked a strong reaction from the civil authorities. In a marxist regime this was a foregone conclusion. Monday, 29 June was the Feast of SS Peter and Paul. As the children were preparing for Mass two vehicles arrived and they were ordered to board them: one was an ambulance. They were packed into this ambulance with their relatives and driven to a psychiatric clinic in Mostar. Here they were treated mockingly, taken for deranged. They were also taken to the morgue, presumably to frighten them. Did Vicka feel fear? 'But I tell you. Not at all. Why should I be afraid? Everyone dies. It's the common lot. I had only one idea: to get into the car and get away.'

Vicka was asked how the drivers felt about all this? 'They thought it was stupid, but what could they do?' And the woman doctor? Her final comment is often quoted: 'The mad ones are those who brought you here. You are absolutely normal.'

Eventually the children got home and reached the place of the apparitions. There they prayed and saw Our Lady. Vicka asked her some questions; 'Dear Gospa, are you happy to see all these people today?' Our Lady then smiled wonderfully. 'It is not enough to say 'happy'; it is impossible to express.'

Vicka put another question: 'Our Lady, how long will you remain with us?' The reply was consoling: 'As much as you wish, my angels.' Again the visionary thought of the people all around and again Our Lady replied: 'There is only one God and one faith. Let people believe strongly and fear nought.' Then the crucial question: 'Will we be able to bear the persecutions which will come to us because of you?' The predictable answer was: 'You will be able to do so, my angels. Have no fear. You will bear everything' she added, 'you must believe and have confidence in me.'

A little child, apparently moribund, was recommended to Our Lady, whose answer was 'Pray much and believe strongly. . .' It would appear that the child recovered. More frightening was the case of a doctor, who had been sent by the authorities to keep the events at Medjugorje under surveillance. She asked permission to touch Our Lady, who made this astonishing reply: 'There are always unbelieving Judases, let her come.' She touched Our Lady's right shoulder and withdrew. Though she was silent at the time she later admitted in Vicka's home before a number of people: 'I felt, at the time, a kind of shudder which went right through my arm.' She was not seen thereafter.

Next day, 30 June, the pressure was still on, but in a different way. A trap was set for the children. Two assistant social workers called on the visionaries and proposed to take them on an outing. They consented and were driven around the countryside. Before long they realised that they had been duped. Then it was their turn to score a point. At about six o'clock, they asked to be allowed to leave the car to pray for a while to Our Lady. They went aside a little and began to pray. They could see Podbrdo where people had assembled to wait for them. When they began to pray, they saw a luminous cloud above the gathering. They knew it was Our Lady. Then they saw her clearly. She came towards them, gliding through the air, her garments waving. Vicka could not find words to express this spectacle. The children recited seven Our Fathers with Our Lady, spoke to her and sang with her. She said goodbye and left them, going to where she had come from.

Understandably, as a result of this episode, unforeseen by the social workers, they were embarrassed and fled.[2] The children made their way back to the presbytery; this was their refuge from the crowd returning from Podbrdo. They felt sympathy for these people. They learned later that strange rumours about them were current — that they had taken flight, were in jail . . .

Vicka admitted that Fr Jozo 'bombarded them with questions', that he asked them how they had been caught. Eventually they reached home about nine o'clock. They were exhausted and when questioned by Fr Jozo were unclear in answering. Vicka could scarcely recall what had happened.

On 1 July Our Lady had a further problem of location. Three of the children were summoned with their parents to a further session with officials from the Ministry of the Interior. The idea was to intimidate the parents. That miscarried. Then while the children were travelling under escort in the police car Our Lady was there before them. Marija and Ivanka were frightened; Vicka not at all. The guards believed the first two to be witches. The three absentees seem also to have seen Our Lady; Ivan certainly did.

On 2 July the visionaries came to the church for the first time and prayed with the people. They were still closely watched by the police and were hesitant to appear in public, so they did not go to church regularly. At times they saw apparitions in the presbytery.

In a very short time these six children — after 25 July only six saw Our Lady regularly — became the centre of popular interest and growing excitement in their community. From his original scepticism and hesitancy the priest in charge of the parish had been won over to them. On one occasion when the police were pursuing them he was praying in the church and distinctly heard a voice say to him: 'Come out and protect the children.' He was once also privileged to share in the vision of Our Lady with them.

Belief gave him fortitude which would soon be his main need. The police had cordoned off the site of the apparitions on the mountain. To what degree this was due to crude anti-religious venom or a fear of an awakening of Croatian nationalism, would be difficult for an outsider to decide. A single target was needed and Fr Jozo was the choice. He was arrested on 17 August. The sisters who lived in the presbytery were locked up and the whole building was ransacked. Money and important documents relating to the apparitions were seized.

The jailed priest was put on trial on 21 and 22 October. The charge was of 'stirring up sedition' and the sentence was three and a half years in prison. It was commuted to eighteen months as a result of protests from abroad. He did not regret his captivity, indeed, he found it spiritually bracing, but he suffered ear damage while working in a furniture factory.

(v)

Who are the children who figured in this exciting chain of events, who were to become so well known throughout the world?

Marija Pavlovic, the eldest of the group, was born on 1 April 1964, one of a family of six, with three brothers who work in West Germany, and two sisters, one married, the other attending secondary school. Her father Philip is a farmer. She is learning to be a hairdresser, and is apprenticed in Mostar. Dark-haired, sensitive, and thoughtful, she is seen every evening about the sacristy, helping the sisters with vestments and altar linen. During the apparition she is absorbed; otherwise she has a quietly relaxed air and shuns publicity — in so far as that is possible — but is lucid and very balanced in the interviews which journalists have persuaded her to give. Her intention is to enter a religious congregation and she has an affinity and friendly rapport with Sister Janja, the Franciscan nun known to English-speaking visitors to Medjugorje; Janja speaks their language which she learned during nine years in New York. Marija is a prayerful person, who reminds one of St Pius X, in that she makes the supernatural look natural.

Vicka Ivankovic was born on 3 July 1964, one of eight children. She is conspicuous in the videos which have been seen around the world, because of her vivacity which seems to increase in moments of ecstasy. An extrovert, sharp-tongued, quick with riposte, she exudes friendliness and is quite courageous. She came through the ordeal of the early days unscathed, showing no effect other than fatigue. Her lengthy dialogue with Fr Yanko Bubalo, some of which has been reproduced here, is informative and a continuous revelation of character.

Vicka's family background is agricultural; grape and tobacco growing. Her two older sisters are married, one is a qualified pharmacist, and the other a graduate from a commercial school.

She also intends to become a religious. For the moment she obeys Our Lady's suggestion that she should remain in Medjugorje so that little Jakov should not feel abandoned. There has been constant talk of serious illness affecting her; a tumour of the brain was mentioned. Friends were at the point of planning a journey to London for treatment at the hands of a specialist. Then early in 1986 Our Lady asked her to make some sacrifices; one was apparently to go without any vision for a period which eventually ran to fifty days. The belief was widespread that during this time she felt no indisposition. The words 'mystical suffering' were pronounced. She has had moments of great pain, headache, when she has been obliged to stay in bed. Our Lady has appeared to her there. She recently underwent surgery for appendicitis.

Vicka is beset by visitors curious for information about the apparitions. Radio, television and press journalists have also been fairly incessant in plying their trade at her expense. She has survived. She has now received nine secrets from Our Lady.

Mirjana Dragicevic was born on 18 March 1965. Her father Jozo works in a hospital as a radiographer; her mother works in a shop. She has one brother. She is of above average intelligence, and is following courses at the University of Sarajevo. She is fair-haired among a dark-haired group. Though the family live in Sarajevo she comes to spend summer holidays with her grandmother, still living in Bijakovici. This explains her presence in the area when the apparitions began.

Ivan Dragicevic was born on 25 May 1965. His background is local agriculture. Gentle, retiring, pensive, he wanted to prepare himself for the priesthood at Drubovnik junior seminary. He was obliged to withdraw as his previous studies were not sufficiently advanced. He still wishes to become a priest, thinks especially of the Franciscan Order. Things have not been easy for Ivan at all times. He is patient and persevering.

Ivanka Ivankovic was born on 21 April 1966. Her father, Ivan, works in Germany. Her mother, Jagoda, died in May 1981. She and her brother and sister live with her grandmother in Mostar. She is pretty and has a serene countenance. She is prepared to marry, is not thinking of religious life as are the others of the group. We shall see later how the apparitions ended for her. She has received the ten secrets, a matter which will also be clarified.

Jakov Colo, youngest of the visionaries, was born on 3 June 1971. His father, Ante, who worked in Sarajevo died recently; his mother died when he was twelve. He is cared for by his uncle, Philip Pavlovic and his family. Lively, yet marked by the loneliness of an orphan, Jakov is prayerful and he is very faithful to the religious exercises, which most boys of his age would find tedious. 'Why' said Fr Yanko Bubalo to Vicka 'did Our Lady choose little Jakov?' 'I don't know', was the answer; 'and no one really knows the little one. One day, at the very beginning, Our Lady said to us; 'You can go, but let little Jakov stay with me. Jakov is an extraordinary boy, as Our Lady knew.' She said later: 'In autumn time of the first year when the others began to go away, Our Lady said clearly to me: 'Remain here with Jakov.' And I have remained. Our Lady knows what she is about.' Jakov refused a request by the Bishop to write down the secrets and leave them with him.

(vi)

Since the secrets have been mentioned, it may be stated that they are an important part of the communications which the children have received through the years. Each will eventually receive ten secrets, some of which have to do with the future of the world. They are part of the message of Medjugorje. Other important communications have been on the subject of conversion, reconciliation and above all peace. The Yugoslav sky above Medjugorje was once a backdrop for the word MIR in golden letters — *mir* is Croatian for peace. Our Lady also recommends prayer, especially the Rosary, and fasting on bread and water.

Such messages have been received by these children to whom Our Lady has also spoken of many other things. Thus on the eve of a lecture tour in Ireland one of the Franciscans especially close to the visionaries, Fr Slavko Barberic, suggested that they should ask Our Lady for a message for that country. The reply was: 'That they (the Irish people) be the messengers of my message: prayer, conversion, peace and repentance and that they may never forget that their Mother loves them and prays for them.'[3] (21 October 1985)

A somewhat similar request was made of Our Lady by Ivan for her blessing on a day of thanksgiving — lectures and prayer — planned and organised by friends of Medjugorje for 12 April 1986 in Queen Mary Hall, London. The reply: 'I am very happy because of this day. I will rejoice in prayer, especially for that day. I will bless them. Let them pray continuously, be united with me in prayer.'[4] (28 February 1986)

To some extent through the action of the civil authorities in 1982, the children were obliged to retreat permanently to the church for their prayer and the apparitions. Vicka is illuminating on the subject:

Bubalo: Our Lady appeared to you first at Podbrdo, afterwards in different places in the village, while journeying, in the presbytery, but when and how were the apparitions changed to the church?

Vicka: Our Lady appeared to us several times in the church from the beginning, but she did not at that time speak to us there.

Bubalo: But since when does she appear regularly to you in the room, identical with the sacristy, where you see her now?

Vicka: I don't know exactly. At the beginning of 1982, I think.

Bubalo: That's right. It began on 15 February 1982. Who had the idea?

Vicka: Fr Tomislav Vlasic.

Bubalo: Why?

Vicka: So that we could assist at Mass and recite the Rosary first with the people.

Bubalo: Were you against this programme?

Vicka: Not at all. Our Lady had told us that we could see her in the church.

Bubalo: You no longer asked yourselves then whether she would come or not?

Vicka: No, she always comes where we are.

Bubalo: Have there been times when she did not come?

Vicka: No, never since then.

Bubalo: It's more suitable, now, in the church at a fixed time?

Vicka: The only disadvantage is that too many people come there. But as soon as we begin to pray nothing disturbs us.[5]

(vii)

As is widely known, Our Lady has spoken to the visionaries of a sign. Vicka gave these particulars:

Bubalo: Where will Our Lady leave this sign?

Vicka: At Podbrdo. In the place of the first apparitions.

Bubalo: Will it be up in the sky or on the ground?

Vicka: On the ground.

Bubalo: Will it appear suddenly?

Vicka: Suddenly.

Bubalo: Will everyone be able to see it?

Vicka: All who come.

Bubalo: Will it be transitory or permanent?
Vicka: Permanent.
Bubalo: Will people be able to destroy it?
Vicka: No.
Bubalo: What do you know about it?
Vicka: Our Lady has told us.
Bubalo: You really know what this sign will be like?
Vicka: Really.
Bubalo: Do you know when Our Lady will show it?
Vicka: That I also know.
Bubalo: Do all of you know?
Vicka: I am not sure. But I think that even we, the visionaries, do not all know it.[6]

In reply to further questioning Vicka said that Our Lady's motive in giving the sign was to assure people that she was there with them. It is one of the ten secrets. 'Alas for those who await the sign to be converted.' People may come, accept it and yet not believe.

Thus the whole phenomenon of Medjugorje looks to the future while conveying a specific programme for the present. It is rooted in the past, drawing meaning and power from it. It is in that context that Our Lady's messages to Vicka about her life on earth are to be understood. Vicka notes these communications but is for the moment forbidden to reveal them; one day she will be allowed to do so. In that context too we may reflect on the message given to Ivan in May 1984 that Our Lady's two thousandth birthday would occur on 5 August that year. Bishop Zanic, as we shall see, has some very amusing (?) remarks on this episode. For the Church celebrates Our Lady's birthday on 8 September. But surely the Bishop knows why the Church celebrates the birth of Jesus Christ of the Virgin Mary on 25 December. Not because that was the exact date but because a pagan festival, *Natalis Invicti*, was taken over.

So the visionaries carry their heavy burden, lightened by faith, for the benefit of the Church and of mankind. In that daily task they have been powerfully assisted by the Franciscans who are in charge of the parish. We have seen that one paid a price for his devotion to the ministry in this new, challenging situation.

Though imprisoned, he was for a while retained as parish priest. Fr Zrinko Cuvalo, associate parish priest, was eventually named to replace him. He was apparently hesitant, if not sceptical, about the chain of preternatural happenings. On his departure Fr Tomislav Pervan was appointed parish priest.

Tomislav has been rightly called the 'rock' that sustains the continuing experience of Medjugorje. Courteous, hospitable, scholarly — Sacred Scripture is his specialty — he remains serene, wise and strong through very testing ordeals.

Fr Tomislav Vlasic has been the discerning, intuitive, spiritual guide of the visionaries through the first three years; he also was their interpreter and protector. He has suffered greatly at the hands of the Bishop as we shall have occasion to see. He is utterly without rancour, bitterness or resentment. He told me that Our Lady's message to him was: *love*. He was not to worry about anything else. How faithful he has been, even under the abominable stress of a vile calumny, despicable and totally groundless! — a 'secret weapon', as the enemy who launched it boasted beforehand, ultimately a boomerang. But the man at the heart of the storm remained serene, steadfast, charitable. There are people who show with blinding clarity that Christianity works.

Another man who found himself in the target area was Dr Slavko Barberic. He was trained in psychological research, is a polyglot. The hope was that he would see through the whole silly game and unmask the culprits. After patient investigation he was convinced that the apparitions are genuine. He then acted as counsellor and as leader in the parochial prayer, giving talks in different languages to pilgrims. Tomislav Vlasic was removed in 1984; Slavko in 1985. Providence mocks the strategies of men. The gifted linguist found a new vocation almost at once; he has embarked on an international lecture tour, eagerly heard by audiences who value his first-hand knowledge of events and are satisfied by his skill as a communicator.

Sister Janja is a link between the visionaries and the public, as between the Franciscans and everyone, parishioners, pilgrims, the lost and found, saints and sinners. She is strong, direct, dedicated, courageous to the marrow of her bones.

(viii)

The phenomenon of Medjugorje is constantly developing. Two events of note deserve attention. On 4 September 1985 Fr Petar (Pero) Ljubicic issued the following statement:

'Mirjana, who was among the first to have apparitions, has told us that for her the daily apparitions ceased at Christmas, 1982. At that time she was promised that she would have apparitions on her birthday (18 March). As she testifies, she has in fact since then had an apparition on every birthday; that is, she has seen the Virgin Mary just as she used to do when she had daily apparitions.

Mirjana also says that for some time now she has been hearing an internal voice — the same voice that she used to hear during the (daily) apparitions. She claims that Our Lady is speaking to her, especially about the secrets. She heard this "inner voice" on 1 and 15 June, on 19 and 27 July, and on 15 and 27 August.

Some time previously Mirjana had told me that I would be the priest to whom she would entrust the secrets; her confidant, that is. After hearing the inner voice on 1 June, she told me definitely that she would confide the secrets to me. She told me that ten days before the occurrence of the secret she would give me a paper similar to a parchment. Three days before the event I am to make the secret in question known to the public. When the event takes place, I will give the paper back to Mirjana and wait for the next secret.'

I add to this report two messages that Mirjana has passed on to me. On 18 March 1985 (during the birthday apparition): 'They too are my children (this refers to those who are far away from God), and I grieve for them, because they do not know what awaits them, if they do not turn back to God. Mirjana, pray for them!'

On 15 August 1985 (given through the inner voice: 'My angel, pray for the unbelievers. They will tear their hair, brother will plead with brother, and they will curse their past godless lives, and repent, but it will be too late. Now is the time for conversion. Now is the time to do what I have been calling for these four years. Pray for them.'

Mirjana emphasises that the time is at hand when the first secret will be revealed. That is why she urges vigilance and prayer in the name of Our Lady.

Mirjana has given this report of a special apparition which she witnessed on 25 October 1985:

'We began to pray at 1.50 p.m. Our Lady came and greeted me with "Praised be Jesus", as always. She at once began to talk about unbelievers. She said that they were her children, that she was sorry for them, and that they did not know what awaited them. She was very sad, and began to pray for them: an Our Father and a Glory-be-to-the-Father. She said we should pray most of all for them.

Then she prayed for the sick and for poor people living alone. We too prayed the same prayer with her. Then she blessed us.

Then she showed me the first secret — like a film running before my eyes. I became sad, and asked her if it had to take place just like that. She said "Yes".

She said that God was not (as I might put it) hard-hearted; but that I should see who today still honours God as his Father and prays to him. She asked me: "How many people come to church as to God's house, with reverence, strong faith and love for their Father?" I could not give any answer. She said: "Very few".

She then prayed twice in Latin over Fr Petar. I was happy that Our Lady also was satisfied that I had chosen him. She said that his heart was open to God, and that he would be rewarded. There followed an Our Father and a Glory-be-to-the-Father for Fr Petar, for a successful carrying out of his mission.

Our Lady was with me for about eight minutes.' (Bijakovici, 25 October 1985)

(ix)

On 6 May 1985 Marija, Ivan, Jakov and Ivanka were present for the apparition. The vision lasted eight minutes for Ivanka, six minutes longer than for the others. During this vision Our Lady entrusted the tenth secret to Ivanka and completed her talk about the future of the world. Our Lady asked Ivanka to wait for her alone the following day.

On 7 May 1985 Ivanka had the vision at her home lasting about one hour. She gave Fr Slavko a paper on which the following was written: 'As on every day, Our Lady came with the greeting "Praised be Jesus". I responded "May Jesus and Mary always be praised." I never saw Mary so beautiful as on this evening. She was so beautiful and gentle. Today she wore the most beautiful gown I have ever seen in my life. Her gown and also her veil and crown had gold and silver sequins of light. There were two angels with her. They had the same clothes. Our Lady and the angels were so beautiful. I don't have words to describe it; one can only experience it.

Our Lady asked me what I would wish and I asked to see my earthly mother. Then Our Lady smiled, nodded her head, and at once my mother appeared. She was smiling. Our Lady said to me to stand up. I stood up, my mother embraced me and kissed me and she said: "My child, I am proud of you." She kissed me and disappeared.

After that Our Lady said to me: "My dear child, today is our last meeting. Do not be sad because I will be coming to you on every anniversary except this year. Dear child, do not think that you have done anything wrong or that this is the reason I will not be coming to you; no you did not. With all your heart you have accepted the plans which my Son and I had and you have done everything. No one on this earth has had the grace which you and your brothers and sisters have had. Be happy because I am your Mother who loves you with my whole heart. Ivanka, thank you for your response to the call of my Son, and for persevering and for remaining with him for as long as he asked you.

Dear child, tell all your friends that my Son and myself are always with them when they ask us and call us. What I have spoken to you these years about the secrets, speak to no one until I tell you.'

After this I asked Our Lady if I could kiss her. She nodded her head. I kissed her. I asked her to bless me. She blessed me, smiled and said "Go in God's peace!" and she departed slowly with the two angels. Our Lady was very joyful, very happy. She stayed for one hour.' (Medjugorje, 7 May 1985)

1. *Je vois la Vierge, Vicka raconte les apparitions et son expérience extraordinaire*, Paris, 1985. The extracts are from p. 19ff. Permission to reproduce them has been granted by Fr Bubalo.

2. One left the country for Germany, the other just disappeared from the locality.

3. The message was read out at Ballinasloe by Fr Slavko Barberic on the occasion of his visit to attend a seminar organised in that town, 29/30 October; this was his first visit to Ireland.

4. I had the great honour of bringing back this message from Medjugorje to our English friends, who asked me to read it out at a packed meeting; as many as came, probably very many more had to be refused applications for tickets.

5. *Op.cit.*, 97.

6. *Op.cit.*, 115f.

4

THEOLOGIANS

(i)

The history of the Second Vatican Council, when it is finally written, will show the important role played in its deliberations and eventual teaching by the corps of theological experts assembled around the bishops. It is already possible to trace the influence of one or other prominent theologian on particular documents; the names of Karl Rahner, Yves Congar, John Courtney Murray, Augustine Bea — both a Council Father and a theological expert — Joseph Lécuyer and others less known recur in such estimates. It is well known that theologians who had lived 'under a cloud', if not out in the rain, in the years immediately prior to the four sessions of the Council were not only brought in to the comfort of friendly consultation, but in some cases given the status of respected elders. Cardinal de Lubac has given an account of his vicissitudes in the bleak period, exaggerated by some commentators into an ice age, at the time of Pius XII's Encyclical *Humani Generis*.[1] At that time his superiors thought it wise to suspend his teaching activity for a while; they were to find that he was never once put under the obligation to retract or alter an iota of his theology. He ended his participation in the Council by concelebrating Mass with Pope Paul VI at the conclusion of the last session. He and another 'new theologian', Jean Daniélou SJ, were named Cardinals.

All this is not to simplify the complex problem of theologians and the teaching authority, any more than the cursory reference to Vatican II need be taken for acceptance of the conspiracy theory, according to which the 'experts' took over the Council and, with progressive journalists aiding and abetting by day and by night — often in Roman *trattorie* into the early hours of the morning — manipulated the bishops to their liberal ends. The point to be made is that bishops are wise to seek the help and collaboration of theologians fully committed to the Church and expert in whatever field they make their own.

Should this rule be followed in regard to alleged apparitions? Most certainly. The choice, however, must be carefully made. In the events leading up to the final favourable judgement on Beauraing, a French theologian, Fr Bruno de Jésus Marie, a Carmelite, editor of the review *Etudes Carmélitaines*, briefly acquired a kind of authoritative status. His review opposed the thesis of authenticity and opened its pages to those similarly inclined. But it was found that he had specialised in mystical theology, had been influenced by a very rigorist opinion held by St John of the Cross — understandably in the circumstances of the time — and had no prolonged acquaintance with the relevant subject; his visit to Beauraing had been brief, superficial and patronising; his mind was made up in the course of an afternoon. The Bishop disregarded his interpretation.

Contrast the singular good fortune of the Bishop of Mostar. From an early stage in the story of the apparitions he has had at his disposal the single greatest authority on apparitions of Our Lady in the Catholic Church at the present time. This is a very large claim. It remains totally exact. Always, as in such judgements, we must rely on the public forum. There may be historians and theologians with vast accurate knowledge and utterly reliable judgement, superior in this regard to Fr René Laurentin. But in their cases we have no adequate evidence to guide our assessment. In his it is massive and unrivalled.

The French theologian, who as a reporter on day-to-day activities during the Council and a regular contributor on religious affairs to *Le Figaro*, the Paris daily, can claim some awareness and discernment of the varying sectors and strata of opinion within the Church, reacts against a hardening of attitudes towards apparitions and similar religious phenomena. He has argued plausibly that if Lourdes were to have taken place at the worst recent moment of scepticism and hypercriticism, it would have been snuffed out. All his initiatives and his sustained support for the visionaries in Medjugorje — as for those who direct them who, because of their priestly office, carry the main responsibility — is designed to avert any such verdict and evil success in the Yugoslav apparitions.

Hostility can be expected in many different places. The press in France as in some other countries was won over by the skilful anti-Medjugorje campaign of the Bishop of Mostar. Fr Laurentin has quoted press articles which played happily on the idea of hallucination, a favourite theory of Bishop Zanic. As a result of this campaign there was the prayer recited in a French church: 'Lord, forgive the Church all its acts of imposture: especially the apparitions at Medjugorje.' Alas, as Fr Laurentin reports, a chaplain in the same church had expressed himself thus: 'Do not expect me to speak about the teachings of the Bishop of Rome on the family, contraception and the rest of it. These positions are out of date.' As Laurentin says, no one asked forgiveness for this scandalous talk.

The man at the centre of the storm sums it up succinctly: 'whoever gets involved in this debate pays a dear price.'

Let it be clear that he is not being considered here merely as an author, one of the many who have written on Medjugorje, a name in the bibliography of the subject. The contention is that because of his unique qualification and of his entire involvement, he is part of the event. At the periphery of this opinion he is the most widely read author on the subject.

(ii)

The impact of the man himself has been much deeper and may be more decisive than this general effect. This is due to three factors:

Firstly, he has an established competence in the whole area of Marian doctrine and devotion. His basic work, *Court Traité de théologie mariale* (*Short treatise on Marian Theology*) which appeared in the early fifties, altered the conventional approach to Mariology and set a model which would ultimately be followed by the Council: a scrupulously honest scrutiny of Scripture and the Fathers, what was called in France *ressourcement* (return to the sources), with a full account of development through the centuries — the teaching authority located in an intelligible context.

This work, continually re-edited, was followed by many other substantial works on the history and doctrinal aspect of Marian theology; two volumes on Mary, the Church and the preisthood; a study of the infancy narrative of Luke, widely consulted; quite recently a massive study, *Les évangiles de l'enfance*, on both Matthew and Luke.[2] In addition it would be necessary to mention the many monographs of the highest quality which have appeared either in scientific reviews or as papers given to specialist congresses. It is especially important to note his continuing contribution to the bibliography of all things Marian: this appears every two years as a *Bulletin Marial* in the French theological review, *La Revue des Sciences Philosophiques et Théologiques* — a Dominican publication.

Secondly, Laurentin's presence on the Medjugorje scene has importance because he has turned aside from general Mariology to scientific investigation of Marian apparitions. Some were surprised that he should undertake research on the events of Lourdes — this is not expected of professional theologians. Few regret his decision. It resulted in six massive volumes with ample documentation and a number of ancillary publications since then; notably *Logia de Bernadette*, a carefully compiled record of all that Bernadette is known to have said on the apparitions or allied topics; and a life for the centenary of her death, 1979.

The Lourdes study was followed by substantial volumes, equally well documented, on the Miraculous Medal — a life of St Catherine Labouré, with a companion collection of the basic documents — and Pontmain, three volumes. René Laurentin showed his mastery of the Guadalupe story in a masterly address to the International Mariological Congress in Saragossa, 1979.

The third reason why this theologian is particularly well-equipped to help in judging alleged apparitions is his experience in the delicate area of cooperation between scholars and the teaching authority. He was an expert at the Second Vatican Council and saw all the aspects of this important partnership. He is a man who can be trusted in research and in loyalty to the Church. When *Les évangiles de l'enfance* appeared Cardinal Ratzinger, Secretary of the Congregation for the Doctrine of the Faith, sent him a letter of commendation which has appeared in subsequent editions.

Fr Laurentin was then the kind of person to whom a bishop faced with the challenge and complexities of the apparitions at Medjugorje would turn for advice and expertise. The only problem might have been: Would he give time to the necessary research and evaluation? Highly qualified people in every walk of life are much sought after.

Here again things could not have been better. The great man was himself drawn to investigate the happenings in Medjugorje. As he has said more than once, he had spent much time studying ecstasies which took place in the past and which, in the sense of past events, were dead. Here before his eyes was the reality, living and continuous. The call was imperative. He first went to Medjugorje at Christmas 1983, gathered a great deal of information and felt justified in weighing the pros and cons of the singular phenomenon. He had found what he has called 'something very different and very new; it has an atmosphere which in many ways is characteristic of the post-conciliar era.'

René Laurentin's first book, translated into English as *Is the Virgin Mary appearing at Medjugorje?* was largely based on the work of Fr Marijan Rupcic OFM, which had appeared in German and French. The Laurentin work is generally considered basic; it has been brought up to date in subsequent editions. It was distinctive in the literature by reason of the full exposition of arguments for and against authenticity.

Laurentin's scientific temper is thus clearly manifest. We should at least list the objections he thinks worth examination: Are there not too many apparitions? Are there not too many words? Are there contradictions? What is to be thought of the phenomena of light? Is the movement about Medjugorje one of political subversion? Do certain aspects of the message imply exaggeration — 'So many hours of prayer, so many days of fasting, is it not too much?' And what, finally, about the tension with Church authority, in particular the case of the two young Franciscans?

How does the author discern favourable aspects of the event, or series of events? There is notable doctrinal orthodoxy; the 'style' is impressively post-conciliar in relation to members of other religions; the ecstasies do not show signs of abnormality; neither do the visionaries; the pastoral approach prompted by the happenings has been exemplary; since the tree is rightly judged by its fruits, the fruits here being good, the tree must also be so.

This summary statement of the position for and against is

made merely to show with what care and scientific precision René Laurentin approached the Medjugorje phenomenon. He became more and more deeply involved, entangled is a better word, in the subsequent development. He was, before long, entirely convinced of the authenticity and felt it his duty to answer criticism, to defend the visionaries.

The controversy between him and Bishop Zanic ensued. The debate was not of his choosing. He has always behaved towards the Ordinary of the diocese with irreproachable propriety. He has pleaded with the Bishop not to make slanderous statements about him. Such as? That he had made a great deal of money on his writings on Medjugorje; that he had practically been 'hired' by the Franciscans to boost their case; that he had been swayed to some extent by the 'charm' of one of the visionaries! Such things have been said in this enlightened age, things that have been ridiculous at the moment they were spoken, and shown to be utterly untenable in subsequent months or years.

Laurentin is courteous and respectful to authority. He is also resourceful and he is tough. In each single case, when he was asked to undertake a campaign of lectures on Medjugorje, he was encouraged by the uniformly enthusiastic audiences. Never in the course of his writing and lecturing career has he met this response. In Brussels, for example, he filled the largest available hall in the city.

The appeal of his lectures has been assisted by all the means open to audio-visual technology. He has built up an extensive library of such material, based on film or photographs taken on the spot by himself or by qualified friends. These he can use to bring home the truth of the visions to his listeners, to reveal the strange things that have been inflicted on the visionaries.

A series of his studies continue the narrative and analysis of the unfolding movement at Medjugorje. Of these publications two merit particular attention. In collaboration with Professor Henri Joyeux of Montpelier University, Fr Laurentin published *Medjugorje, Études medicales et scientifiques* to describe and explain the highly sophisticated experiments carried out on the children, with their consent, in the moment of ecstasy. Here is theology joining forces with science and technology in an area of concern to the Church.

That this specialised research should be conducted was

admirable; that a theologian should be present to show how the separate disciplines can exercise their autonomy and achieve mutual enrichment was fortunate for the Church and for the faithful who accept Medjugorje as a divine intervention. The work is unique in the literature of apparitions.

The second decisive contribution to the Medjugorje literature made by the French priest was a detailed examination of a work reproduced textually in this book, the critical memoir composed and distributed throughout the world by the Bishop of Mostar, *Medjugorje à l'heure de la désinformation, Autopsie des fausses nouvelles*.[3] This remarkable essay is drawn on elsewhere in the present work. It is mentioned here as an example of René Laurentin's tenacious efforts in the service of truth about Medjugorje.

The service of truth is a necessary apostolate, for souls risk being damaged by error in what concerns the faith. Any apostolate entails suffering. René Laurentin is no exception. He has suffered at the hands of the ecclesiastical authority in Mostar, and at the hands of the civil authority. On the occasion of his first visit to the country he was subjected to an interrogation and a search of his luggage which lasted two hours. It ended amicably, but was followed by what he calls 'a discreet surveillance.'

When Fr Laurentin arrived at the frontier with the intention of observing and reporting on Professor Joyeux's investigation he was turned back and forbidden entry; he waited a while and came in by another road. On 29 December 1984 he was taken to a police barracks, stripped naked and fined heavily. He was also forbidden to enter the country for twelve months. The charge against him was 'bringing books into Yugoslavia.'

(iii)

Fr Laurentin has had support from other theologians within the Church; from none more prestigious than the Swiss writer, Hans Urs von Balthasar. The intervention of this giant among contemporary theologians caused much surprise. He had just come to prominence as the first recipient of the Paul VI prize for theology; it was conferred in Rome by the Pope and was an occasion for recalling Fr von Balthasar's achievement over a long lifetime, in many branches of theology, anthropology, the theology of history and patristics as well as in aesthetics, especially musicology.

Against such a background, already firmly marked but now suddenly illumined by the double papal accolade, any statement of Fr von Balthasar would draw attention. His close personal and literary links with Cardinal Ratzinger would prompt still more consideration in any area of controversy. Disturbed by the trend set in the post-conciliar international review, *Concilium*, he had, with Ratzinger who was still immersed in writing and teaching theology, launched a new review, *Communio*, which has had much the same international impact as *Concilium*. The two men remain close to each other in thought, though Ratzinger was taken from the academic scene to operate in the pastoral domain, first as Archbishop of Munich and then as Secretary of the Congregation for the Doctrine of the Faith.

It is difficult to think that Fr von Balthasar would have written this letter to the Bishop of Mostar — after the famous *Posizione*, without consulting his friend in the high Roman office, where the Cardinal is the 'watchdog of the faith'.

'My Lord, what a sorry document you have sent throughout the world! I have been deeply pained to see the episcopal office degraded in this manner. Instead of biding your time, as you were advised to do by high authority, you thunder and hurl thunderbolts like Jupiter. While you denigrate people who are renowned and innocent, deserving your respect and protection, you bring out accusations which have been refuted a hundred times over.

I am naturally also extremely pained by the declarations of the Episcopal Conference (the exact terms of which I have not been able to read), but I can understand them in the context of the political situation, and only that, of your country. I would wish that all the members signed in good conscience.

I hope that you are praying sincerely to the Lord, and his Mother to bring this sad drama, one so important, to an outcome that will be fruitful for the whole Church. Join with all those who pray with such fervour at Medjugorje. Yours in the Lord, Hans Urs von Balthasar, Basel, 12 December 1984. '

Some months later, Fr von Balthasar heard of the restrictions imposed on the Franciscans and the visionaries by the Bishop of Mostar. Acknowledging to John Hill, Director of the Boston

Center for Peace, receipt of material relating to Medjugorje which John had sent him, he dealt with the latest episcopal action:

'Dear Sir, Many thanks for your huge package relevant to Medjugorje. But can you do something to bring to the attention of your large public the absolute tragic *events which are currently taking place there? Priests removed, the children forbidden to come to the church, the ban on preaching etc., etc. Zanic is out to destroy (*annihiler*) the whole thing. He gives the impression of one working with the atheistic government. People should be informed about all this. Yours sincerely in the Lord, Hans Balthasar. PS. The work of the commission set up by Zanic is scandalous. The other bishops do not intervene.'*

The Swiss theologian was in London in November 1985 and gave an interview on the subject of Medjugorje to Fr Richard Foley SJ, spiritual director of the London Medjugorje Centre and a frequent commentator on the whole subject in the Catholic press. The great theologian's verdict: 'Medjugorje's theology rings true. I am convinced of its truth. And everything about Medjugorje is authentic in a Catholic sense. What is happening there is so evident, so convincing.'[4] The speaker saw the importance of the *sensus fidelium*, what he called the uncomplicated response of the faithful, at times a genuine test of truth. He was also impressed by the beneficial effects of the message on so many lives, the fruits which tell of the tree.

It is refreshing to find the man who conceives theology on such a vast scale, one of whose creative intuitions is *Theodramatik* — the drama of love continuing between God and man — at the same time so close to the faithful who make up the Church.

We rejoin Laurentin here. He has publicly stated that the response from readers of his book on Medjugorje has been overwhelming. With touching modesty he pointed out on the same occasion, that of his eighty books the only one which has made people change their lives, face conversion, was that on Medjugorje. His conclusion: he had nothing to do with it. Our Lady was the one.[5]

Cardinal Ratzinger is also on record on the same theme of the faithful as God's messengers. In the interview given to the Italian monthly review, *Jesus*, in November 1984 (the basis of his work, *Report on the Faith*, which has been widely translated), the Cardinal spoke thus about Medjugorje: 'Revelation was completed by Jesus Christ, who is himself our revelation.

Nevertheless we cannot deny that God could speak to our own age, even through humble or simple people and through extraordinary signs, to expose the shortcomings of a culture imbued with rationalism, as is the case with ours.'

I do not have to mention all the theologians who have brought their expertise with integrity to the subject of Medjugorje. The books of one, Fr Robert Faricy SJ, of the Gregorian University are widely known. He is Professor of Spirituality in that great centre of theology.

1. Cardinal de Lubac dealt with the events surrounding *Humani Generis* in a lengthy interview in *La France Catholique*, 19 July 1985.

2. Paris 1982. The work had a sensational success considering that it deals with a biblical subject scientifically: 3,000 copies were sold in a month and it was reviewed favourably right across the theological spectrum, which in France is wide. *Le Monde*, exceptionally, carried its review on the front page; the work was awarded a prize by the French Academy.

3. Paris 1985.

4. Interview published in *Catholic Herald*, 22 November 1985. Fr von Balthasar's letters have been available through John Hill, Boston.

5. Statements made at the London meeting on Medjugorje, 12 April 1986.

5

SCIENTISTS:

MEDICAL TESTIMONY

(i)

It is evident from Vicka's narrative that the visionaries were from the very beginning subjected to medical examination. It is a conclusion already drawn from the summary review of the history of public apparitions by Our Lady that those at Medjugorje are distinctive in this regard. The image on Juan Diego's tilma preserved in the Basilica of Guadalupe has been studied scientifically by experts from the Massachusetts Institute of Technology. This is a welcome initiative and has had fruitful results; but it is separated from the event by four centuries.

At Medjugorje the encounter with modern science on its own terms has been immediate. It began three days after the first apparition. The children were examined by Dr Ante Bijevic in Citluk. He did not think it necessary to detain them. On the 29 June they were brought to a psychiatric clinic in Mostar. They were also questioned by another doctor for two hours.

A number of doctors came independently to Medjugorje from 1982 on, and studied the children carefully during the moment of ecstasy and in their normal life. Before this Fr Slavko Barberic OFM, who was later to become well-known as the visionaries' spiritual guide, had examined them in the light of his specialised studies in social psychology — he has a doctorate in this field. He had concluded that the children behaved independently of one another and that there was no sign of hallucination. A Yugoslav doctor, Stopar, a specialist in psychiatry, hypnotherapy and parapsychology found the children 'to be absolutely normal.' A French doctor, Philippe Madre, founder and director of a clinic for research on the interplay of somatic, psychological and supernatural forces, went to Yugoslavia in August 1983. He could only form a summary judgement as the authorities expelled him from the country before his research was completed. He found the children healthy, both physically and psychically.

In 1984 Italian medical practitioners or professors came frequently to Medjugorje. They sometimes visited Archbishop Franic and shared their opinions of the phenomena with him. Some are on written record as to their professional judgements. Dr Maria Frederica Magatti studied the reaction to stimuli in the moment of ecstasy and concluded that the ecstasy was genuine and the neurological condition of the children was one of absolute normality. Dr Lucia Capello summarised her impression of the visionaries as follows: 'They appeared to me discreet, orderly, clean, careful in their dress, in their words, with complete respect for the milieu.'[1]

The same doctor noted three synchronous movements of the children at the time of the ecstasy: they fall to their knees at the same moment and then though their lips move they are not heard speaking; the sound of the voices return simultaneously to take up the *Our Father* at the third word, the first two having been intoned for them; their heads are raised and their eyes turned upwards at the end of the apparition all at the same time. She concludes: 'The first synchronous movement could be (I say 'could be', not 'is') explained by natural causes; the second and third, especially the second, are not naturally explainable and imply causes perceptible only to the visionaries and not to those observing them.'[2]

In March 1984 Dr Mario Botta, a cardiac surgeon, took a cardiograph of one of the seers, Ivan, at the time of the ecstasy. He concluded that the ecstasy does not alter normal physiology, but transcends it, lifting the visionary on to a higher plane, which renders it impossible to apply the ordinary techniques of medical diagnosis. The conclusion: the phenomenon calls for openness of faith directly related to the Blessed Virgin, whom the visionaries see.

In the following month, Dr Enzo Gabrici, a neuro-psychiatrist, had some interesting comments to make. He examined Vicka and Jakov particularly. Vicka he found a normal, relaxed young person, not in need of emotional support, not a victim of human misunderstanding or of previous traumatic experience. She is not tired by the ecstasy, but seems to be invigorated by it; fatigue generally sets in after a hysterical trance. Dr Gabrici saw that

Jakov, tired after the long church ceremony which follows the apparition, went off spontaneously to play with friends of his own age.

In general, the psychiatrist found no sign of hallucination, epileptic syndrome or any disorder which could change consciousness. The visionaries differ from those subjected to hypnosis by the fact that they remember exactly what takes place during the ecstasy, whereas people who are hypnotised forget what happened during their trance. They are not like spiritualistic mediums, who feel that they are taken over by another personality; on the contrary they retain their identity and manifest it in what they say.

This same note of personal independence was observed by Dr Anna-Maria Francini, who was in Medjugorje at the same time. This is so though they are drawn to an external object. She said that she had never seen attention and interest manifested to such a degree of intensity.[1]

(ii)
Dr Giorgio Sanguinetti

In the following year a psychiatrist from Milan, Dr Giorgio Sanguinetti, spent three days in Medjugorje — 26, 27, 28 April — and drew up a report which is reproduced in full, with his permission:[2]

This commentary relates to my experience in Medjugorje, in Yugoslavia on 26, 27 and 28 April, 1985. The young people, the 'visionaries' whom I got to know were Vicka, Marija, Ivanka, Ivan and Jakov.

At a meeting which took place in Jakov's house as well as one in the presbytery, where the visionaries go through their supernatural experience, I tried to draw on, as much as possible, my experience and knowledge as psychiatrist to observe the circumstances which I shall describe in a simple, clinical perspective, which will have nothing savouring of magic or any special emotional conditioning. I believe that, without too much difficulty, I succeeded in that.

The first thing to strike me both after individual conversations which I had with these young boys and girls, the 'visionaries', and after observing them continuously before, during and after their 'vision', was that I did not find anything psychopathological of a delirious, hallucinatory or hysterical kind in their gestures, their behaviour or their words.

In cases of delirium, a syndrome which I know very well because of the numerous paranoid delirious people with a mystical bent seen at the Clinic, there always follows, though in different ways, a surge of 'omnipotence', not necessarily expressed with noisy insistence or displayed fanatically, but coming across with a quiet, complacent silence: this hides the sense of triumph through a privileged relationship with the transcendant: an illusion. Besides that, a mystical delirious idea is a constant conviction of these patients. It distorts their critical attitude to reality, tainting it with subjective interpretation, with religious practices that are often incongruous, irrational, of a rigid pattern. This conviction is accompanied by a scarcely veiled aggressiveness, distrust and proneness to irritability, and it is sustained by a rigid, one-track thought process.

Generally the relationship of a delirious person towards others is altered, with no genuine ability for spontaneous communication; the interests of such a person are paltry or non-existent, since his whole being hinges on an imperative and overwhelming sense of religious mission and a relationship with the supernatural. Although these individuals declare themselves in different ways to be God's servants, it seems that, with an apparent show of humility, they identify themselves with God. If their delirious state is criticised or called in question they react resentfully and without restraint, intolerant of any contradiction. Their expression is never calm, but shows either an emotional state of tense anxiety and aggressiveness, or in the ecstasy of delirium, a lifeless immobility, which reminds one of a doll's eyes.

A person who manifests a conviction (which he himself considers more or less real) of a privileged relationship with the transcendent, as a defence or compensatory mechanism, hysterical in nature, is not such a clear-cut pathological case. In these cases a mystical conviction appears to be less rigid and less cohesive and it is easily intensified by the presence and participation of others. The person could then adopt extravagant behaviour as of mystical fervour, with theatrical gestures. These phenomena can be displayed, even when the person is alone, but there may be a secret intention of attracting other people's attention. If such a person is asked about his(her) mystical experience, he(she) will strive to heighten curiosity in the person making the inquiry or in the public, either by giving a loquacious account of the facts, or by taking on an ecstatic and dreamy pose, or again by withdrawal and capricious silence.

Such a person will, however, give expression to an emotional state that is incongruous: either supreme joy or over-emphatically expressed suffering, or again a slightly snobbish detachment from the mystical experience (the belle indifférence *of the hysterical subject). He certainly fails on the other hand by a too marked emotional vacuum about the events which he is experiencing. We must remember that mystical exaltation of a hysterical nature can easily be induced by an individual to whom the patient attributes a certain authority, and who exploits the deep suggestibility of the hysterical person. This suggestibility, which is found to some extent in all of us but especially in the immature and in those particularly sensitive to highly emotional stimuli, can induce collective hysteria, wherein, through mutual conditioning, the whole group passes into a state of mystical exaltation; this ends in their having perceptual experience which is hallucinatory.*

Here I consider it of fundamental importance to emphasise that in all my contacts with the young 'visionaries' in Medjugorje I have never discovered, on any occasion, any thought, look, conversation, attitude or behaviour similar to these pathological states which I have listed.

First of all it must be made clear that the 'visionaries' live a normal life; they are integrated in their community and in their families and are treated by others (relatives, friends, priests) as if they were not visionaries; they themselves relate to others as if they were no different from other people, or from themselves before they became 'visionaries'. The phenomenon of collective suggestion which I mentioned earlier is not present. They differ from others only in the time they give to the practice of religion and to the visions; all this is done in a very natural way, without piosity (apparent fervour) or complacency; their behaviour is by preference discreet and, politely, they try to shield themselves from the overpowering pressure of pilgrims, when this is possible. They are quite open to conversation and seem patiently resigned to always having to answer the same questions; in this they are not effusive, nor are they withdrawn or exhibitionist. On the contrary they look calm and peaceful and gentle. They do not try to convince one, and they do not exceed what is asked of them; their smile is not smug or malicious, and it is not artificial. Their movements reflect only kindness and good will. They certainly are not looking for attention or for an audience; they do not offer interpretations or personal opinions about their mystical experiences; all they want to do is to report the facts and admit that they are happy.

At the time of the 'vision' they gather in one room in the presbytery, which is filled with a variety of objects (it serves as a bedroom and study for one of the Friars). On one wall there are several religious pictures —

not very remarkable. By this I mean that even the environment where the 'visions' take place is free of all decorative elements which could favour a special feeling of religiosity. Anyone there with the 'visionaries' finds that he has only the company of a Friar; I found him serene and taciturn, a little abrupt, very much against anything that would tend towards magic or the supernatural. Others present can be admitted for the purpose of research or scientific assessment, but the number is limited (in my case three people).

The Friar and the 'visionaries' sit down on little stools, and recite the Rosary in a thoughtful, recollected manner. Suddenly, at exactly the same time, which is amazing, the young people stand up and line up in front of one of the walls of the room. All of them gaze upwards at the same time, without ever looking at each other, and they seem to stare intensely at something that is outside the room and very far away. They keep their hands joined in prayer, and some of them move their lips, but their voice cannot be heard. After approximately one minute of time (on the occasion I was there), and again, amazingly all together, they give signs of a fleeting bodily tremor, and all withdraw from the place where they were standing. The expression on their faces becomes like ours. Behaving quite normally and with no haste, but deliberately, they go towards a table, do not speak to each other and each taking a pen and a notebook wherein their names are written, they sit down, and again without talking to each other, write down quickly, without pausing, the message which was given to them during the 'vision'. The length of the text differs from one to another. When they have finished, they leave the notebook and the pen, and with a quick handshake they greet us and leave the room, each going about his or her own business.

I know that this description of the 'vision' has already been given by other witnesses; however, I considered it useful to describe it after I had sketched pathological mystical behaviour so that the reader can compare these and take account of the psychic normality of the young 'visionaries'.

Something unusual, extra-ordinary exists but it seems to be strictly limited to the short period of the 'vision'. However, nothing authorises us to say that the 'visionaries', because of this experience, manifest any personality disorders. They seem to be in a world beyond the perception of others and, for what concerns them, to have left our sphere of perception.

(iii)
Dr Henri Joyeux

Together with this considered judgement of a psychiatrist we should also take into consideration the detailed examination of the physical organs affected by a vision (brain, eyes, ears) which was carried out by Professor Henri Joyeux of the prestigious Medical Faculty of Montpelier and some of his colleagues. The different phases of this thoroughly professional investigation and the final report — phrased in strict scientific terms — are dealt with in detail by René Laurentin and Professor Joyeux in their joint work, *Études medicales et scientifiques sur les apparitions de Medjugorje*, which was published in 1985. Marshal McLuhan said that the medium is the message. The fact of this book is itself a message, part of the richly varied phenomenon of Medjugorje. Nothing at all so complete, so patently objective and rigorously scientific has ever been accomplished and made available to the public on a preternatural happening with deep religious import.

The essentials of this study were given to readers of *Paris Match* in the summer of 1985 by Professor Joyeux and are here reproduced in an edited version:[3]

Paris Match: How did you, as a professor of medicine, come to be interested in the apparitions in Medjugorje?

Prof. Joyeux: It was providential. A friend of mine asked me to read Fr Laurentin's book so that he could obtain a scientific view of these supernatural events. During the first weeks of the apparitions, in June 1981, the visionaries had been examined by two Yugoslav doctors to see whether they needed psychiatric treatment. The doctors honestly testified to their psychological and psychiatric fitness. Apart from my being a neurologist or neuro-psychiatrist, I am interested in all phenomena which science finds inexplicable.

The main purpose of our first medical expedition was to take observations only. In March 1984 four of us drove there from Montpelier. I was the only doctor in the group;

a friend, who is an electronic engineer, M. R. Dubois-Chabert, accompanied us. On 24 and 25 March 1984, I witnessed the phenomena of ecstasy, as it has been occurring every day since 24 June 1981. I had expected to see the young people in a particular state of ecstasy: rigid and tense. But the five of them — one does not receive any more visions — Ivanka, 17 years old, Ivan 18, Jakov 13, Vicka 19 and Marija 18, seemed very natural and normal. They certainly did not fall into ecstasy as one would from a ladder. They enter slowly into an ecstasy. No violence or abnormality could be seen in their behaviour. The first two ecstasies I witnessed lasted for less than two minutes. During this time they appeared to be talking to someone we did not see; they articulated words we could not hear. Only towards the end we heard them again praying the 'Our Father'; the Virgin Mary, they explained, usually starts the first words of the 'Our Father'. . . At the end of the ecstasy their gaze followed upwards and one or more said '*ode*' which means 'She is going.'

Paris Match: And then you went back?

Prof. Joyeux: On coming back to Montpelier, I immediately contacted some of my colleagues, specialists in neurology, neuro-psychiatry, sleeping disturbances, neuro-physiology, opthalmology, otorhino-laryngology and cardiology. We decided to conduct a full investigation of these supernatural phenomena. Not all of my colleagues agreed to it, some being reluctant to deal with sacred events, others worried about getting into trouble. We decided, considering the difficult circumstances of the situation in Medjugorje (a communist country, 1200 miles from Montpelier, language) to make several expeditions taking plenty of time. They took place on 9-10 June, 6-7 October, 28-29 December 1984.

Paris Match: Did the children agree readily to being
                    examined?

Prof. Joyeux: When we first arrived in June, we could not
                    get them to agree straightaway. First they could
                    not see the purpose of it, but most of all they
                    felt guilty about disobeying Our Lady since
                    after Doctor Botta, from Milan, did some
                    investigations, they asked her what she thought
                    about these experiments and she had stated: 'It
                    is not necessary.' But young Jakov, because of
                    our insistence, ended the discussion by
                    suggesting, 'We'll ask Our Lady as we are
                    going to see her anyway.' At the end of the
                    ecstasy on 28 June 1984, the young people all
                    agreed that Our Lady's answer was: 'It is good
                    you thought of asking me. You may have it
                    done.' For us who do not see the Virgin, we
                    had the impression that it was the wall in front
                    of which they knelt that had changed their
                    minds completely. They had been against it,
                    but now they had become like lambs, ready to
                    accept whatever we asked.

Paris Match: Which experiments did you perform?

Prof. Joyeux: None of them gave scientific proof that the
                    Virgin is appearing to the visionaries and this
                    is impossible to achieve. These many
                    experiments (polygraphy) can be repeated or
                    multiplied, but I consider that the results we
                    have obtained up to now allow us to draw some
                    important scientific conclusions. With Professor
                    Jean Cadilhac we did, before, during and after
                    the ecstasy an electro-encephalogram (brain-
                    waves recording) and an electro-oculogramme
                    (movement of the eyes). With Doctor J.
                    Philipott we proceeded to study the visual
                    function experimenting with ordinary reflexes
                    in the eyes (reflexes of contraction of the pupil
                    reacting to light, reflex in blinking when the
                    eye is exposed, screen-test consisting in setting

a cardboard screen in front of their eyes during the ecstasy).

We have also studied with Doctor F. Roquerol their hearing faculty by recording the effect of a measured sound injected into the ear of one of the visionaries (70 decibels before the ecstasy and 90 during it, which corresponds to the noise of an internal combustion engine at high speed). Ivan did not hear this noise, though he had reacted to a feeble noise before the ecstasy. This proves that during the ecstasy Ivan is as if disconnected from the outside world, though his hearing faculties function normally. We have also recorded their blood pressure and heartbeats. As I said, the main video-recordings have been examined with the greatest accuracy, especially by Professor J. Cadilhac.

On returning in October the young people objected to being tested again. They again asked Our Lady if they should submit themselves to it. The answer was clear: 'You are free.' So after some explanations of the experiments, they agreed to them.

Paris Match: What questions did you put and what results did you get?

Prof. Joyeux: We needed to know if the cerebral function, the sight function, the hearing and phonation were subject to modifications during the ecstasy in comparison with the period before or after. It was strictly necessary to answer the following questions: Is the ecstasy a state of sleep, a dream-state, an illusion, an illness such as epilepsy, hysteria, a cataleptic state, a nervous disorder, or a pathological ecstasy? The main purpose of our work was to obtain very accurate scientific data by observing how the main organs were functioning . . .In this case you need to rely on ordinary common sense and

medical common sense. As a matter of fact,
there is no need to be a doctor to recognise that
the young people are normal and sane in body
and mind.

Paris Match: In the end, what results did you get and what
                 are your conclusions?

Prof. Joyeux: The phenomena of the apparitions at
                 Medjugorje cannot be explained scientifically.
                 According to experiments carefully conducted,
                 we can affirm that there has been no
                 pathological modification in the parameters
                 which have been investigated. In one word,
                 these young people are healthy and there is no
                 sign of epilepsy nor is it a sleep or dream state.
                 It is neither a case of pathological hallucina-
                 tion nor hallucination in the hearing or sight
                 faculties connected with an abnormality in the
                 functioning of the peripherical sensorial
                 receivers, the hearing faculty or sight. Neither
                 are there any paroxystical hallucinations as
                 testified by the electro-encephalogram nor
                 delirious hallucinations nor acute mental
                 confusion. It is neither hysterical nor a nervous
                 disorder nor a pathological ecstasy because the
                 visionaries show no signs of these conditions
                 in any of the clinical examinations. It cannot
                 be a cataleptic state, for during the ecstasy the
                 facial muscles are operating in a normal way.
                 We can also ascertain that the intentness of the
                 movements of the orbs of the eyes of all the
                 visionaries is in perfect timing with each other
                 at the beginning and the end of the ecstasy.
                 During the ecstasy there is a perfect
                 convergence of their eyes and there is a strong
                 feeling of a face to face encounter between the
                 visionaries and a person we cannot see.

                 Their behaviour presents no pathological
                 signs. During the ecstasy they are in a state of
                 prayer and inter-personal communication.
                 They are not drop-outs, dreamers or people

who are tired or distressed. They appear to be free and happy, well-rooted in their country and the modern world. At Medjugorje, the ecstasies are not pathological or a trick. They do not belong to any scientific denominations. It is more like a state of deep, active prayer, in which they are partially disconnected from the physical world, in a state of contemplation and sane encounter with a person whom they alone see, hear and can touch. We cannot reach the transmitter but we can ascertain that the receivers are in a state of sane and good working order.

Paris Match: So you really believe that the Virgin Mary is appearing to them?

Prof. Joyeux: As scientists we can reach no conclusion in such a matter. This can be answered only by competent people such as the local Bishop and the theological commission which is advising him. In Lourdes the Catholic Church did recognise the eighteen apparitions of the Virgin Mary to Bernadette. At Medjugorje, if the Virgin Mary is appearing, she will have appeared more than 1500 times . . .(In June 1986 it will be over 1800 times) it would not surprise me if one day the Church does recognise these apparitions.

Paris Match: If the Virgin Mary was not appearing, could it be a trick?

Prof. Joyeux: Through the many experiments we have made, we can exclude this. Crowds of people have been there from all over Europe, the United States, and even Japan. . . Most of the French people I have met there, or even those who have been there and whom I have met back here, have been transformed; they feel peaceful and happy and eager to return there. I could not state that the Virgin Mary is appearing in Medjugorje, but if God exists, why should this not be possible?

(iv)
Dr Marco Margnelli

To this judgement, which speaks for itself, may be added the
verdict of an Italian neurophysiologist, Marco Margnelli;[4] he
is a specialist in ecstasy and altered states of consciousness, author
of a work, *La Droga Perfetta*, in which he seeks to establish a
parallel between changes in consciousness induced by chemical
means and by religious experience:

'I am a non-believer', he says disarmingly, 'and therefore I
went to Medjugorje in a critical spirit, ready to welcome any
(evidence of) what would contradict it or show up a fake. In so
far as I am concerned, that is from my studies on change in states
of consciousness in the children, I must say that I have, with
my instruments, verified and documented a genuine state of
ecstasy.'

'Certainly, as far as my opinion goes, there is no lying, and
certainly the children enter a different state of consciousness,
that which is scientifically called the ''alfa'' state. If they then
really see the Madonna, or if it is a case of suggestion
phenomenon inexplicable to us, is a matter for theological
competence, on which I cannot express myself.'

'Certainly', the expert continued, obviously troubled as the
interviewer notes, 'we were in the presence of an extraordinary
phenomenon. Since my return from Yugoslavia, I continually
think of it, and I confess that I also ask myself questions which
are not scientific, and I question myself on the meaning of all
that.'

Dr Margnelli explained that he had not done an electro-
encephalogram, as the French investigating team had already
done this. 'It was also because the three ecstasies at which we
were present were rather brief: 75, 55 and 45 seconds. Probably
our presence somewhat disturbed the children, for their ecstasies
are normally longer.'

The neurophysiologist made several other medical checks and
concluded: 'As a scientist I can only declare that the children
pass really into another state of consciousness, a condition which
one can also reach by the use of meditation practices, such as
auto-training — though not so profoundly; and they are not
lying, otherwise they would react to tests of a sensory and painful
kind.'

And as a man, what did he think? 'As a man the events surrounding this phenomenon also surprise me. There is the videotape of a colleague which records our work, in which one can see the absolutely synchronous movement with which the children act, their looks which all together follow the apparition; there are films taken by people I know and who appear to be honest, of the cross which dominates the hill nearby, which disappears; there is the absolute silence of the birds which gather before sunset in the square (the ecstasies for four years now take place every evening at 18.45 and they go silent, all together, suddenly as soon as the apparition begins.)

'A lady living in Milan, and who seems to me to be a very responsible person has told me a curious fact. Gravely ill with leukaemia, she had gone to Medjugorje, wishing to be embraced by the Madonna; at the end of the ecstasy, one of the children ran to embrace her, among hundreds of people present, saying to her: ''That's the embrace you wished from the Madonna.'' She is now healed of her illness. Another doctor from the Mangiagalli of Milan, Luigi Frigerio, to whom we were indebted for the organisation of our journey, tells that he was singled out in the same way by one of the visionaries who asked in a loud voice, in Croatian: ''Where is the doctor from the Mangiagalli in Milan. The Madonna asked me to tell him that she is pleased with the work he is doing.'' The conclusion of the specialist in ecstasy as a psychic state: 'If anyone had told me these things before my journey here, I would have laughed at it. We are certainly in the presence of an extremely interesting phenomenon. Whether we are dealing with an authentic apparition or something else that we cannot explain, I cannot say; it is a question I prefer not to put myself.'

There is another conclusion: Dr Margnelli, quoted here as saying that he was a non-believer, is now a practising Catholic.

1. References in René Laurentin, *Études medicales et scientifiques sur les apparitions de Medjugorje*, Paris, 1985, 18-26.

2. Dr Sanguinetti's report was communicated to me by Fr Slavko Barberic; the translation is by Olivia de Pasquale. Dr Sanguinetti is a psychiatrist attached to the Institute of Criminology, Milan University.

3. I give the edited version of the interview given to *Paris Match* by Dr Joyeux from Peter Batty's most informative *MIRecorder*, St Joseph's (feastday), 1986, 4-6; the translation is by Ghislaine Raby.

4. Dr Margnelli's interview was given to Viviana Kasam; it appeared in *Corriere della Sera*, 1 November 1985. A team of twelve medical and scientific experts with René Laurentin as adviser, met in Italy and Medjugorje in September 1985. Their findings, in the form of a report, have been forwarded to Rome. It is known that they are favourable to the apparitions.

6

BISHOP PAVAO ZANIC

(i)

Bishop Pavao Zanic is Ordinary of the diocese of Mostar, successor to the heroic Bishop Cule, the second ruler of the diocese who is not a Franciscan. Before his appointment as Auxiliary Bishop in 1970 he worked in parishes in his native diocese of Split and was appointed Rector of the seminary; he was not a professor. His appointment was due in large part to the other bishop we shall have to consider at length, Archbishop Frane Franic, Ordnary of Split and Metropolitan of the area which, incidentally, does not include Mostar.

Bishop Zanic has had worldwide publicity, which does not disturb or dismay him. He is a tough Croatian — in his case the usual Croatian toughness is reinforced. The apparitions occurred during his episcopate and in his conduct ever since his character has been increasingly made known. He is strong-willed, self-assured, combative, uninhibited to the point of recklessness in his judgement of others, expansive in expression, skilful in the use of the media; he is also a very considerable puzzle.

Here we shall let him speak for himself. Comment will be quite clearly separate. The first document is the official statement by him which appeared in the Croatian Catholic paper, *Glas Koncila* (*The Voice of the Council*), 16 August 1981, within two months of the first apparition:

1. The public awaits a statement from us about the events at Medjugorje, where the children assert that the Virgin has appeared to them and continues to appear to them. When those who report on these events are atheistic journalists who believe neither in God nor in the Virgin, it is normal that they should deny any truth in what the children are saying. For us, however, believers, this way of treating the events is offensive and unacceptable. Without any proof they are accusing the children of being manipulated.

2. *The articles which are appearing in the press are written by people who, starting out from a position of power, approach questions of faith and religion with irony and suspicion and make accusations without any proof. Among the numerous insinuations they accuse the priests of 'gathering these small children and teaching them, without the knowledge of their parents, to pretend that the Virgin has appeared to them in human form'.*

3. *It is equally false to say that the ecclesiastical authorities have taken a stand against the events at Bijakovici, declaring them to be superstitious. We also regret that the Church of Hercegovina is accused of mixing in politics and desiring to fool the public.*

4. *Concerning apparitions and miracles in general, we must say that, for us believers, they are possible. We cannot deny Jesus Christ or the lives of the Saints. On the other hand, it is well known that the Church has always been very prudent before offering a positive judgement concerning the apparitions and miracles at Lourdes, Fatima and elsewhere.*

5. *It is true that pious people have often asserted that they saw apparitions when these were rather hallucinations, personal psychological experience, or pure imagination.*

6. *What can we say about what is happening at Bijakovici? One thing is certain: the children are not being urged by anyone, least of all by the Church, to make untruthful statements. For the moment, everything leads us to the conviction that the children are not lying. The more difficult question remains: are we dealing with a purely subjective experience on the part of the children or with a supernatural event?*

7. *We read in the Acts of the Apostles that, when the Jews tried to silence the apostles, a teacher of the law, one highly regarded by all the people, Gamaliel, said to the whole assembly: 'for if this plan or this undertaking is of men, it will fail; but if it is of God, you will not be able to overthrow them.'* (Acts 5:38-39).

The Bishop did not quote the next sentence spoken by Gamaliel: 'You might even be found opposing God' (*ibid.*)

Bishop Zanic showed the same moral fibre in a letter addressed to the president of the Federal Republic of Yugoslavia, Sergej Kraiger, dated 1 September 1981:

'Mr President,

In the newspapers, on the radio and television, the news was given us that on 17 August, 1981, there took place at Citluk a meeting of the communal conference of the Socialist Union of the Working People of Citluk.

At this meeting the events taking place in the parish of Medjugorje were discussed and the following text was released to the press: 'It was decided that it is necessary to explain again to the people more clearly that what the priests Jozo Zovko of Medjugorje and his colleague Ferdo Vlasic, Pavao Zanic, the Bishop of Mostar, and other extremists intend and desire is nothing other than to bring about the dream and project of the terrorist Ustasa organisation. All of this constitutes the gravest abuse of religious sentiment. (Taken from the radio-television news of Sarajevo, 17 August 1981, and from the newspaper *Vecernji List*, 18 August 1981).

I consider it my duty and my right to protest forcefully against such calumnies totally devoid of any foundation. As a Catholic Bishop and the Ordinary responsible for the Diocese of Mostar, for my own part and for that of the priests who have been implicated, I am saddened by these irresponsible calumnies and these attacks whose bad taste will in no way help to ssess serenely the events which have taken place in the parish of Medjugorje.

By such proceedings the fundamental rights of a man and a citizen are violated.

I ask you to accept my protest, which I address to the person who holds the highest responsibility in Yugoslavia, and I ask you to react firmly against such attacks.

I ask you to accept this expression of my respect.

Pavao Zanic, Bishop of Mostar

(ii)

Without prejudging any question, but solely to help the reader understand the next document to be quoted, some history is needed. The Bishop of Mostar, though not a native of the diocese, inherited the complex problem inherent to its government. The Franciscans, as has been seen, were the bulwark of the faith during the centuries of Moslem domination. They were so with their characteristic genius for understanding and meeting the needs of the people.

When the change-over to secular clergy was being effected the faithful were hurt, felt deprived and in places resisted: they refused to accept the ministrations of the secular clergy, going so far in places as to wall up the churches to keep them out.

Bishop Zanic directed a major application of the new policy, building a cathedral in the diocesan city and taking over — with the approval of the Franciscan authorities — three quarters of the city.

Opposition was widespread and intense, masked for the most part, seething in places, smouldering elsewhere. Two ardent young Franciscan priests, probably not much different in outlook and reaction from their brethren, chose, in contrast with the behaviour of these, to show their sentiments publicly. They were Fr Ivica Vego and Fr Ivan Prusina.

That made them marked men. They compounded their manifest dissidence by enlisting the help of the visionaries of Medjugorje. It is only a ten mile run from Mostar and they were at home with their Franciscan brethren, who still minister to the parish. They were now suspended by the Bishop and expelled from their Order by their own superiors. They sought some words of consolation from one of the visionaries, the smiling extrovert, Vicka. They received good measure: a message that allegedly came from Our Lady herself. She approved their decision to remain in Mostar; this had been their policy thus far, on conscientious grounds, since they thought they should not abandon their flock.

Our Lady is also alleged to have censured the Bishop, saying that he had been too severe in his dealings with those she thought innocent. It has been suggested that all this could and should have been kept from him. It is very difficult to understand how this should be. The way in which he learned of it has its own piquant touch. He sent a Jesuit friend, hostile to Medjugorje to do some investigating.

The Jesuit, Fr Grafenauer, changed his mind as he studied the Medjugorje phenomenon on the spot. He was informed about the Madonna's messages concerning the Bishop and on his return to Mostar spoke to him about them. He unfortunately gave the prelate the impression that he had read these damaging comments in a diary kept by Vicka.

The Bishop wanted to lay hands on this diary. It seemed to become an obsession with him. Several times in the course of the year 1983 he tried, during visits to Medjugorje, by letters or by summoning the pastor, then Fr Tomislav Pervan, to his episcopal office, to get hold of the offending document.

He was told that it was non-existent. The spiritual director of the children, Fr Tomislav Vlasic, first repeated what had already been said: that there was no diary. To reassure the Bishop he swore this on a crucifix. For his pains he was to be branded a perjurer throughout the world.

This is the background to the Bishop's change of heart towards Medjugorje. A letter written early in 1984 to a French priest shows just how much he had changed:

Thank you, Father, for the pamphlets. I think that your judgements are right.

I have not the time to translate the materials, I send them to you in French, Italian and English. The propaganda for Medjugorje is terrible. We are preparing for war. It is a struggle for the position taken up (l'affirmation) by a group of Franciscans. In my diocese 80 per cent of the faithful are in the parishes of the Franciscans, they must leave some parishes to the diocesan clergy, they do not want to and from that comes much hurt (mal). The Franciscan Fr Provincial and the government of the Province do not believe in the apparitions and the entire diocesan clergy do not believe in them. The supporters (défenseurs) are disobedient and I must await the judgement of the commission. I am sure it will be negative. All yours in Our Lord and Our Lady, Pavao Zanic. (PS) R. Laurentin is wholly for Medj. (sic). . . If you wish you may publish this letter.

(iii)

In that year, 1984, I went for the first time to Medjugorje, spending a week there from 28 October to 4 November. On my return, after due reflection and recalling all that I had heard on the spot from many people, including Fr René Laurentin, Kevin Devlin of Radio Free Europe, and the Franciscans, and recalling also an interview with Archbishop Frane Franic, I sent a letter in French to the Bishop of Mostar. Here are the important extracts:

I believe that it is my duty to write to you after a week's visit to Medjugorje. I do so without any intention of meddling in things which concern you as Bishop of your diocese, but as a witness to a movement which extends more and more through the Church. I am not a young enthusiast, I am seventy-three years of age. . . (I here gave an account of work I had

done in the field of Marian theology, mentioning that I was a
member of the Pontifical Marian Academy, of the French Society
for Marian Studies and an Associate of the Bollandistes) *I have
specialised in the history of certain apparitions, at Knock in Ireland —
my book on this subject is to appear shortly in France — and at Banneux
in Belgium, where I work every year with the handicapped.*

*My Lord, after having studied the facts of Medjugorje in books and
on the spot I am entirely convinced of the authenticity of these apparitions.
I consider this event one of the most important in the history of modern
Marian devotion. I consider it a dazzling, undeniable sign of the power
of the Virgin Mary, Queen of Peace, a providential sign, merciful at this
moment when mankind appears to be rushing towards the abyss.*

*My Lord, you have here doubtless a role to play. You can accept this
role and be assured of the gratitude and prayers of all those who turn to
the Virgin as their Advocate, as men have always done in moments of
great crisis. Time is of the essence. I know that in many countries devotion
to Our Lady of Medjugorje is growing in fervour, that souls faithful to
the Church and the Virgin await from you a favourable reply to their prayer.
Medjugorje is now a world phenomenon; I do not think that its growth
can be halted. Inevitably your judgement will have a worldwide repercussion.
I know that this is a heavy responsibility, but what prayers ascend to heaven
for the one who carries this responsibility. The Church and the world need
prayers, fervent prayers enlivened by confidence, as I have been able to observe
them at Medjugorje. I counted eleven countries represented there, from as
far away as Reunion, Canada, Mexico, from every European country.
Except in Poland and at Lourdes I have never seen people pray with such
fervour. People will be thankful to you to pronounce on the authenticity
of the apparitions which inspire such fervour. How fine it would be for
Croatia, which we all love and admire, how splendid it would be for the
Church, how consoling for the Holy Father. Abroad people wish to show
great respect, great delicacy towards the Church in Croatia. People only
want one thing: that the will of God our infinitely merciful Father, made
manifest by the Virgin Mary, be entirely accomplished.*

*I beg you My Lord, to kindly accept the expression of my most respectful
good wishes in Our Lord.*

The Bishop replied by a short note dated 24 November, as
follows:

*Thank you for you kind letter. . . but I ask you to publish entirely or
in summary 'Posizione attuale. . .' you will be able to see at once how
things stand. Thanks. I greet you cordially, most faithfully in Christ.*

Along with this letter the Bishop sent a copy of the long memorandum which he calls the 'Posizione attuale. . .'. As he asked, I now publish it entirely. Commentary and extracts from replies by those competent to do so will follow:

(iv)
THE PRESENT POSITION (NON-OFFICIAL) OF THE BISHOP'S CURIA OF MOSTAR WITH REGARD TO THE EVENTS OF MEDJUGORJE

1. Reasons why the Bishop's Curia intervened

The parish of Medjugorje, which belongs to the diocese of Mostar in Hercegovina, Jugoslavia, has become well known throughout the world. The presumed apparitions of Our Lady, described by the press all over the world since June 1981, have become an attraction which creates excessive enthusiasm in many, whilst others fear negative judgement on the part of the Church. The faithful on the whole don't usually know much about theology. They are sometimes inclined to associate their own faith with private revelations and apparitions. Sometimes, they don't even know that not even the Holy Father can oblige people to accept Lourdes, Fatima and other places of heavenly apparitions. Therefore, those who fanatically accept the events of Medjugorje as authentic can regard as enemies of the faith those well-meaning Catholics who do not believe in the 'apparitions' of Medjugorje. Since this creates tension and division amongst the faithful, the Bishop's Curia of Mostar is obliged to intervene even prior to the final opinion formed by the Medjugorje Commission to warn the public about the unwise propaganda and the irresponsible organisation of pilgrimages to Medjugorje. Such things can do more harm than good to the Church, because there is real reason to fear that all this might disgrace the Church and the Catholic faith and might greatly delude religious people.

Furthermore, the Bishop's Curia of Mostar is aware of its great responsibility before God and man in publishing this text. From the start, the Bishop has invited the Franciscans of Medjugorje, both in spoken and in written form, not to indulge in wild propaganda and not to prevent the Church from reaching a judgement. The desire to assert themselves in order to defend

their position in the notorious 'Hercegovina case' as well as
important material gain has eliminated all barriers and
consideration. Various bits of information and articles in
newspapers and magazines, news bulletins, booklets, books,
articles by well-known but irresponsible theologians, TV films,
video cassettes, superficial journalists, exalted charismatics. . .
have created an all-round euphoria that has forced the Bishop's
Curia to make its present position public as regards the events
of Medjugorje, even though this position is not yet official.

2. Suspects and doubts
The Bishop, Mons. Pavao Zanic has followed the events of
Medjugorje right from the start and thought to himself: If the
scandalous 'Hercegovina case' (re the Franciscans' disobedience
with regard to the Decrees of the Holy See concerning the
parishes) that has been going on for years in Hercegovina has
not been resolved by man, then perhaps God has chosen to send
us Our Lady to encourage the disobedient to be obedient and
show love towards the Church.

During the first weeks, when the influx of people to Medjugorje
started to increase, the local Bishop had a conversation with the
'visionaries' (on 21 July 1981). Even at the beginning certain
things sounded like lies (for example, the reasons why the boys
and girls went to Podbrdo, the place of the 'apparitions', differed,
i.e. to round up the sheep, to pick flowers, to have a cigarette
or because the watch was slow etc.) but the Bishop didn't consider
that this was of any importance. But, he asked the 'visionaries'
if Our Lady had said anything about the 'Hercegovina case'.
They answered that Our Lady had told them that everything
would soon be solved. Then when they asked her if it was
necessary to pray for this to happen, She replied: There's no
need to! Later the boys and girls repeated the question to Our
Lady a second time and a third time but the answer was always
the same.

After the seventh 'apparition' that took place not in
Medjugorje, but in Cerno (a few kilometres from Medjugorje,
where the 'visionaries' were taken by car by state officials), the
boys and girls told the parish priest the same evening that Our
Lady had said that there would be three more apparitions: on
Wednesday, Thursday and Friday, i.e., on 1, 2 and 3 July

(1981). The last apparition would be on Friday. Some priests were also present at this last 'apparition' which took place in the parish house of Medjugorje. When the 'apparition' was over, the 'visionaries' said: This is the last apparition! So, how can one explain the fact that the 'apparitions' continued and still haven't finished?

At the beginning, the 'visionaries' were very excited, exalted and even fainted. A hallucinatory state was even transferred to the pilgrims, many of whom 'saw' various things and people and told each other ridiculous stories. It was very difficult to ascertain the truth and the falsity of such stories. At the end of summer 1981, when serious doubts arose as to the authenticity of the apparitions, it wasn't easy to explain how everything had started, what the meaning of the events was, and what truth was to be found in the descriptions of the light phenomenon and the presumed healings. But there were also many reasons to doubt the authenticity of the apparitions and to seriously consider hallucination. In fact, Our Lady was 'seen' for the first time by Ivanka Ivankovic, whose mother had died a few months beforehand; she wanted to know what had become of her mother. Then, in the apparition at Cerno, again Our Lady first 'appeared' to her.

The Bishop was right to have had serious doubts about the 'apparitions' even before having the famous extract from the diary of the main 'visionary', Vicka Ivankovic (in February 1983). In fact on 14 January 1982 the following persons came to see the Bishop: Vicka Ivankovic, Marija Pavlovic and Jakov Colo. They told the Bishop that Our Lady had said that he had been hasty in his decisions regarding the Friars. The Bishop asked several times if there was anything in the 'apparitions' that could interest him (The Bishop, in fact had heard about Our Lady's 'messages' to the two Friars of Mostar from a member of local government). But the 'visionaries' categorically denied having any other message.

But on 3 April 1982, Vicka Ivankovic and Jakov Colo came to see the Bishop having 'been sent by Our Lady'. Vicka said textually (recorded with tape-recorder): 'Our Lady reprimanded us because last time we didn't tell everything. She spoke about this case (the Hercegovina case) and burst out laughing and said that "She, alone, would sort out everything." I haven't the slightest idea what it's all about. Then she began to laugh. Then Jakov and I had fits of laughter. The people asked us: why are you laughing? We said that we were laughing because she told us to laugh. She told us about these Friars, that they, like everyone else, like working for the Church and celebrating Mass. The priests are not guilty at all. She also mentioned their names, I didn't know who they were, than later I saw them — Prusina and Vego. She says they are not guilty at all. She repeated this twice. Jakov heard, and Marija was also present'.

The Bishop: She told you these things, concerning them, before 14th January 1982 when you last came to see me, so, did she reprimand you for not having referred these things to me?

Vicka: Yes, for this reason she reprimanded me three times because I didn't come and because I didn't tell you.

The Bishop insisted further: We're still not getting through to each other. The last time you came to me was on 14 January. Before this date, had Our Lady told you to give me the message about the chaplains from Mostar?

Vicka: Yes, but I didn't pass on the message and so she reprimanded me for not having done my duty. I spoke too much and I couldn't remember.

Yet the Bishop had asked her explicitly about the chaplains!

Furthermore, three days before the above-mentioned date, i.e. on 11 Jauary 1982, Vicka had written the following in her secret diary: 'We asked again about the two chaplains from Mostar. Our Lady repeated twice what she had previously said'. We must remember that Vicka had spoken to 'Our Lady' about the same topic on two previous occasions, i.e. on 19 December 1981 and on 3 January 1982. Therefore her behaviour betrays an obvious contradiction and lie!

Let us add some other factors that have made us seriously doubt the 'apparitions' of Medjugorje.

Towards the end of 1981 and during 1982, various 'miracles' and absurd things happened. People spoke about them a great deal. Some of the gossip was even put into writing. For example, Vicka, in her diary, of which we have a copy, writes that they, the 'visionaries', had also seen on several occasions, alongside Our Lady, Friar Jozo Zovko, the parish priest of Medjugorje who was in prison. They had also seen Ivan Dragicevic who was in a Franciscan seminary in Visoko. In this same diary, we find fantasies concerning Brother Jozo Zovko in prison, like for example: the guards turn off the lights and lock Zovko's cell door, but the light comes back on and the door opens of its own accord! Or something else like this: 'Friday 4 September 1981. Today, we waited for Our Lady at Marija's house. Marija, Ivanka, Jakov and I (Vicka) were there. We started to pray at 6.20 pm. Our Lady immediately appeared. We asked her about the Friars and nuns from our parish. We asked about the man who saw Jesus along the road when he took the people in his car. He met a man who was covered in blood — this man was Jesus — and he (Jesus) gave him a handkerchief soaked in blood and told him to throw it into the river. Driving on further, he met a woman, it was the Blessed Virgin Mary, and she asked the driver for the blood-soaked handkerchief. The man gave her a handkerchief that belonged to him, but Our Lady asked for the blood-stained handkerchief. When the man gave her the blood-stained handkerchief, Our Lady said: "If you hadn't given it to me, it would have been the last judgement for everyone!" Our Lady said that this was true. This is what Vicka writes in her diary and this is also what the 'visionaries' have told in various interviews.

The Bishop asked the 'visionaries' who it was who had told them to say seven Our Fathers, a Hail Mary, a Glory Be to the Father and the Credo. Some answered: Our Lady, others said: our grandmothers, and others said: this is how we pray in Hercegovina. All this makes one seriously doubt the authenticity of the 'apparitions'.

3. The 'big sign'

Right from the beginning of the 'apparitions', the 'visionaries' said that Our Lady would leave a sign, visible to all, as proof of her apparitions. In connection with this sign, Vicka wrote the following in her diary: In explaining when the sign would happen, Our Lady said the following:

'It will soon come' (27 August 1981)
'Just a little more patience' (29 August 1981)
'Come on, just a little more patience' (31 August 1981)
'Again, just a little more patience' (3 September 1981).

Vicka told someone who in turn told the Bishop in confidence that the sign would happen before her Dad came home from Germany. And he was due home at Christmas 1981. This sign, which attracted the pilgrims, was mentioned to the public several times: at the feast of the Immaculate Conception in 1981, at Christmas during the same year and on New Year's Day 1982. Obviously, when nothing happened, the 'visionaries' said 'we didn't say anything about it!'

With a decree of 11 January 1982, the Bishop nominated a Commission to collect and examine the material concerning the events of Medjugorje. The Commission held some meetings. At the second meeting on 10 May 1982, the Bishop asked two members of the Commission to go to Medjugorje to ask the 'visionaries' to describe and give the date of the 'big sign'. The description had to be written in two copies: one for the Bishop's Curia and one for the 'visionaries'. The copies were to be put in envelopes, then closed and sealed with the seal of the Bishop's Curia of Mostar. But the 'visionaries' replied that Friar Tomislav Vlasic ordered them to ask Our Lady for permission to write it. But Our Lady categorically forbade anything to be written down. (Brother Ivan Dugandzic, a member of the Commission, later admitted having informed Friar Tomislav Vlasic of what the Commission and the Bishop were planning to do). Then, the two members of the Commission went straightaway to Sarajevo to ask the 'visionary' Mirjana Dragicevic the same thing (she has a telephone at home). She said that she had asked Our Lady who had forbidden that anything be written about the 'sign'. Then, a member of the Commission went to Visoko to ask the 'visionary' Ivan Dragicevic the same thing (the seminary telephone is under the control of the local state authorities). This 'visionary' described everything, without the least hesitation, and his envelopes, sealed with the seal of the seminary, are to be found in the seminary and in the Bishop's Curia of Mostar.

Then on 3 August 1982, the Bishop summoned all the 'visionaries' to Mostar. In the presence of some members of the Commission, he asked them, separately, to describe the sign, to indicate the date of its appearance and just place the answer in an envelope stamped with the seal of the Bishop's Curia and then take it home without leaving a copy at Mostar. And when the 'sign' takes place, the envelope could be opened to see if the prophecy corresponded to the facts. But the 'visionaries' refused to do so. Then the Bishop asked Ivan Dragicevic if Our Lady had reprimanded him for having described the 'sign' at Visoko. He replied: 'No!'

The Bishop had the cassette of the recorded speech of the 'visionary' Mara Jerkovic from Medjugorje, but she doesn't belong to the group of six 'visionaries'. She says that one day a big sanctuary of Our Lady will rise on the hill of the apparitions because of the extraordinary presence of God and Our Lady. There will be a big church with a big statue of Our Lady in front of it. There will be a big lake, surrounded by red and white roses. There will be stone steps from the Church down to the village below.

4. The 'prophecies' of the charismatic people

A special insertion Number 11 (1981) published by Lucy Rooney SND (Fr Robert Faricy's secretary) includes the following passage: 'In May 1981, an international conference for the leaders of the Charismatic Movement took place in Rome. One of the leaders present from Jugoslavia was Fr Tomislav Vlasic OFM. During the conference he asked some leaders to pray with him for the welfare of the Church. One of the leaders that was praying with him, Sister Briege McKenna, had a mental vision of Fr Vlasic sitting down surrounded by a big crowd; a stream of water was flowing from the chair. Another, Emile Tardif, OP, said as a prophecy "Don't worry, I am sending you my Mother". And so, Fr Vlasic returned to Jugoslavia. Two weeks after his return, Our Lady started to appear to a group of boys and girls in the Franciscan parish of Medjugorje. New Life is flowing.'

One has to wonder who on earth is this Fr Tardif who can send Our Lady wherever he wants?

Right from the beginning, the events of Medjugorje were in the hands of the charismatic people: Friar Jozo Zovko, Friar Tomislav Vlasic and others. People often say that the 'messages' of Our Lady are evangelical. They obviously are evangelical, at least those that were propagated the most. They had to be such, because they were composed by Fr Tomislav Vlasic who is familiar with theology and knows what to say. It can be very effective to appeal for prayer, penance and conversion. Those that came to Medjugorje were so struck and enthusiastic about the praying and confessing that many of them became converted because they believed Our Lady appeared. *But such facts are not proof of the authenticity of the apparitions!* It's well-known in the history of the Church that behind the heretics and schismatics there were masses of followers doing great penance and having pity, sharing all with the poor, walking barefoot, remaining celibate etc. But such signs were not proof that the heretics were on the right track! It's also well-known that people pray in just as devout a way both in front of a false relic and an authentic one, both in places where Our Lady has appeared (like Lourdes and Fatima) and elsewhere where there was just hallucination.

Our people didn't know much about similar places of 'apparitions' like for example Garabandal in Spain where Our Lady 'appeared' to four girls from 1961 to 1964. There the same thing happened as in Medjugorje — the invitation to prayer and penance and to conversion, threats to the world if it didn't become converted, and especially a 'big sign' because of which everyone believed that Our Lady really did appear. After four years of such 'apparitions' one of the 'visionaries', Maria Cruz, said: 'I have never seen Our Lady!' There was no trace of the 'big sign'. The Commission, nominated by the Bishop of Santander, declared that the apparitions were not supernatural.

The same thing happened in San Damiano in Italy. For years, those who propagated the 'apparitions' of Garabandal and San Damiano didn't heed ecclesiastical discipline and the local Bishops' decisions. Finally, the world accepted that the 'apparitions' were mere hallucinations.

5. In agreement with the Holy See

The Bishop of Mostar tried to inform the Holy See of all the events of Medjugorje. He spoke to the Holy Father twice about this. The Pope recommended him to be very cautious ('to proceed with great caution'!) On 2 June 1982, the Bishop went to Rome again and presented the Holy See with a report. He was warned not to be hasty in judging because time would bring new pros and cons. However, the 'apparitions' are still happening, and something new will probably happen. It wasn't possible not to do anything since propaganda has done its work and has had its effects — they wanted something concrete to put before the Bishop and the Commission: here you are, see for yourselves, there are masses that pray and that are being converted, there are healings etc.

The Bishop continuously warned the Franciscans of Medjugorje not to propagate the authenticity of the apparitions, not to go against the Church's judgement. And he repeated this sentence: If Our Lady makes an authentic sign, those who don't believe in the 'apparitions', above all the local Bishop, will come to Medjugorje and deny what they previously said. But if one day we come to the conclusion that the apparitions are not authentic, what will those who now propagate Medjugorje say to the people?

6. The diary of the 'apparitions'

What the Holy See said when it suggested going about things cautiously because time would produce new pros and cons came true to a certain extent at the end of January 1983. In fact, a Slovenian Jesuit, Fr Radogost Grafenauer, who introduced himself as an 'expert in discerning spirits' became interested in Medjugorje. He came to the Bishop's Curia in Mostar in January 1983. He stayed there for three days: he listened to tapes of the interviews and things told by the 'visionaries', he took note of several things and said at the end: 'I'm not going to Medjugorje. Nothing happens there'. The Bishop replied: 'Do go and see what there is!' So he went. He arrived there and stayed for some time, he questioned the 'visionaries' and came to the conclusion that 'Our Lady' didn't appear there. But during the conversation with Fr Tomislav Vlasic, he became totally converted and accepted the authenticity of the apparitions. When the friars saw that he firmly believed in them, they gave him the chance to have a look at the diary of the main 'visionary', Vicka Ivankovic, and at the chronicle of the apparitions kept by Fr Vlasic. Fr Grafenauer copied from the chronicle and compared what was written in the diary with all the messages that Our Lady had had for the local Bishop. On 16 February 1983 the priest himself sent the Bishop Our Lady's 'message' concerning the two chaplains from Mostar, Friar Ivan Prusina and Friar Ivica Vego who had been expelled from the Order, suspended from the priesthood and suspended *a divinis* (on 29 January 1982). The following are the extracts from Vicka's Diary:

19 December 1981 - Saturday
I asked about the Hercegovina problem and especially about Fr Ivica Vego.
Our Lady said that the guiltiest person in this affair is Bishop Zanic. She said that Fr Ivica Vego isn't guilty and that the Bishop has all the power. He told him (Fr Vego) to stay in Mostar and not to go away.

3 January 1982 - Sunday
All of us visionaries asked Our Lady about Ivica Vego. Our Lady answered: 'Ivica isn't guilty. If he is expelled by the friars, may he be brave! I say every day: Peace, peace and there is more and more anxiety. Ivica is not guilty. Let him remain!' She repeated this three times. All of us heard and we told him about it. 'The Bishop isn't regulating things and therefore he is guilty. He won't always be Bishop. I will show justice in the kingdom'. This lasted ten minutes and everything referred to Ivica.

11 January 1982 - Monday
We asked again about the two chaplains from Mostar. Our Lady repeated twice what she had said before.

20 January 1982 - Wednesday
We asked what Fr Ivica Vego and Fr Prusina will do now that they are expelled. (They weren't yet expelled! Note from the Bishop's Curia). Our Lady replied: 'They are not guilty. The Bishop has been hasty in his decision. May they stay, may they pray a great deal and may the people also pray for them'.

16 April 1982 - Friday
I (Vicka) asked some questions concerning Ivica Vego and Ivan Prusina and Our Lady herself answered some of my questions. 'Our Lady — the newspapers say that Ivica and Ivan have been expelled by the Friars.'
She answered: 'They haven't been expelled!' Then she smiled. 'Tell them to be calm and brave. There are many trials. They must persevere. The newspapers can write what they wish, they (the two expelled Friars) mustn't pay any attention to them, because it's not important'.

'Our Lady, give us peace once and for all, so that Ivica and Ivan won't have any more problems.'

Our Lady answered: 'I will grant peace in everything'. She also mentioned some Friars from Mostar but added 'never mind, I will get the chance to talk to them, there are three principals'.

Our Lady, what will happen to the Bishop? Will he change his attitude?

Our Lady answered: 'I don't want to hurry. I'm waiting to see if he will give in as a result of my messages sent to him by you.'

But for me (Vicka), this is something very difficult. It's all too much for me, and for Ivan and Ivica as well!

Yesterday, while we were with Our Lady, we asked her if we could say an Our Father for the two of them.

She at once said: 'Yes'. And she began to pray. When we finished, she smiled and said to me: 'The only thing you think of is those two Friars'.

I replied: 'Yes, I can't think of anything else!'

26 April 1982 - Monday

The Bishop has none of the real love of God for those two. May Ivica and Ivan be calm as regards the Bishop, since he has burdened them with a great weight in order to free himself of this weight. He has begun with the younger ones and intends to proceed onwards little by little. I know that this is a big shock for them. But they mustn't worry at all. They must forget about the whole thing. May they learn to suffer for justice. What the Bishop is doing is not the will of God: innocent, blameless, and punished in this way! God would not allow this, but the Bishop does not act according to the will of God, and can do whatever he wants. But one day justice will be seen that hasn't been seen for some time. I will start to sort everything out, little by little and a lot of Friars will be enlightened by immense happiness'.

End of August 1982

Vicka told us more or less the following:

Our Lady told me that Ivan and Ivica mustn't leave Mostar!

29 September 1982 - Wednesday

Friar Ivica asked: 'Must we leave Mostar or stay here?'

Our Lady answered: 'Stay!'

Having heard about these 'messages', the Bishop asked Friar Tomislav Vlasic who was then chaplain of Medjugorje and the visionaries' spiritual guide how it was that they had hidden these messages for over a year from the Bishop of the district?

Fr Vlasic: We didn't want Medjugorje to be burdened with the Hercegovina case.

The Bishop: If you think that these messages in the diary, addressed to the Bishop, have really been pronounced by Our Lady, then why hide their content from the public? The faithful can and must know about them. Why not publish them?

Fr Vlasic: I am convinced that those words have come from Our Lady. But I wanted to have respect for the Bishop. . . You publish them!

The Bishop: I will publish them when I consider it right to do so!

Therefore, at that time (February 1983), Fr Vlasic was convinced that the words and messages contained in the extract from the diary were really from Our Lady. It didn't occur to him to deny the existence of the diary. But later it occurred to him and to other brothers to make sure that Our Lady's verbal attacks against the Bishop constitute the strongest proof of the authenticity of the apparitions. Therefore, a few months later, he and the others began to claim that that extract had been copied from some sheets of paper that had been given to Vicka, *but that the diary didn't exist.*

With an official letter dated 12 April 1983, the Bishop asked the parish priest of Medjugorje and Vicka Ivankovic to bring him the diary. On 7 May 1983, Vicka wrote to the Bishop, and apart from other things, made this important statement: '*I have recently found out that typed extracts from my diary have been distributed — my diary is private and written exclusively for myself from the very start of the apparitions of the Blessed Virgin Mary at Crnica in the parish of Medjugorje.*' (Fr Vlasic said before the Commission on 25 May 1984 that this same letter was written by a priest and given to Vicka to sign.) (It just goes to show how these manipulations all come out in the end!) But we are interested in assessing the truth. In the above sentence, Vicka confirms having the diary, having written it for private use, and says that the published extracts are from her private diary! *Not really very private! It has been shown to Fr Grafenauer!*

On 17 May 1983, the Bishop wrote to Vicka again asking her to bring him the diary of the apparitions. Vicka came to the Bishop's Curia on 27 May 1983 bringing an agenda of the apparitions, covering those during February and March 1982, about thirty days. But this agenda was got together 'ad hoc' to deceive the Bishop. From then on, even Vicka began to deny having written the diary! 'That's all there is to it', she said, contradicting what she had written to the Bishop on 7 May 1983.

On 16 June 1983, the Bishop wrote to the parish priest of Medjugorje for the third time asking him to bring him the chronicle of the apparitions and asking Vicka to bring him the diary. They didn't bring the chronicle or the diary but started to say that the diary didn't exist!

On 16 November the Bishop went to Medjugorje to ask for the chronicle of the apparitions and Vicka's diary again. He finally managed to get four volumes of the chronicle. The diary? The principal person behind Medjugorje, Fr Tomislav Vlasic, was prepared to swear on the cross that the diary didn't exist. The Bishop showed him the letter from Vicka Ivankovic (of 7 May 1983) and the letter from Fr Grafenauer (of 14 November 1983), from which it is clear that the diary exists! But he declared that he was willing to swear all the same.

When he got back home, the Bishop started to look at the chronicle. From a first glance it was clear that the chronicle had been 'edited' and certain words that were unsuitable had been eliminated or wiped out. But he was surprised when he came across something that had escaped the attention of the writer, Fr Vlasic. The following was written:

16 March, 1982. Today I spoke with the visionary Vicka for slightly longer. Since she hasn t brought *her diary of the apparitions* to me for quite some time, I felt it was necessary to question her for longer. The essential elements are as follows: She records eveything *in her diary* in chronological order. . .'

How about that! But that's not all. Fr Vlasic, perhaps forgetting what he had written on 16 April 1982, swore on the cross in the presence of the Bishop on 14 December 1983, using the following words:

'Thus may God Almighty, the Father, the Son and the Holy

Ghost help me! *I have never seen the hidden diary* which the Bishop talks about, nor am I aware that Vicka's diary exists. I have done my best to find out from Vicka in a very sincere way if it exists and from her conversation, I am persuaded that *this diary does not exist.* During this period, I suggested to Vicka that she write a diary and from what I can gather, she hasn't written it. I know nothing else about this diary. Amen!'

Sapienti sat!

Furthermore, relistening to the recorded conversation with Vicka on 3 April 1982, Vicka's words can be heard: *'I have the diary at home. Every day, the date and everything is recorded'.* But Fr Vlasic goes his own way!

7.   *The two ex-chaplains of Mostar, Prusina and Vego*

In September 1980, the Bishop of Mostar, Mgr Petar Cule resigned and his auxiliary, Zanic, took over the running of the diocese. At that time the new cathedral parish was formed, which replaced the Franciscan parish of Mostar (this change was brought about by order of the Holy See and through an internal agreement with the Franciscans), the only one to exist in a city of about 25,000 Catholics. But the friars didn't accept the fact that their parish was being divided. A very big quarrel broke out. Two Franciscans, chaplains of the Franciscan parish of Mostar, Fr Ivan Prusina and Fr Ivica Vego, who were amongst the most stubborn and contumacious, behaved in such a way that they were hit by the severest of all ecclesiastical sanctions: suspension *a divinis,* expulsion from the priesthood, expulsion from the Franciscan Order. This decision was reached after eight serious warnings by the General Curia of the Friars Minor of Rome. The decision was made on 29 January 1982. But such a decision didn't prevent the lawless behaviour of the two ex-friars. Up till now they have lived in the Franciscan convent of Mostar and have continued their priestly activity in the area of the newly created cathedral parish.

These two disobedient ex-Friars, Prusina and Vego, have been protected and defended by 'Our Lady' of Medjugorje from 1981 onwards, according to the messages contained in Vicka Ivankovic's diary, which we have described at length in the preceding pages.

These two ex-Friars, out of gratitude to 'Our Lady' of Medjugorje, together with the friars of the parish of Medjugorje and other Franciscans who are not very interested in peace and obedience to their superiors and to the Church, come forward as tireless propagators of the 'apparitions' of Medjugorje! These two ex-Friars even came to Medjugorje often to hear people's confession, as though they had been rewarded and not suspended *a divinis!*

8. The Commission was enlarged

The initial Commission of four members, nominated on 11 January 1982, to examine the events in the parish of Medjugorje, was extended at the beginning of 1984 to include twenty people, including the nomination of ecclesiastics chosen amongst experts in theology in the various Faculties of Theology in Croatia and Slovenia and representatives of medical sciences.

This Commission met for the first time on 23 and 24 March 1984. The members had about 180 pages of various material useful for their discussion on Medjugorje. The commission declared that it was against priests and laymen organising pilgrimages to Medjugorje. But the defenders of the 'apparitions' increased their propaganda especially on the 'miracles'. Until then, people had spoken of about 200 'healings'. The Bishop had asked the Friars of Medjugorje to present a medical report on the healings. They brought about ten certificates, but they were just ordinary certificates that are given when someone is discharged from hospital, and nothing else!

The Commission met again last May and then on 10 and 11 October last. During the last meeting a statement was issued which said that there was no scientific documentation of the presumed healings, that the Commission disapproved of the organisation of pilgrimages to Medjugorje, that it has decided to continue investigating the events but 'already sees certain difficulties of a disciplinary and theological nature in the messages of Medjugorje'.

Let us also add the following Declaration of the Episcopal Conference of Jugoslavia, made on 12 October 1984:
'The Bishops have considered the development of the events in Medjugorje, Hercegovina. Judgement on the meaning of the events in this place will be made when the experts' inquiries have

been completed, and these inquiries are to be made exclusively by competent ecclesiastical authorities. Therefore, official pilgrimages to Medjugorje must not be organised; the judgement of those who are responsible for the life of the Church must not be prejudiced'.

9.   'Love of the truth' by René Laurentin

Unfortunately, the well-known French Mariologist, R. Laurentin, has greatly contributed to the uncontrolled propaganda of the Medjugorje events. He came to Mostar before Christmas 1983 and asked the Bishop why he didn't believe in the authenticity of the apparitions. The Bishop replied:

— According to the entries in 'Vicka's diary', 'Our Lady' speaks out against the Bishop saying that he is responsible for all the problems concerning the 'Hercegovina case'. She defends the two Franciscan chaplains, expelled from the Order and suspended *a divinis*! But they are continuing to carry out their damaging activity in the diocese. 'Our Lady' recommends that they stay here!

— Then the Bishop explained to Fr Laurentin about the visionaries' lies and Fr Tomislav Vlasic's perjury re Vicka's 'private' diary.

When he heard these things, R. Laurentin advised the Bishop not to publish them because it would be damaging with regard to the numerous conversions amongst the pilgrims. This advice scandalised the Bishop. He wondered if such an attitude was compatible with scientific investigation worthy of a famous Mariologist!

Then when Fr Laurentin came to visit the Bishop again on 9 August 1984, while he was talking he denied having advised the Bishop what is mentioned above, much to the surprise of the Bishop! But the Bishop answered him in this way: If Our Lady appears in Medjugorje, then lies, perjury and twisting of the truth aren't necessary for this to happen!

In the meantime, Laurentin, together with Fr Lj. Rupcic, a Franciscan from Hercegovina, a professor of Franciscan theology in Sarajevo who was co-author, published a book on Medjugorje. It was written in French and later an Italian translation was published. The book cost 76 French francs, and, as he himself says, 75,000 copies were sold in four months (approximately

$600,000 - six hundred thousand dollars). Fr Laurentin widely advertised his book, first in France then in Italy.

His articles, originally published in *La France Catholique*, were translated into Croatian and appeared in *Glas Koncila* with specific descriptions of the 'visionaries'. But what was most unexpected on the part of this Mariologist was the defamation of the Bishop of Dubrovnik, Mgr Severin Pernek, who together with the superiors of the seminary, supposedly pressurised the seminarist 'visionary' Ivan Dragicevic to such an extent that he no longer felt at ease in the seminary. When the superiors and the Bishop reacted, each in his own way, R. Laurentin said that his articles had been badly translated into Croatian! He wasn't thinking about the Bishop of Dubrovnik, but about the Bishop of Mostar! Instead, the Bishop of Mostar has never said a word in the presence of the seminarists of Medjugorje!

In the Italian edition of Laurentin's book, *The Virgin Appears in Medjugorje*, Queriniana, Brescia, 1984, pages 167-168, the author says that the fifty-six cases published by Fr Rupcic were referred to Dr Mangiapan, chairman of the Medical Bureau of Lourdes. He divided them statistically and according to their 'value'. But Fr Laurentin omits referring to the very negative judgement expressed by Dr Mangiapan: "To conclude, if we are to adhere to the rules of the Medical Bureau, then all of this "dossier" is really of very little value. . . and *as such* is of no use. . . nor can it support a valid argument in favour of a place of apparitions". (International Medical Association of Lourdes, Nos 205-206, April 1984, page 14). After being judged in such a way by the competent Medical Bureau of Lourdes, one would expect the Italian edition not to refer to the 'healings', or at least not to refer to the 'healed' people who had since died!

Anyway, Fr Laurentin has tarnished his fame as a Mariologist by leading wild propaganda for the authenticity of the apparitions of Medjugorje!

10. *47 other 'visionaries'*

The Bishop of Mostar has listed the names of forty-seven of the 'visionaries' outside Medjugorje, resident in other parishes of the diocese. All boast of similar 'visions', but since their parish priests don't support them, several no longer have such 'apparitions'. These too, spoke of 'ten secrets', a 'big sign' etc.

One of the 'visionaries' said the following to the Bishop, which was registered: 'I wanted very much to see Our Lady. One day, in my room, first a light then Our Lady appeared. Some days, I see her all day, wherever I go, in the house, in the field, in the bus, in the church. . .'. These are signs of typical hallucinations.

The book entitled *Vraies et fausses apparitions dans l'Église*, lists 230 places of great importance and miraculous events over the last fifty years. But Banneux, Beauraing and Syracuse in Sicily are the only places that have been approved of from an ecclesiastical point of view. One could ask of the other 227 places — How did it begin? Why did it begin! How is it that some people have visions and others don't? One thing is certain: Our Lady isn't there!

11. Attempts to influence the Bishop by intimidation

The 'visionaries' as well as the Franciscans of Medjugorje, should have worked in strict and sincere collaboration with the Bishop and should have informed him of all the 'messages' right from the beginning. We can now make this statement: the biggest novelty of the apparitions of Medjugorje consists *in declaring the local Bishop responsible* for all the problems caused by the disobedient Friars, and *in claiming* that the two chaplains, who have been expelled from the Order and suspended *a divinis, are innocent.* All the rest is like what happens in other apparitions, whether true or false: prayer, penance, conversion.

Now one wonders why the 'visionaries' and their spiritual fathers, the Franciscans of Medjugorje, kept Vicka's famous diary a secret from the Bishop for over a year? Vicka's diary contained a record of the above-mentioned 'message' and events. Perhaps they were expecting the Bishop to declare the apparitions authentic and then they would come out with their 'weapons'!

The fact that the 'visionary' Ivan Dragicevic, the ex-seminarist, intimidated the Bishop is symptomatic. This intimidation was expressed in a letter written on 21 June 1983 and sent to the Bishop of the district:

On 19 June 1983, Our Lady appeared to me, together with the visionaries Jakov, Marija and Ivica. First she answered some of my questions about the sick people, then she began to speak about you, Bishop. This is what she said to me:

'Tell the Bishop that I am asking him urgently to approve of the events in the parish of Medjugorje, before it's too late. I want him to approach the events with great understanding, love and a great sense of responsibility. I don't want him to cause opposition amongst the priests or to draw attention to their negative attitude.

The Holy Father has told all the Bishops to carry out their duties in their dioceses and to solve problems and quarrels. The Bishop is the principal father of all the parishes in Hercegovina. He is the head of the Church in Hercegovina. Therefore I am asking him to accept these events.

I am sending him a second-last warning. If he doesn't accept these events and behave properly, he will hear my judgement and the judgement of my Son, Jesus. If he doesn't heed my message, then this means that he hasn't found the way of my Son, Jesus!'

Our Lady has asked me to pass on this message to you.
Bijakovic 21 June 1983

Yours sincerely,
Ivan Dragicevic

Even though the letter was hand-written by Ivan Dragicevic, ex-seminarist who missed two school years in Visoko and in Dubrovnik, we still cannot say with certainty that it was composed by him. But who is it that attributes absurd threats to the Blessed Virgin, on her part and on the part of her Son, if the Bishop doesn't accept the authenticity of the apparitions? According to the Catholic faith, no one is obliged to believe in apparitions and private revelations! How is it that the Bishop will be judged by Our Lady if he doesn't believe in these apparitions? Perhaps all the others will be judged as well — the other Bishops, the priests and the faithful, even the Holy Father himself?

But the Bishop has had no regard for these 'threats'. He passed on the 'message' to the Holy See. Then Fr Vlasic wrote another letter in a different tone to the Bishop. Our Lady replied in a gentle way through Ivan, Jakov and especially through Marija Pavlovic:

'I have sent the Bishop a lot of messages. But he hasn't wished to accept them. I have also sent you. But not even in this way has he listened to the Queen of Peace, because there is anxiety in his heart and this anxiety has come to stay'

Anyway, at this rate, Vego and Prusina are still not guilty. The Bishop is guilty. We have to pray for his conversion. Jelena Vasilj (22 January 1984) says the same thing. Since the Bishop

hasn't become 'converted' to the events of Medjugorje, Fr
Tomislav Vlasic has thought out something new, something very
exciting. On the hill during the night, one of the people present
prayed for Bishop Zanic. 'From the eyes of Our Lady flowed
a big tear. It ran down her face and disappeared into the cloud
under her feet. . . Our Lady started to cry and rose up to heaven
crying'! (22 August 1984)

12. New ideas from Fr Vlasic
For quite a while now, it's a well-known fact that Fr Vlasic, the
chaplain of Medjugorje from 1981 to last summer, tries now and
then to make Medjugorje more exciting so that the influx of
pilgrims doesn't drop.

Thus a big sign was announced. But nothing happened. In
addition, he publicised the arrival of Fr Tardif OP, a magician.
On the first day he is said to have 'cured' about twenty people
of sclerosis, of cancer and of paralysis, and on the second day
another twenty, but he gives no names or surnames and there
is no documentation of this. But news of the 'healings' have
spread all over the world.

Recently something extraordinary was done to create fresh
enthusiasm: a change in Our Lady's birthday, again according
to Our Lady's messages. Our Lady's birthday was no longer
to be on 8 September but on 5 August! This year we had to
celebrate the 2000th anniversary of the birth of Our Lady. This
is what Our Lady supposedly told little Jelena Vasily, who
doesn't have 'visions' but merely 'internal locution'. When Fr
Vlasic came to the Bishop with this news and these proposals,
the Bishop of the district forbade him to propagate such anti-
ecclesiastical feelings. But after a while the whole world knew
and was writing about it. Fr Vlasic asked little Jelena to ask Our
Lady to explain all this again, because the Bishop was against
the whole thing. So Our Lady 'said': 'Let the Holy Father know.
If he confirms this, celebrate it as I have told you'. If he doesn't
confirm it, insists Fr Vlasic, how can we tell the people? 'Then
pray and leave the rest to me. I'll sort everything out'. (Letter
sent from Fr Vlasic to the Holy Father on 2 June 1984, and a
copy sent to the Bishop). The Holy Father obviously didn't reply!
But on 4 and 5 August there was a big gathering of people in
Medjugorje to participate in the miraculous events and the

important conversions, etc. Journalists spoke of a 'star' that was seen! The people came home disappointed.

When we compare this fantasy on the part of Fr Vlasic and little Jelena with what is written in the chronicle of the apparitions, we find the following information, hand-written by Fr Vlasic himself: *8 September 1981:* 'Visions: The boys and girls met Our Lady. Young Jakov wished her *happy birthday*. She was delighted and said that that day was one of the happiest. . .' Then a year later Fr Vlasic himself recorded in the chronicle: *8 September 1982:* 'Mirjana and Ivica were not present amongst the visionaries. Other were there. They had the vision. Our Lady was particularly solemn. The boys and girls wished her *happy birthday*'. Now, this year Our Lady celebrates Her birthday on 5 August and this is precisely the 2000th birthday! Because of this, perhaps we should expect 'Our Lady of Medjugorje' to change the Feast of the Immaculate Conception as well, from 8 December to 5 November?

Let us describe further fantastic information used to spur up enthusiasm: the number of the pilgrims. On 24 and 25 June 1983, according to some newspapers, there were 200,000 faithful present in Medjugorje. In the chronicle Fr Vlasic wrote: those who believe that there weren't many people present say there were between 40,000 and 50,000 people there, instead those who believe that there were a great many people present say that there were 200,000 there. The visionaries asked Our Lady what the precise number was. Our Lady answered: 110,000! You don't have to be an expert to calculate the number of pilgrims. During those days, 3,000 cars came to Medjugorje and about 70 coaches. If you add another 15,000 pilgrims that came on foot, you reach 30,000. Enough said!

We find that a great deal of manipulating is going on. And it really is a pity to be so light-hearted with the most saintly and human person in the Catholic Church — that is to say, the Blessed Virgin!

13. *Unfulfilled promises*

The unfulfilled promises concerning the 'healings' make one doubt the authenticity of the apparitions. 'Our Lady' is said to have promised many sick people that they would be healed. Let's give some examples:

In 1981, there was a promise made concerning a child from Grude suffering from leukaemia — that he would get better, certainly and unconditionally. There are written descriptions of the case. But he died towards the end of 1981.

The Franciscan Brother Ivan Dolan suffered from cancer. His mother went on foot from Rama to Medjugorje to ask Our Lady to heal her son. The 'visionaries' said that Our Lady promised to heal him. Several months later, the brother died.

A girl called DB also got cancer. The doctors advised her to have a mastectomy. She went on foot to Medjugorje, to seek health. The 'visionaries' turned to Our Lady who replied that there was no need for the operation. But the girl died, following terrible suffering, on 24 December 1983.

Amongst the miraculous healings described in the book by Fr Rupcic, there is the case of Venka Bilic-Brajcic from Split. When her doctor saw the book, he protested outright against the affirmation that she was cured. She delivered her medical certificates on 8 September 1982 and she died in June 1984. And so on.

The last case was that of a heart patient, Marko Blazevic from Buna near Mostar. According to the letter from the Archbishop of Belgrade, Mgr A. Turk, sent to the Bishop's Curia of Mostar on 3 June 1984, Marko was admitted to hospital to the Cardiology Department where the above-named Archbishop was also a patient. Blazevic told the Archbishop that he was due to undergo a risky operation, but that he was sure of the success of this operation, 'since he and his family had asked the boys and girls from Medjugorje where the Holy Mother of God appears and that a boy (he said "boys" to the others) had asked the Virgin Mary whether he should undergo the operation. And the Mother of God replied that he should have the operation and not worry about it because it would certainly be a success as long as prayers were said'. But the patient didn't wake up after the operation; he died.

The Bishop of Mostar sent the letter to Medjugorje, asking for an explanation. Fr Vlasic made enquiries with the 'visionaries' about the above-mentioned case. They replied *that no one had ever asked them anything whatever*. Then the Bishop called the daughter of the deceased man Blazevic. She had probably been instructed by Fr Vlasic and confirmed that she had been to Medjugorje and had asked about her father. But the 'visionaries' replied that it was necessary to pray during the operation, but said nothing as to the success of the operation! So, where does the truth lie!

14. Diana Basile's 'healing'

In mid-August last year, Dr Luigi Frigerio from the 'Mangiagalli' hospital in Milan came to the Bishop's Curia in Mostar, bringing with him a report on the 'miraculous healing' of Signora Diana Ferro née Basile. The Lady was supposedly cured of multiple sclerosis and of blindness of the right eye in Medjugorje on 24 May 1984. The world press and especially the Italian press wrote a great deal about this case last summer. Even the Archbishop of Split-Makarska, Mgr F Franic, reported this news in his episcopal bulletin Number 4/1984. Recently we found an article on this case in a magazine called *Gioia* of 29 October 1984.

The Bishop of Mostar thought it was best to send the above-mentioned report to the Medical Bureau of Lourdes, the most competent authority for such cases. The president of the Bureau, Dr Theodor Mangiapan, replied on 13 September last with a detailed letter. The main points of his letter are:

— Multiple sclerosis is a real challenge to doctors nowadays as far as a *positive and objective* diagnosis is concerned.

— The President wonders what this Institute of Specialisation in Milan really is. Most of the doctors and 'witnesses' connected with this 'healing' are associated with this 'boutique'.

— In order to judge the permanent nature of this healing, the case required time, i.e. at least 3-4 years.

— We want to let the Medjugorje Commission know our 'reservation in this matter' concerning the 'healing' of Signora D.B. Ferro.

— Dr Mangiapan advises the Bishop responsible for Medjugorje, not to let himself become too involved, not to accept or refuse this apparent miracle too soon!

This is how the President of the Medical Bureau of Lourdes expressed himself. Time will advise us best.

15. Conclusion

a) The Bishop of Mostar, having personally studied the case and with the help of a suitable Commission, has after all this time, in a responsible way and with moral certainty come to the conclusion that the events of Medjugorje are a case of collective hallucination. This has been cleverly exploited by a group of Franciscans from Hercegovina who have made the presumed 'apparitions' and the contents of the messages seem serious, manipulating the sincere desire for the supernatural on the part of the people and their deep love of Our Lady. The greatest responsibility belongs to the mystifier and charismatic wizard Fr Tomislav Vlasic who, in this affair, risked perjury to defend his position.

b)   The real aim of this group of Franciscans — in fact many of the members of their own order condemn their behaviour — is to point out to the simple people and to the people abroad, with the authority of Our Lady, that they are in the right while the Bishop and the legitimate Superiors of the Province and of the Order are in the wrong, in so far as the famous problem of the division of the parishes is concerned. The sad case of the two ex-chaplains of Mostar, expelled from the Order for their faults and then defended by 'Our Lady of Medjugorje' despite the Decrees of the Holy See and of the Franciscan Order is clear proof of their exploitation of the affair.

c)   Thus we can understand why Our Lady's 'messages' contain attacks against the condemnation of the Bishop, of the Franciscan Provincial authorities and also of the Holy Father himself. The presumed visionaries are the ignorant pawns in a game that is way beyond them and by now they behave like domesticated 'robots'.

d)   The incredible propaganda campaign set up by very many newspapers and Catholic magazines abroad, especially in Italy, is set within this context which damages the truth and the seriousness of supernatural facts and even the credibility of the Church. You just have to follow what is published in *Sabato*, *Avvenire*, *Jesus*, *Madre di Dio*, *Domenica del Corriere*, etc.

e)   The episode concerning Fr René Laurentin is particularly serious. He abuses his authority on apparitions and in order to make quick and easy money, has gone beyond the legitimate authority of the Church and with books, articles, cassettes and conferences has publicly defended the authenticity of the 'apparitions' of Medjugorje.

What has become of the professional ethics of this priest and journalist?

f) But the greatest danger lies in the fact that all this emotional excitement over Medjugorje is destined, sooner or later, to fizzle out into nothing, like a balloon bursting or like soap bubbles and then there will be great disappointment and disgrace for the authority of the Church, who, with some of its responsible people, have favoured hope and have considered the apparitions authentic without waiting for the official judgement.

To avoid such damaging consequences we are publishing our present attitude with regard to the Medjugorje affair.

Mostar, 30 October 1984.

This text is signed by Bishop Pavao Zanic and stamped with his Bishop's seal.

(v)

Fr Rupcic, the first one to write substantially on Medjugorje, composed a reply to this episcopal broadside. He has allowed me to reproduce it, which I do in full.

An overall view
Everything began unexpectedly when, on 24 June 1981, six boys and girls between the ages of eleven and seventeen, saw Our Lady on Mount Crnica, in the vicinity of Podbrdo which is in the parish of Medjugorje in Hercegovina (Yugoslavia). This they still claim to this day.

Since then Medjugorje, which throughout the centuries has been unknown to the outside world, has come to the attention of the press. By now, news of all that happens in the town has spread worldwide. People have reacted very differently to this news. Right from the start, there was above all doubt and scepticism, mixed with curiosity, but then, little by little, as time passed, doubt gave way to faith. This is mainly due to the apparitions which have taken place continuously since then as well as the healings and other unusual events that happen on the mountain where the apparitions take place and in the surrounding areas.

At the same time, much has been asked about the origin and truth of these facts. Such questions have had various different answers. From the beginning, the reasons and explanations given were on the whole influenced by *ideological* motives. The first medical-scientific investigation excluded mental disease and the influence of outsiders from the apparitions. The fact that the first people to investigate were mostly, though not all, of materialist-marxist orientation is of considerable importance. And even though everything pointed towards the authenticity of the apparitions, the Church, because of her traditional caution, not only showed lack of interest *in the events* but even opposed them. The parish priest, Fr Jozo Zovko, and the chaplain, Fr Zrinko Cuvalo have tried in every way to keep people away from these facts. And it was only when it became clear to them as well that there was something serious behind it all, did they include these extraordinary events in the pastoral theology and liturgy, leaving the rest to God and time so that everything can be explained, little by little.

Meanwhile, the apparitions and the messages, accompanied by miraculous healings, have continued to happen and have increasingly attracted people to Medjugorje. Thus a continuous flow of pilgrims from all over the world has been formed. In this crowd, people of different ideas, politics and social background have been brought together — believers and non-believers, young and old, healthy and ill, white people and coloured people, simple people and highly educated people, workers and intellectuals, secretaries of world democratic parties and humanitarian movements, representatives of religions and of the sciences, princes and princesses, priests and bishops. Many of these people who, through faith, conversion, prayer and fasting have heard Our Lady's message, have discovered a personal depth and peace. Of the almost four million pilgrims who have visited Medjugorje so far, it can be said that no one went away disappointed. Many people have said that, on coming to Medjugorje they realised that they had entered what could be called an extraordinary *magnetic field* in which both their adhesion to the faith was justified and their desire for inner peace became reality. For this reason, many have come back several times to Medjugorje from faraway places to strengthen their faith even further, to make thanksgiving and to obtain the necessary strength with which to continue their lives.

Now since the Medjugorje affair has become more and more important both at home and abroad, the problem concerning its origin and truth has become even more urgent. For this reason, many specialists in the natural sciences (such as medicine, psychology, sociology) and in theology, mostly from Italy, France and Austria, either individually or in groups, have tried to explain this problem. Conscious, on the one hand, of the seriousness and responsibility of their position, and aware, on the other hand, of the limits of science, they have proved to be open-minded towards the supernatural — in so far as the above-mentioned facts are concerned. They have confirmed all this as experts and as technicians while as believers they have heard, in various different ways, the message of God through Our Lady.

For this reason, the dissent expressed by the Bishop of Mostar, Mgr Pavao Zanic, whose diocese includes Medjugorje, comes as a surprise. Wanting to lead world opinion in the wrong direction, in the opposite direction away from truth, he has defined his attitude in the circular letter mentioned above that was sent to the biggest and best-known institutions in the West, both ecclesiastical and non-ecclesiastical. If the Bishop, on his own, is not infallible in this matter, his statements are worth whatever his evidence is worth. For this reason, everyone has the right and in this case also the duty to examine and verify this evidence, because as evidence it claims to have a certain strength, and also because the compelling character of its conclusions has a deep influence for truth and Christian life in general.

The following is an explanation of how things stand at present.

How the Bishop approached the events
During the first two months of the events, the Bishop visited Medjugorje five times. After this, he went there twice — once for Confirmation ceremonies and on another occasion to get news from the parish church. For anyone who wishes to get acquainted with the many events that take place in Medjugorje and their dynamics, it is necessary to be on the spot and to be interested in these events. Whoever considers he has the right and duty to judge the affair cannot be satisfied with other people's accounts of the facts, must see for himself and must verify things in Medjugorje itself. The Bishop has deliberately kept some distance from the facts.

Because of insufficient direct contact with the events of Medjugorje the Bishop has turned towards stories and invented 'facts', half-truths, misinformation and false interpretations. All this has created a sort of 'Medjugorje' versus 'Medjugorje' to such an extent that what is correct has been set aside, and decisions and opinions have been formed which are based on falsehood.

Furthermore, the Bishop has become unjustifiably involved in the natural sciences; he has incompetently, without even examining a single case and without valid argument, 'responsibly' and 'with moral certainty' — as he himself says — claimed that 'the events of Medjugorje represent a case of collective hallucination'. He has thus systematically entered into conflict with what is happening and with the findings of the numerous conscientious specialists in the natural sciences such as psychologists, psychiatrists and other medical specialists mostly from Italy and France, who have, on several occasions, and with the help of modern equipment, examined the visionaries, the people and the events of Medjugorje.

Not only do these specialists oppose the opinion of the Bishop; they explicitly exclude individual or collective hallucination as being the cause of the Medjugorje events. In the field of science one cannot pass for an expert without evidence for one's statements; science does not recognise affirmations without proof. We are therefore amazed at Bishop Zanic's presumptuous claim to resolve serious problems concerning science and faith with simplifications: this shows incompetence. It shows that the wrong use of authority not only is possible, but is also, as in this case, self-destructive.

When the Bishop uses hasty and unfounded denials and does not pronounce judgement on the facts, doubt is the only method left him to prove or disprove the facts. He expects us to consider doubt, and not facts, as valid proof. But doubts can never constitute proof, even a thousand 'serious' doubts are not worth one single argument that demonstrates the truth or falsehood of something. To affirm something as true, it is necessary to have irrefutable reasons. Doubt can only act as an incentive to investigate, not as proof of the truth or falsehood of any statement. The Bishop's method of argument is full of cleverly constructed doubts and is utterly worthless. For example, he tells us that the visionaries do not agree as to the reason for their going to the Podbrdo district just before the apparition, since some of them say they went there to get the sheep in, others say they went to gather flowers and others say they went to light a cigarette. It is quite obvious to anyone with a minimum of common sense that these statements made by the visionaries, do not represent any contradiction at all. These reasons fit together very well; they prompted the visionaries to go out for a walk or for recreation.

In the same way, the Bishop, remembering that Ivanka Ivankovic had lost her mother a few months beforehand and wanted very much to know where her mother was, and remembering too that she was the first one to have seen Our Lady, obviously wants to create doubt and attribute the apparition to Ivanka's grief and also, though he doesn't actually say so, to her confused mental state. Having expressed this doubt, the Bishop went on to say, untruthfully, that Our Lady first appeared to Ivanka, also at Cerno. Besides, it is hard to understand how Ivanka's 'reasons' became reasons for which the other visionaries saw Our Lady. It is even harder to understand why Ivanka hadn't seen Our Lady earlier on when she was even more grief-stricken. The fact is that neither mental illness, had this been the case, nor the mere doubt expressed in a very exaggerated way, can be used as reasons not to believe in the apparition and vision. Proof against the apparitions should be looked for and found elsewhere.

One of the main reasons for this incorrect approach to the Medjugorje affair has been the Bishop's *heretical a priori* position — 'according to the Catholic faith, no one is bound to believe in apparitions and private revelations'! If we do not exclude on principle the possibility that God can reveal and communicate himself to men other than in the Sacred Scriptures, then it is wrong to claim that apparitions and 'private' revelations do not bind anyone. In other words it would be absurd to admit that it is possible for God to communicate and demand something and then say that people do not have to listen and accept. Can God perhaps speak in vain? Or is man autonomous compared to God? For this reason, whoever has received an authentic revelation from God, or has heard his word, is bound to accept it. What is more, man has the duty to be responsible and open-minded towards everything, and one who is quite certain about any concrete revelation from God has the duty to accept it in a responsible manner. We are bound to do this in the same way as we are bound to accept what our conscience dictates; this is said to be, in some way, the voice of God. If we do otherwise, we commit sin.

This position, based on a false conception of the 'private' nature of the revelations, gives the Bishop the chance to degrade, discredit and deny the Medjugorje apparitions and to declare as 'absurd' the messages about conversion and peace. What is more, it is easier for him to deny these things rather than examine them, and it is more 'profitable' for him to refuse them rather than put them into practice.

The messages of Our Lady are so clear and, according to Ivan, invite the people 'to approach all that is happening in Medjugorje with deep understanding, love and great responsibility' and again, 'I wish (these are the words of Our Lady) that he (the Bishop) may not create opposition amongst the priests. 'The Bishop does not consider these messages as binding. He has pointed out the questionable character of the messages by stating, but not in any way proving, that Ivan could not have written them himself because he had not studied much at school. This statement, apart from the fact that it was not proved, is a contradiction of the other statements made by the Bishop in connection with Ivan. The Bishop first said that the messages were 'absurd' and later said that they contain wisdom that is beyond Ivan's capacity. For the same reasons and with the same certainty, the Bishop also refuses the message that Our Lady sent to him on 22 August, 1984, through Marija Pavlovic, as she herself claims. The Bishop, again without proof, attributes this message to Fr Tomislav Vlasic. Here too, he has invented a doubt instead of giving proof. The Bishop obviously thinks that with a mere doubt he has proved everything.

With this procedure and with this method people have been unable to approach the facts of Medjugorje let alone know the truth about their origin and meaning. An unlawful and unacceptable judgement has been made by someone who doesn't know or doesn't want to know what he is talking about. But it is above all an unacceptable and offensive judgement to make with respect to the people, not only because they have their own opinion but because, in this case, they also have the real proof to support it. So, not only without proof, but even in the face of known facts and indisputable evidence, the Bishop claims that the visionaries are liars, that they as well as the pilgrims are the victims of hallucination, that theologians of world fame are irresponsible, that experts are ignoramuses, that charismatic people are fanatics, that the Friars of Medjugorje are criminal manipulators, and, furthermore, that Fr Vlasic is a hoaxer and a perjurer.

One has to admit that these men will wonder if the person who has made these 'compliments' with such talent is sane and responsible. How awful it is when a man thinks he 'knows' as much as God himself!

Question of principle
It would be wrong to think that the Bishop has always had such a sure and clear appreciation 'on principle' with regard to the Medjugorje affair. He has had other appreciations 'on principle' as 'sure' as that just mentioned, even though they contradict each other. The Bishop, as he himself has said, had already visited Medjugorje and had spoken with the visionaries on 21 July 1981. Before the interview, they had taken an oath to say that they would tell the truth about the things he asked them. At the end of the interview, the Bishop came to the conclusion which he expressed in these terms: *'I am firmly convinced that no one has influenced the boys and girls who claim to see Our Lady.* If there was just one boy or girl involved, one could say: This person is so stubborn, not even the police could make him speak. But six simple, innocent young boys and girls, if induced, would say everything within half an hour. *I declare and guarantee that none of the priests has had any aim whatsoever in this affair, nor has any of them tried to influence the boys and girls for any ulterior motive. I am equally convinced that the boys and girls are not lying; the boys and girls are saying exactly what they feel in their hearts. . . It's certain, the boys and girls are not lying'.* (Bishop's sermon, 25 July 1981, recorded).

Later, the Bishop described the same events and the same people as despicable. Despite the fact that he had said and solemnly repeated three times that the boys and girls weren't lying, after a certain time, he declared: 'Right from the beginning you could tell that there was something untruthful underneath it all: for example, the boys and girls all went up to Podbrdo, the place of the apparitions, for different reasons.'

Similarly, their previous declarations — saying that the apparitions would last until 3 July 1981, were later interpreted by the Bishop as doubts, even lies, considering that the apparitions continued afterwards. Previously, even though the Bishop was aware of all this, nothing had prevented him from saying; 'It is certain, the boys and girls are not lying'. The accusing statements made about the visionaries came about in the following way: when the parish priest Fr Jozo Zovko, realised that the visionaries were not sufficiently instructed in the faith and in the problem that they were now faced with, he gave them some prayer books and some rosaries and in addition to these, he gave Mirjana a book called *Gospina ukazania (The apparitions of Our Lady)* written by Bozo Vuco and published in Makarska in 1974. As well as that, he tried to convince the boys and girls to move to the parish church for the apparitions. In this way, he hoped to discourage people from roaming on the mountain and lingering round the visionaries' houses. But the boys and girls were not keen on moving to the church — in a way, they would have preferred to be alone, without people. With reference to this, Mirjana said to Fr Jozo: 'There is no reason for us to move to the church, because the apparitions will finish next Friday'. Fr Jozo asked if it was Our Lady who had told her so. Mirjana answered: 'It was not she who told me, I read it in the book that you gave me. That is what happened in Lourdes and that is what will happen here'.

The boys and girls had probably calculated from what they had read in the book that the apparitions of Our Lady would come to an end, and once they were convinced of this, had discussed the matter among themselves. So, on 3 July, after the apparition, they declared that it was all over. But on the following day, a Saturday, even though they had not expected it and did not go up on the mountain, each one had a vision wherever he or she happened to be at the time. So the Bishop was mistaken in saying that it was Our Lady who had spoken about the end of the apparitions. Nor was he right in saying that there were some priests present during the last apparition on 3 July because Fr Jozo was actually the only one present at that apparition.

In the same way, despite his previous statement: *'I declare and guarantee that no priest has had any aim nor has he tried to convince the boys and girls for some ulterior motive'*, the Bishop later declared 'Right from the beginning, the Medjugorje affair has been in the hands of the charismatic priests Fr Jozo Zovko, Fr Tomislav Vlasic and others. It has often been said that Our Lady's messages have an evangelical character. It is true that they have an evangelical character especially those that have been sent out all over the world, since they have been written by Fr Tomislav Vlasic who is familiar with theology and knows what to say.'

Here the Bishop not only contradicts himself but also goes against well-known facts. It is an undeniable fact that at the beginning, Fr Zovko as well as the chaplain Fr Zrinko Cuvalo were strictly opposed to anything in the way of a vision or apparition, whereas Fr Tomislav Vlasic, whom the Bishop insults even more than the others, and in such a brazen way, was at that time working permanently at Capljina, which is about thirty kilometres from Medjugorje. The Bishop, despite the fact that he had previously stated that the boys and girls were not lying, and going against well-known facts, suddenly declares that those responsible for having started the whole thing and for having manipulated the events and the people were the very ones that he had at first guaranteed as being excluded from the events. The fact is that either they were against things that they are now being accused of, or they were not even in Medjugorje at the time.

In the same way, the Bishop's judgement of the boys and girls is self-contradictory. On one occasion he says that 'no one has influenced the boys and girls' and on another occasion that 'they are unaware that they are pawns in a game that is way beyond them', and that 'they behave like trained robots', that of course they are being manipulated by the brothers and especially 'by the hoaxer and charismatic wizard Fr Tomislav Vlasic'. How can these two opinions about the same boys and girls be compatible, and how can Fr Vlasic be considered innocent and guilty at the same time? Above all, how can Fr Vlasic be considered guilty, considering that the visions, the messages and the Bishop's opinions about the boys and girls took shape a long time before Fr Vlasic came to Medjugorje to start work there as a chaplain? This was when Fr Jozo Zovko was arrested on 1 August 1981. These judgements expressed by the Bishop are contradictory and show clearly that it is the boys and girls, the apparitions, the brothers, the pilgrims, the readers, even logic and truth that are being manipulated.

Any intelligent person would, at this stage, wonder: when has the Bishop told the truth? And which of his explanations must one listen to, seeing that they contradict each other? There is nothing certain about them, except that the Bishop contradicts himself and invents things, without taking into account the real facts.

The reasons for the contradictory interpretations

In the illogicality of the contradictory, though none the less ingenious, interpretations made by the Bishop about the events of Medjugorje there is however a strange kind of logic. Let us listen to the Bishop himself, who, as he has personally said, followed the Medjugorje events from the start and thought to himself: 'If the scandalous "Hercegovina affair" about the Franciscans' disobedience with regard to the decrees of the Holy See concerning the parishes has been going on for such a long time and has not been cleared up by man, perhaps God has chosen to send us Our Lady to persuade the disobedient to be obedient and to love the Church'. For this reason, when the Bishop met the visionaries for the first time on 21 July 1981, he wanted to know first and foremost if Our Lady had said anything about the 'Hercegovina affair'. The Bishop later said that they answered saying that 'everything would soon be cleared up'.

The Bishop does not mention the other messages, nor is he very interested in them. His worry was not so much how to settle the problem, but how to settle it in the way he liked best. He had not even considered, let alone permitted, that the matter be settled in any way other than that which he himself thought right. And yet one of the instructions and fundamental requirements of the Holy See regarding this problem was the following: that the controversy created by the Bishop of Mostar be resolved by mutual agreement; but the Bishop has never paid much attention to this instruction, he has stubbornly and selfishly tried to get his own way. For this reason, he has come into conflict not only with the Franciscans but also with the rest of the faithful. No conspiracy will ever be able to hide these essential facts and truths. The scandalous result of all this can above all be seen in the unjust division of the Parish of Mostar and the problem of the two chaplains Fr Ivica Vego and Fr Ivan Prusina which has thus arisen, as a 'case' within a 'case'.

Meanwhile, since only the spiritual messages were being proclaimed in Medjugorje, especially messages on conversion and peace, and the promise that 'everything would soon be cleared up' repeated by the visionaries was taking longer than expected to come true, the Bishop became impatient. Realising that things were not working out well and that he was not able to get his own way in the 'Hercegovina case', he thought it best to intervene as quickly as possible, especially when he considered that the multitude of pilgrims coming daily to Medjugorje could make the whole thing more and more famous. When the Bishop suddenly noticed an unwelcome 'prestige' on the part of the Franciscans who are in charge of Medjugorje he decided to complicate everything with insinuations and interpretations, despite the obvious and extraordinary spiritual growth of conversion and of peace and of deep faith, not to mention the miraculous healings and other amazing facts which hundreds of thousands of people have witnessed. He has often modified these interpretations himself, whenever he felt the need, because hardly anyone was prepared to accept them. And they were, in fact, unacceptable because they were unreasonable and self-contradictory. The Bishop first claimed that no one had influenced the boys and girls in connection with the visions and messages, later he said that the Friars and especially Fr Vlasic were behind it all, then he said Satan was responsible and finally, that the whole thing was hallucination. When interpreting the facts, the Bishop has been very emphatic on each separate occasion.

Since, as the Bishop said 'those who came to Medjugorje were very impressed and enthusiastic about the prayers and confession, and many were converted', he then found no way out and no way of denying all this other than by saying that the Medjugorje affair was the 'work of Satan' He repeated this statement everywhere and even two Italian journalists who visited him with Fr Masetto, a Jesuit, were authorised to spread this message all over the world. The Bishop as usual, did not prove his statement. Perhaps this should have been clear to all, but just what we have seen is what Christ says: 'You will recognise them by their fruit'; this is quite the opposite to what the Bishop claims, since 'a good tree cannot produce bad fruit, neither can a bad tree produce good fruit'. (*Mt 7:17-18*) It is absurd to say that prayers, conversions, confessions, communion and other good works done by millions of people are the works of Satan, because that would mean using Beelzebub to drive out Beelzebub. 'If Satan is really divided in himself, how can his kingdom last?' (*Lk 11:18*) Each conversion by its own meaning, implies removal from and not a call to Satan. And when people are converted, especially hardened sinners as in Medjugorje, Christ 'drives out the evil spirits with the hand of God' and shows that 'the Kingdom of God has come'. (*Lk 11:19-20*)

But if the Bishop considers despite all this (what Christ judges as impossible) that Satan can bring about conversions, confessions, communion and prayers far more than anywhere else in Yugoslavia, and what is more, for a greater length of time, it is hard to understand what makes these same things happen elsewhere — though they happen elsewhere to a lesser extent. What criterion can be used to establish that in one place certain events are the works of God, and in another, that they are the works of Satan? Is what is happening in the Franciscans' parish in Medjugorje perhaps different from what is happening elsewhere? It is strange, however, that the Bishop should say that Satan is responsible for everything that is happening at Medjugorje and that he is trying to deceive the people and cause greater damage to the Church later on.

Even though Our Lady has purposely not resolved the 'Hercegovina case' in the way that was hoped, she has nonetheless resolved it in the best way, by inviting conversion. Conversion creates a new man and thus a new situation around him and within him. His eyes are opened to see things that he has not seen beforehand and he gets the strength to carry out that which he has previously been unable to carry out. In this way only can injustice be turned into justice, hatred into love and problems resolved. Everyone is invited to be converted. It is unacceptable for some to be converted and for others only to observe as outsiders, as sin is not found only in lowly people. 'If we say', and here John the apostle also includes himself, 'we haven't sinned, we are deceiving ourselves and there is no truth in us' (*1 Jn 1:8*). And, 'whoever commits sin, violates the law' (*1 Jn 3:4*). If we do not recognise our sins, not only do 'we make God a liar' (*1 Jn 1:10*) but we render ourselves incapable of reaching a just and lasting solution. According to the Bishop, the only ones responsible for the 'Hercegovina case' are the Franciscans. But they, as well as everyone else know that this problem did not arise when the Franciscans stayed in Hercegovina for centuries as spiritual pastors when the Bishop had fled from the Turks. The 'Hercegovina case' did not even exist when the Franciscans, who were still on their own, created the diocese, nor did it exist when they became independent of the Turks and the doors were opened to secular clergy. Should the Franciscans perhaps repent of their past and regret that they are stil alive? But even if they all became canonised saints, the 'Hercegovina case' would, when seen, interpreted and settled by the Bishop, still continue to be scandalous.

However, this problem *is in no way connected with the apparitions of Our Lady at Medjugorje*. It has been violently and abruptly inserted in these events. Since the apparitions have not brought the solution to the problem that the Bishop very much wanted, he has declared them non-authentic.

In any case, both the apparitions and the most important messages happened a long time before a connection was seen between them and the 'Hercegovina case'. Therefore, whatever its origin, the 'Hercegovina case' cannot affect the authenticity of the apparitions. This was clear to the Bishop when he openly declared that 'the boys and girls are not lying' and that 'no one has influenced them'. It was so certain that even Archbishop Frane Franic who is familiar with the 'Hercegovina case' declared: 'I think these events (i.e. the Medjugorje events) are of supernatural origin'.

The reason for opposition to the supernatural origin of the Medjugorje affair is partly because Our Lady, through Vicka. let the Bishop know that in his behaviour towards the two chaplains of Mostar he acted rashly. He understood this gesture to be a '*crimen laesae majestatis*'. The Bishop was so angry that one day he sent Vicka away with these words: 'Go away! And when your Lady pronounces a swear word against God, come and tell me about it'! Why cannot Our Lady say that the Bishop has been rash? How awful it is, when man considers himself 'faultless', and incapable of sin, as God is incapable of sin.

Other facts and how they were interpreted

For the above-mentioned reasons, all the facts were to be used, above all, to justify the validity of such an interpretation; so some had to be modified, others weakened, others ignored, and others invented so as finally to interpret them 'responsibly' and with 'moral certainty'.

The 'big sign'

Vicka, in her notes, in the entry made on 27 August 1981, wrote that Our Lady said the 'big sign' would happen 'soon' and that meanwhile, they had 'to be patient' (29 and 31 August, 3 September 1981). The Bishop tries to make out that this is a lie, since the promise has not yet come true. But in the case of prophecy, one has to take into account the kind of language that prophets usually use. They express themselves in a literary-prophetic style and sometimes a thousand years can mean just one day. When Vicka uses the word 'soon' this shouldn't create doubt any more than what other prophets have said. Similarly, who would dare to doubt the word of Christ with regard to his coming again 'Yes, I will come soon' (*Apoc. 22, 20*)? The Bishop tries to associate the word 'soon' with the return of Vicka's father from Germany for Christmas or for the feast of the Immaculate Conception in 1981 or for the New Year holiday in 1982, but there is no mention of this in Vicka's notes nor did the visionaries mention this. This attitude on the part of the Bishop became clear when two members of his 'Commission' were given the duty of making the visionaries write down when the 'big sign' would happen. Since the visionaries refused, the members of the 'Commission' tried to convince Mirjana, who was in Sarajevo, to do so, but she refused (and the Bishop, just because she has a telephone in the house, tried to insinuate that she phoned the other visionaries to make an agreement with them). Then the members of the 'Commission' tried the same thing with Ivan Dragicevic, who was at Visoko at the time. When they insisted, Ivan behaved differently and, according to the Bishop, described what he was asked to describe; the Bishop added that later he asked Ivan Dragicevic if Our Lady had reprimanded him for having described the 'big sign' at Visoko, and he answered 'No!'. But Ivan gives his own version of all this, and says that just when he was about to write down the answer he felt an inner warning not to do so; so he did not write the answer but simply sealed the envelope and handed it back. Apart from that, he says that he had been to the Bishop only once, and was in the company of others, and that in connection with the written description of the sign, the Bishop did not ask him anything, nor did Ivan give him any information.

To diminish the importance of what the visionaries say about the 'big sign' and to file it all as part of 'day-dreams', he puts forward a statement made by a certain Mara Jerkovic who is not one of the visionaries and whose gossip cannot be considered valid in this affair.

Comparison between Medjugorje on the one hand and Garabandal and San Damiano on the other
The Bishop mentions the events of Garabandal (1961-64) and presents them in such a way as to make people think that something similar is happening in Medjugorje. But first one has to point out that being similar does not mean being identical and this cannot be used as proof against Medjugorje; secondly, none of the visionaries of Medjugorje has ever declared that he or she has not seen Our Lady, which, according to the Bishop, happened with Maria Cruz of Garabandal. To strengthen his position, the Bishop later declared that 'the same thing happened at San Damiano, in Italy. At the end, public opinion accepted the apparitions as mere hallucinations'.

But if the same thing happened at Garabandal and at San Damiano, and if a Commission which in itself is not infallible declared that 'the apparitions are not supernatural', there is no logical reason why, without documentation, one can automatically claim the same thing for other visions. In which case, one would involve not only Medjugorje, but also Lourdes and Fatima.

The 'diary of the apparitions'
Among the alleged arguments against the apparitions of Medjugorje, 'Vicka's diary' is of special importance. This diary *is absolutely non-existent*. But the Bishop insists that 'The Friars have hidden it, and now they say it does not exist. They are afraid of something'. This is what he wrote on 12 December 1983 to Fr Radogost Grafenaeur, a Jesuit, adding that some

articles in the Chronicle and in the diary constitute 'the key to the understanding of Medjugorje.' Later, when he spoke to Fr Vlasic, who swore on the Cross that the 'diary' was not in his house and did not even exist, the Bishop did not change his mind and called Fr Vlasic a perjurer and liar; later he spread this version of his both in written form, and orally, all over the world. In connection with the existence of the 'diary', he first refers to Fr Grafenauer. But Grafenauer, in a letter to Fr Ljubicic dated 7 October 1984, writes: 'You know what he (the Bishop) has been telling everyone abut this diary, and how he has publicly put Fr Tomislav to shame. . . This same person swore on the Cross that he had not even seen the diary, but he says that Vicka showed it to me. He considers me a witness against Vlasic. I have heard all this from Mate Zovkic, who sent me the Bishop's circular letter. I immediately let the Bishop know, through Zovkic, that I had not seen Vicka's diary. He cannot consider me a witness against Tomislav in this affair. I also sent a photostat copy to Tomislav. In this letter I explained to the Bishop in what way I had spoken about and written about Vicka's diary. The Bishop did not take into account my extracts about Tomislav in the chronicle, because he does not believe in the chronicle. He only believes in the diary. . . Alas, at that time, I had not the courage to write and tell him that I had never seen the diary. At least from then onwards the Bishop knew how things stood. . . Even though I communicated these events to the Bishop, until now, from what I am told, he has not withdrawn what he originally declared. And he continues to write in foreign newspapers and refer to me as a witness as regards Vicka's diary. I am sorry that people are getting confused ideas about the Medjugorje apparitions and that the Bishop is impugning the honesty of Our Lady's witnesses'.

In the same letter Grafenauer goes on to say that in connection with all this, he has drafted a letter to an important German person, whom he asks to inform the Pope or Cardinal Ratzinger himself: 'With reference to all this, I have prepared a letter — writes Grafenauer — though in the eyes of the Lord, it honestly appears to me that the Bishop is getting an undue amount of importance. But why say nothing when the Bishop is making his "honest" opinion — the only one — heard all over the world? Why can not people use this *"corpus delicti"* to show what kind of honesty is underneath the whole thing? It is time for everything to be brought out into the open. Many people have suffered because of the Bishop's haste, but he himself does not consider that he has been hasty, let alone dishonest'.

At this stage, there is little else to add. We are faced with the logic of facts: The Bishop refers to Vicka, Grafenauer and Vlasic as the only witnesses to the fact that the hidden 'diary' exists, whereas the witnesses Vicka, Grafenauer and Vlasic — who even swore before God — all claim 'it does not exist'! And now the Bishop, on the basis of their collective witness, comes to this conclusion: Vicka *wrote* the diary, Vlasic *hid it* and Grafenauer *saw it* and *copied* some of Our Lady's messages from it. No matter how muddled this seems, the Bishop sees as 'key to the understanding of Medjugorje' things that don't exist and considers as 'key' witnesses people who witness the non-existence of such things; he considers the whole thing to be the result of 'collective hallucination' and this *whole thing actually cannot even exist*. So, he does not judge Medjugorje from what is happening there, but on the basis of things that have been invented, and things that have been fabricated elsewhere and that he has wanted, at all costs, to include.

The chaplains of Mostar

The Bishop, using this same style, also contests the authenticity of the Medjugorje apparitions from the fact that Our Lady has 'protected' the two young chaplains Fr Ivan Prusina and Fr Ivica Vego, who, as he states, have been suspended *a divinis* from the Order. He says that they did not obey his veto by which he instructed them not to carry out their spiritual activity in the part of the parish of Mostar which he had included in the new Cathedral parish. Their case has become part of the 'Hercegovina case'. But, without going into details as to blame and punishment of these two chaplains, serious and competent legal experts say that in their case canonical procedure was not respected. This is an important factor when weighing the validity of the punishment and decisions pertaining to them. But, what is even more important is the fact that their case was inserted in the Medjugorje events at a very late stage. Quite some time beforehand, Our Lady had already appeared and had already given her most important messages. Now, whatever happened afterwards cannot have retroactive effect to make us doubt the apparitions and their authenticity. The Bishop himself had said that the boys and girls were not lying.

Furthermore, it is known to all that such a decision is not *ex cathedra*, neither can it be considered merely an involuntary mistake and, in connection with this, the message of Our Lady that speaks of over-haste on the part of the Bishop, is quite precise. Since a juridical or moral error cannot be excluded either theoretically or practically, it would be in favour of truth and justice if everything were to be re-examined in depth, because man is of greater value than law. So far, the chaplains have made more than thirty pilgrimages to Medjugorje, covering a distance of about thirty kilometres on foot from Mostar to Medjugorje. If no one is trying to recognise them as innocent, their good will and devotion cannot be denied. They themselves are deeply convinced that though they have been punished they are absolutely innocent, and that they have not had the opportunity to prove it. They are behaving according to the principle: *Non est poena sine culpa* (There is no penalty without blame.). They are still willing to discuss this problem with the Bishop but until now, he has not summoned them. They have appealed to the Generalate of the Order but so far have'nt had an answer.

The Bishop's communication to the Generalate of the Order and to the Holy See, with regard to this affair, is neither convincing nor justified because these authorities have known nothing about the problem independently of the Bishop, nor have they had any direct knowledge of it. Any judgement (and therefore even this one) depends on whether there has been blame and whether the witnesses have spoken the truth. And this is just where the problem arises: is it not perhaps cynical to invoke the Holy See and the Generalate of the Order, when these, without the Bishop, knew nothing of the existence of these chaplains, let alone their offence? Anyone would agree that either side could have made a mistake. Is not mercy, rather than law the very substance of the Gospel? And in the Gospel itself, are there no other solutions to be found, knowing that Christ has never refused anyone who has turned to him humbly and sincerely? Therefore, there is no one to whom one cannot grant the love, the mercy and the peace of Christ.

A great number of 'visionaries'

The Bishop tries to use the great number of 'visionaries' as proof
that the apparitions of Medjugorje are not authentic. The forty-
seven 'visionaries' that he claims to have discovered outside
Medjugorje in other parishes, and that have had similar 'visions'
are, the Bishop would have us believe, all false. First of all, here
again, being similar, if there really is similarity, doesn't mean
being identical. And neither can we, from one vision, claim the
existence or non-existence of another vision. Furthermore, the
apparitions that many visionaries have had, in many different
places, are not necessarily a reason to doubt the truth of such
apparitions: above all, each case has to be examined on its own
merits, before making a judgement, because one case does not
give us any information about another. It remains a fact that
none of the visionaries, outside Medjugorje, mentioned by the
Bishop, has ever been examined scientifically. Therefore they
cannot be used to prove anything against the visionaries and
apparitions in Medjugorje be they authentic or otherwise. There
is the possibility that they are all true or all false, or that one
vision is authentic and the others false. But what exactly is
underneath them all can only be established by using serious
scientific tests. If some visions were found to be false, that would
be no reason to reject them all: as one false pearl doesn't exclude
the real ones, neither do false apparitions exclude authentic ones.
It is known that along with the apparitions at Lourdes recognised
as authentic, in the vicinity of Lourdes and even in places further
away, about fifty other 'apparitions' were registered. However,
they did not undermine the authenticity of the recognised
apparitions and visions. If one wants to make a comparison
between the apparitions in Lourdes and those in Medjugorje one
may note the following: both those in Lourdes and those in
Medjugorje happened before the so-called 'visions'; both in
Lourdes and in Medjugorje the parish priests and the Bishops
were opposed to these events. But the apparitions in Medjugorje
are also different from those quoted by the Bishop from the fact
that the 'visionaries' outside Medjugorje 'no longer have such
visions as the parish priests do not support them', whereas the
apparitions of Medjugorje still continue despite the fact that the
parish priest not only did not support them (at the outset) but
opposed them vigorously.

How many pilgrims are there?

Very many pilgrims were present in Medjugorje on 5 August 1984. It is really difficult to establish exactly how many there were, or even give an approximate number. Those who were there do not agree on the number. The Bishop was obviously disturbed by their number, so with an 'imaginary' calculation of the pilgrims, he creates imaginary proof. He hasn't counted them either of course, but for his 'purpose', says that there were about 30,000 people. He reaches this number assuming that there were about 3,000 cars and about 70 coaches. 'If', he says, 'we add 15,000 more that came on foot, we come to 30,000'. This reckoning is no doubt fairly exact, if we really do add the Bishop's 'if'. But if we add another 'if', then even the other reckoning is precise. In any case, whatever the number really was, perhaps 30,000, are they not many, considering that the Bishop had forbidden organised pilgrimages? Perhaps this multitude is saying something to make us reflect?

The 'false' healings

According to the Bishop's theory on Medjugorje and his false judgement as regards 'private' revelations, miracles should not and 'could not' happen. Therefore the Bishop rejects them outright. But even here he refers to doubtful witnesses and to cases that were not examined. He refers to a certain child from Grude, in Hercegovina, who suffered from leukaemia and whom Our Lady promised to heal but who, instead of getting better, died. This case was not sufficiently examined: we do not really know whether or not the visionaries passed on this message. On the other hand, in no other case, as far as we know, have the visionaries ever promised a healing without conditions. As in the case of young Daniele Setka, from Vukodol, near Mostar, who was cured — his parents were told to believe, pray and fast. It is not certain and it is not easy to believe that things were different in the case of the child from Grude or in the case of Ivan Dzolan, whose mother prayed to Our Lady and asked her to cure him, but he died. Here there are also other reasons for associating Our Lady with the sick; because of this, one would have to examine the above-mentioned cases in an unbiased way, and not merely accept written texts as evidence, especially those written by people who, because of ignorance or ideological reasons, are against the apparitions of Medjugorje. It is possible that the sick children's parents, because they very much wanted their children to get better, distorted Our Lady's promise or overlooked the condition under which such a promise was made.

Even though the above-mentioned cases are not clear, the others mentioned by the Bishop including the case of Desa Busic and of Marko Blazevic are presented in an extremely false way. The Bishop's Curia of Mostar, in its letter addressed to the parish of Mostar (No 636/84) says that Desa had asked Our Lady if she should undergo an operation or not, and that Our Lady, through the visionaries, replied that it was not necessary, but then the patient died. The deceased woman's sister Maria, who was very attached to her sister especially during her illness, replied to the Bishop's Curia, in connection with this misinformation. These are her words: 'With reference to letter No 636/84 from the Bishop's Curia date 8 June 1984, addressed to the Parish of Medjugorje, in which my sister's death is connected with declarations made by the visionaries of Medjugorje, I hereby declare that what is mentioned in this report is totally inaccurate'. Despite this, the Bishop continues of his own accord, and claims the contrary, even though he has no evidence relating to the deceased woman Desa Busic.

What happened in the case of Marko Blazevic is almost the same: according to what the Archbishop of Belgrade Alois Turk writes to Bishop Zanic, Mr Blazevic said that he had to undergo a serious operation but that he was sure it would be a success, 'because he and his family had turned to the visionaries of Medjugorje and a boy (to the others he said: the boys) had asked Our Lady if he should undergo the operation. And the Mother of God replied that he should undergo the operation and not be worried because it would certainly be a success, as long as he prayed'.

But, with all due respect, Monsignor Turk's declaration does not contain the truth since apparently Blazevic first said 'a boy' had asked Our Lady, and then said 'the boys'. Anyway, apart from this, this is what happened: Marko didn't ask either 'a boy' or 'the boys', neither did his daughter Melania. She merely implored Ivan Dragicevic to recommend the sick man to Our Lady, which he did. This is exactly what happened, but the story continues to be spread. Perhaps we need to ask ourselves, where

people like Bishop Zanic are concerned: 'Where is the truth?'.
One thing is still not clear: why does the Bishop continue to
uphold what first-hand witnesses like Ivan and Blazevic's
daughter expressly deny? What is the meaning of that sentence
that does not prove anything and that is not proved (according
to which the daughter of the deceased Blazevic declared to the
Bishop that nothing had been said about the success of the
operation) other than 'she was probably instructed by Fr
Vlasic. . .'? Obviously anything can be declared as true, the only
thing that does not prevail is the truth!

Furthermore, in my book entitled *Apparitions of Our Lady at
Medjugorje* I have reported the doctor's diagnosis and the
statement made by Venka Bilic-Brajcic, who was suffering from
a tumour. The Bishop, in connection with this case, said: 'When
her doctor saw the book, he vigorously protested against the
declaration that she was cured'. It is not clear to whom the
aforementioned statement about the healing is attributed, because
in my book I only referred to the doctor's diagnosis and to what
the patient had said. Now, after Venka had turned to Our Lady,
the diagnosis was as follows: 'The patient has improved, she feels
well, there are no signs of changes due to metastasis in the bones
and in the organs'. Therefore, if, as the Bishop said, it's true
that Venka's doctor protested against something, he could only
protest against himself.

With reference to this, I consider it important to draw attention
to the false interpretations, some of which are given deliberately,
of the extraordinary healings that I have referred to in my book.
In this book, I have openly warned that all the cases of healing
mentioned are spoken about freely and described personally by
those who felt cured. It is simply an account of their own
experience and evidence. Likewise, I have clearly stated that this
healing like the others (and there are many important healings)
are open 'to the researches of natural, medical and theological
sciences and to the examination of faith'. So, these healings,
instead of being labelled, must be explained, and until they have
been scientifically examined in every aspect and in a responsible
way (which until now has not been done), no one has the right
to judge them 'by appearances' and above all no one has the
right to deny personal evidence given in a sincere way, by honest
people, as regards these events.

The most interesting case of healing so far is that of Diana Basile from Ferro, near Milan — not only because it is the most important among the healings in Medjugorje but because it is the one that has been most thoroughly examined. Diana suffered from multiple sclerosis. She couldn't get up or move. For a long time she had been treated for her disease in a clinic in Milan but despite treatment from highly qualified specialists, her situation got steadily worse. She had become completely blind in the right eye and for many years had been unable to see with it. For this reason, she had decided to go on a pilgrimage to Medjugorje to where she was accompanied on 23 May 1984; she assisted at the apparition of Our Lady in the church, in the little chapel near the altar. Immediately after the apparition, *she was instantly healed, she could see again and she stood up alone.* The next day, she went on foot from the Bigeste Hotel in Ljubuski where she was staying to Medjugorje (12 kilometres) and she went up to the mountain where the apparitions occur. A report on her disease, therapy and healing has been scrupulously drawn up by the same doctors who had treated her. This report was sent by them to the Parish of Medjugorje, to Bishop Zanic and to Archbishop Franic of Split. After this, the Bishop of Mostar says that he asked the opinion of the Medical Bureau of Lourdes. Dr Theodor Mangiapan, the director of this Bureau, answered him. Unfortunately, the Bishop doesn't refer to the original reply, so it is not possible to use it as a basis for criticism. Anyway from what he says we come to the conclusion that as regards this healing, it will be necessary to wait three or four years before being able to give 'a judgement on the permanent character of the healing'. This and everything else referred to by the Bishop is only Mangiapan's opinion, who is really freeing himself from any responsibility, regardless of the truth or otherwise of the healing described. This way of behaving is easier than examining the healing, as is his duty.* However, supposing that the answer

---

*It is known that the Medical Bureau of Lourdes has a rule whereby it considers as miracles the cases that have been examined by this same Medical Bureau. Diana Basile, an employee of the 'Mangiagalli' hospital of Milan, was treated for years in this hospital, but the Medical Bureau of Lourdes does not have a record of the tests she underwent. So perhaps Dr Mangiapan meant to say this in his letter: 'With reference to Diana Basile's case, we are not pronouncing judgement because we do not possess the case-history made out by us and we cannot form an opinion based on tests done by other hospitals.'

was made in good faith, we realise that Manigiapan has not a clear concept of what a miracle is, seeing that he gives instructions to the Bishop as to how to behave when accepting a healing as a miracle. A miracle is a special grace from God, and because of this, goes beyond medicine. It can be known only through revelation and faith; thus it has a theological explanation and not a medical or merely scientific one. Its essence and value lie in its capacity to act as a sign, and not in the specific light of its 'supernatural content'. God can make even the things of nature turn into 'signs', that is to say, miracles; therefore the 'naturalness' is not in itself proof that a thing or event can't also be a miracle, sometimes. But when this really happens, it is not the task of medicine or the other sciences to judge it.

If that is the way things are, medical science can examine every healing but can not legitimately ascertain if and when any one of these is really a miracle. When medical science has done all that it can, and has reached the limits of its medical aim — that doesn't mean that it has reached the limits of reality and therefore it must remain open to this. We do not understand why it is necessary to wait so long to confirm Diana's healing and that only then can one speak of a miracle. Why three or four years and not more, or less? If this was the criterion used for the healings of Jesus as told to us in the Gospels, then not even one of them could have been proved or could have been recognised as a miracle, at least as long as Jesus remained on earth. Instead the Gospels tell us that the people present noticed and at once recognised these miracles and for this reason were converted. The real meaning of a miracle is this: that it helps men to believe. This is why it is performed and it must therefore be recognisable immediately. At the same time, every science has the right to look at the miracle from its own point of view and to observe the particular aspect that belongs to it.

Even a superficial examination of the many healings that have taken place in Medjugorje show that the people cured and many others, like those of the Gospel, have considered their healings as a message from God and have replied to this with faith, thanking God and Our Lady. Because of this, it is very important to be able to recognise miracles. If we leave all else aside and consider that Diana Basile had been blind in the right eye for years and that in Medjugorje she suddenly began to see again,

It was in this way that on 2 June 1984, N. Bulat, a member of the 'Commission' came up behind the visionaries during an apparition and pricked Vicka twice in the back with a needle. Apart from the aim of this gesture, the manner in which it was carried out was irresponsible. Firstly, it is immoral to treat a person without his or her consent, like a guinea-pig on which to demonstrate one's hypotheses. Secondly, it is dangerous and thus even more immoral to prick someone with a non-sterilised needle in the back, which is such a delicate place and expose him or her to dangerous infections. Furthermore, from a theological point of view, this test brings us back to the medieval 'ordeal' and to the 'temptation' of God. But no one can expect God to provide, when ordered and commanded, the proof that he or she wants, because it is God who gives us the proof that he wishes. Therefore, in this affair, everyone must examine what is before him, and not what he 'orders'. Otherwise, with this method and these requirements, where would the whole thing lead to? Seeing that Vicka didn't react to the prick of a needle, the inquisitor could have tried to pull her head off, to see if God or Our Lady would have put it back on. And thus the inquisitor would feel confident that God was, or wasn't at work, through the girl.

However, the declaration repeated by the Bishop several times: 'I am the Commission' had already made the 'Commission' and its work seem superfluous. When it met again in October 1984, it examined some of the visionaries only in a formal and superficial way, while most of its time was spent drafting a new 'statement' that is actually no different from the previous one in its form or content. Perhaps one or two suggestions were phrased in a slightly different way. Some more enlightened members of the 'Commission' were very much opposed to this orientation and did not agree with the text that was later issued on behalf of the entire 'Commission'.

From the fact that the Bishop chose the members of the 'Commission' using a personal criterion and not according to their competence, that he was the President (which doesn't happen in such cases), that he made it use his 'data' and his 'records' and that he edited its 'statements' for the public, we can clearly see that it was merely a tool in the hands of the Bishop. Not only that but he preceded it by giving his own judgements

about the events of Medjugorje before it had made 'its' official
opinion known. In this way, the present 'Commission' has
become a problem in itself, not a solution.

Conclusion

In contesting the supernatural character of the events of
Medjugorje, Bishop Zanic hasn't used *a single valid piece of evidence*
against them. He has expressed only doubts, invented 'facts',
half-truths and false interpretations. He himself has confirmed
that such evidence is worth nothing because both the facts and
his own opinion on Medjugorje have been radically changed by
him several times. Even though he refers to the same things and
to the same events, this doesn't prevent him from declaring them
on one occasion true, on another occasion as lies on the part
of the Franciscans and the visionaries and on a third occasion
as hallucinations on the part of the visionaries and millions of
pilgrims and lastly as works of Satan.

Furthermore, the Bishop improperly entered the field of
science, and as a layman, opposed facts and specialists in
medicine, psychology, psychiatry and theology. He denied things
without giving reasons, doubted things without warrant and
affirmed things without proof. Thus his interpretation of the facts
of Medjugorje as 'collective hallucination' is *senseless* from a
scientific point of view and *irresponsible* from a human point of
view. Fortunately, the facts are mightier than their interpreter.

He has declared things that are non-existent as being the 'key'
to the understanding of Medjugorje, whereas he has purposely
and unjustly associated other things with Medjugorje such as
the 'Hercegovina case' and the problems of the two chaplains
from Mostar that are in no way connected. Still, his criticism
has in no way affected Medjugorje and what is more, right from
the beginning, even beforehand, he had kept a certain distance
from the visionaries, the Franciscans and the pilgrims.

Just how much all this is in contrast with the events of
Medjugorje has been confirmed by Archbishop Franic in his
statement that 'the events of Medjugorje are of supernatural
origin' and 'Medjugorje in three years, has done more for the
faith than all the pastoral activity carried out in forty years in
our local Church'. He is totally convinced of Medjugorje and
of all that is happening there and since he is not oppressed by

the things that outsiders are at all costs trying to introduce, can see even more easily than at Lourdes or Fatima the message of God, through Our Lady. His declaration is confirmed by the Christian lives of millions of pilgrims, by the conversions and by the miraculous healings.

Medjugorje with its message of conversion and peace is greatly opposed to any attempt to turn it into a shooting-range for any battle other than that against sin, especially all individual effort and what is in favour of peace.

Everything, up to now, makes us think that God and Our Lady are at work in Medjugorje, and that in this time of crisis, by their presence they are continually trying to teach, enliven, uplift and direct humanity towards peace and salvation.

No one has the right to make a private monopoly of Medjugorje and use his power against it, making God's action through Our Lady futile. Unfortunately, Zanic has attempted this to such an extent that he has, despite an explicit warning from the Holy See, been hasty in giving a personal judgement. This unhappily is not evidence against Medjugorje, but only against himself.

(vi)

Fr Rupcic's opinion of the Bishop's memorandum should be supplemented by the detailed reply to the document made by Fr Laurentin. Instead of drawing on his rare expertise, so generously available to him, the Bishop launched a personal attack on this scholar. When Newman was attacked he composed one of the great documents of Church history, the *Apologia pro Vita sua*. Laurentin did not issue such a manifesto. But he took up the Bishop's submission point by point. The overall effect is damaging, not to say damning. It is not merely an instance of superb dialectician dealing with a less gifted man. The French theologian rightly criticises the whole orientation, tenor and character of the Bishop's document.

The preliminary question is that of the commission. The Bishop surprisingly named himself first member and president of the body: Laurentin notes that the Bishop of Lourdes in a similar circumstance did nothing of the kind; nor did the

Archbishop of Tuam, in whose diocese Knock is situated. It is more serious that despite the advice given by Rome — which the Bishop himself recalls — to proceed with caution, he still rushes into print before all the media. The letter was circulated far and wide.

The aim of the document is frankly and pitiably polemical whereas one expects from a Bishop in the post-conciliar Church respectful dialogue, sympathy with other people's feelings and a willingness to use the best elements in every situation constructively.

It is deeply disturbing, shocking even, to see the reckless attacks on two persons of singular merit, the Franciscan Tomislav Vlasic, a man whom Fr Hans Urs von Balthasar once called a saint and Fr René Laurentin, one of the greatest apostles of the spoken and written word of our time.

But, as this same writer contends 'the strangest thing about the document is that everything is brought back to the quarrel between the Franciscans (sole religious ministers in the diocese until 1881) and the secular clergy who have to establish themselves there and find difficulty in doing so. This local quarrel, for which Rome has been seeking a solution in vain for forty years, encroaches on everything in the document and thrusts the apparitions into the background.

Our Lady was brought into the continuing wrangle when the young Franciscans sought her opinion through one of the visionaries: she was asked for her opinion thirteen times, so much so that she made a riposte to Vicka 'You think of nothing but these two.' One may disagree with Laurentin who says that the question should not have been put to Our Lady. I once asked him what Our Lady would have replied if she were approachable directly when Joan of Arc was condemned to be burned as a witch by a Catholic bishop! The simple painful fact is that since Our Lady took the part of two young men severely punished by Church authorities, we are asked to believe that the entire Medjugorje phenomenon lacks credibility.

The methodology then was to look for any and every argument which would help demolish the phenomenon. The two which were chosen were to prove disastrously brittle. The visionaries were the victims of hallucination; they were manipulated by the Friars.

The word hallucination occurs too often in the literature on Medjugorje, and possibly also in this book. The thesis is without foundation. Laurentin quotes Professor Emilio Servadio 'Genuine hallucination (not to be confused with optical illusions or mass hysteria) is always an individual fact. It is untenable that several people repeatedly, without ever failing, should have had identical hallucinatory experiences and that they should at the same time give no evidence of psychic anomalies. It is altogether astonishing that a bishop should make a diagnosis psychiatric in content, using criteria which are incorrect from a psychiatric point of view.'

Anyone who, like the present writer, has spent his whole life with young people will find the idea of manipulation practically absurd. I have written elsewhere that it was singularly unfortunate that such an insult was offered to these admirable witnesses to the apparitions at Medjugorje during International Youth Year. On the one hand the Church praises young people, encourages them to dedicate their splendid qualities to Christian ideals; on the other, when they give to the whole world a shining example of prayer, penance, gentleness and availability, they are dismissed as victims of manipulation. Who could manipulate a group of young people in their twenties (as all but one of them are), evening after evening, to pray for hours, to receive day after day in their homes visitors, the curious, the insensitive, with unfailing courtesy, with unwavering testimony to the supernatural world which they are privileged to observe?

Bishop Zanic went further. Whereas at the outset, before the question of the young Franciscans was raised, he thought that 'everything leads to the conviction that the children are not lying', he changed this favourable judgement later. He said bluntly in an interview given to the Italian review *Sabato*: 'they are little liars.'

The prelate got the children to contradict themselves and though this would have been due to the pressure on them he makes much capital of it. Laurentin quotes a Jesuit from Split: 'Bishop Zanic uses improper methods, by which the young visionaries, intimidated by his authority and the tape-recorder, end by stammering and saying what he wants them to say. The apostle Peter, upset by a momentary crisis, ended by denying Jesus. These are the methods of brainwashing which recall what cardinal Mindszenty had to endure. . . The Bishop should behave like a father desiring to defend, to correct, not as a judge, or worse still as a politician trying to trip up those who believe in the apparitions, especially the young visionaries.'

If the visionaries were too hasty in their expectation of the great sign, Laurentin rightly comments that the early Christians were mistaken in anticipation of an immediate end of the age; St Paul, who may for a while have shared the view, was obliged to correct them. The Bishop also complains of the fact that he had to deal with forty-seven 'visionaries'; as Laurentin points out, there were some fifty in Lourdes about the time of the genuine apparitions! The wheat can be sifted from the chaff.

The reader must go through the work of Fr Laurentin if he wishes to have the detail. A selection must be made here for reasons of space. Bishop Zanic says, for example, that Fr Laurentin advised him 'not to publish these things (i.e. the 'lies' of the visionaries and 'Fr Tomislav Vlasic's perjury') because it would be damaging with regard to the numerous conversions among the pilgrims.' Fr Laurentin's comment: 'This is a total misrepresentation of my remarks. I pointed out to the Bishop the disadvantage of displaying before the public the sordid quarrels which distress his diocese, on the principle that one washes one's dirty linen within the family. But especially I urged him not to publish ''inexactitudes''. Out of courtesy and respect I did not use the words ''lies'', ''calumnies'' or ''slanders'', hoping that he would better understand mollifying words. But I urged him not to publish so many false accusations against Tomislav Vlasic.'

Laurentin, who was once warned by the Bishop to keep away from Medjugorje at the risk of losing his reputation, discovered that this was not advice but a threat. The Bishop ends his memorandum with the outrageous assertion that 'he (Laurentin) abuses his authority on apparitions to make quick and easy money.' Earlier he had given the impression that the French author had made $600,000 on the sale of his book. A naïve conclusion which, as Laurentin remarks, will give a laugh to any writer. With what must be given to booksellers, and to the publisher, the writer is fortunate to get 10 per cent — for which he must wait. At the time the Bishop made his extraordinary statement, the Frenchman was still out of pocket on expenses,

different journalists come to see me. I have already told some of them what I think of the announcement by the bishops that official pilgrimages should not be brought to Medjugorje. In that I am united with my brother bishops. I think that by that announcement, they wanted, more than anything else, to refrain from final decisions before the Church investigation is completed. I am against slowing down the movement of pilgrimages, but I do not favour official pilgrimages. . . . I express my opinion — privately as a believer, not as a bishop — with personal conviction, that these events are of a supernatural origin. I conclude this from their fruits, which no one can deny; this is seen by the increase in prayer, penance and conversion, the way Our Lady recommends to peace.'

The Archbishop spoke from strength; he had met countless people who had been pilgrims to Medjugorje:

'Almost every day I meet hundreds of Italian pilgrims, among whom there are professors, medical doctors and other intellectuals. Actually, the other day, 3 December, the president of the Christian Democrat party, Piccoli, was in Medjugorje; he climbed the hill, followed the stations of the Cross, and went to confession. Now shall I say to all these intellectuals, theologians and experts, that all this comes from the devil, when they go to confession there, pray and are converted? To me that would be absurd. I also think that it is absurd to demand that the pilgrimages be stopped before the Diocesan Commission establishes whether these apparitions are from God or from the devil. Actually if these pilgrimages, these prayers, these conversions were stopped or suppressed, and if all this were to die out, then no one would be interested in finding out if it was from God — the interest would no longer exist. The only thing that would interest us then would be whether it died out by itself or if it was suppressed in an illegal way. Many of us are trying to explain these events theologically and scientifically, and I am one of the least of these. I am only a witness to my inner convictions. But many world experts, scientists in all fields of human interest, . . .go there to investigate.'

The Archbishop had a salutary word for the Diocesan Commission set up to investigate and report on the case. He thought that they 'should be thankful to God that they have so much literature about the case which they are investigating, and that they could hear the voice of the world's theological and scientific experts.'

There was practical advice on procedure: 'If the members of the Commission wish to treat this scientifically, they have to use scientific methods, and that is to study the sources and the literature. That is the basic methodology of a scientific investigation. The sources are the children who are the visionaries and their messages; the devotion of the pilgrims, the feelings of the faithful — *sensus fidelium* — and the literature that is being written about it. One has to interview, to talk with the pilgrims, to see their belief or disbelief.'

Dr Franic asked that allowance be made for the age of the visionaries and the possibility of error in what they report. It is well known that in a genuine vision the recipient may make an error of interpretation. One case, not the only one, is that of St Catherine of Siena who thought that Our Lady told her that she was not conceived immaculate. 'This means that this holy woman was following the suggestions of her Dominican teachers who, at that time, before the dogma was pronounced, held this theological opinion. The suggestion was so strong in her head that even in her mystical rapture, she could not sufficiently immerse herself in God to overcome the suggestion. Therefore all messages should be investigated one by one.'

Archbishop Franic was also informed on the alleged miracles. Italians had told him that documentation on healings stood at 139 items. 'Out of fifty cases with records they have separated twenty-five for more detailed investigation.'

Questioned on the advisability of measures against the gathering of the children in the room off the sanctuary, or against their leading the congregation in prayer Archbishop Franic could not refrain from the riposte: 'Shall the Bishop of Mostar forbid Our Lady to appear in the sacristy and forbid the children to lead the faithful in the Our Father? I do not know.'[1]

(iii)

In the course of our conversation with Dr Franic there had been the question of the Pope: Was he interested in Medjugorje? Did he believe in the authenticity? The Archbishop had no doubt about the answers to these questions. He hoped that the Pope would intervene. He was in Rome early in December of that year and discussed the whole matter with John Paul II. He has been discreet on the exchange of opinion. But it was significant that within a week of his return to Yugoslavia he visited Medjugorje and spent two days there as guest of the Franciscans, 16 and 17 December. He gave a lengthy interview to one of the Franciscans, Slavko Barberic, who questioned him on many aspects of the Medjugorje phenomenon. He saw the children twice during the visions and he visited them in their homes. He had interesting remarks to make about them; he stated that as a result of this contact his conviction deepened.

Dr Franic paid tribute to the Franciscans: 'You are considered to be directing the faith of the people and the pilgrims for your material gain and for your prestige in order to remain the leaders of the people, as in the past, without having to share that role with the Bishop and the secular clergy. I have observed none of these qualities in the Franciscans of Medjugorje; your only goal is to respond to the call which you feel in your souls to conversion, for the glory of God. I have seen great piety in you. Last night I told a Portuguese priest here that I found the Franciscans polite, pious, self-denying, working only for the glory of God and the salvation of souls.'

On 17 December the Archbishop celebrated the thirty-fourth anniversary of his episcopal ordination by leading the Mass as principal celebrant — on a previous visit he had remained among the congregation, receiving Holy Communion with the faithful wearing a scarf to veil his identity. This time he was possibly recognised and preached. He tells one incident with touching simplicity: 'Marija does express a greater depth in her relations with people, a greater kindness, or it may be that her behaviour pleases us more. Her gentleness is completely feminine and wholly Christian. She also gave me a prophecy. On 17 December, the anniversary of my episcopal ordination, she asked Our Lady a question. On that day, very privately, I celebrated the thirty-fourth anniversary of my episcopal consecration with a Mass which I led at Medjugorje. I was completely incognito. (?) No one mentioned that I was an archbishop but I was simply, a priest among other priests. I asked Marija if I would be imposing too much if she were to ask Our Lady if there was a message for me. I expressly said that I would be happy if she would give me some admonition for my conversion, if she would point her finger at my weaker points and tell me where I need to be careful and where I need to improve. However, the word I received was that from now on I should expect greater sufferings to be asked from me, and that Our Lady will be with me in those greater sufferings. It will probably be a reaction to the stand I have taken in regard to Medjugorje. I have already seen this in Rome and at home also. However, we shall see what will happen.'

Dr Franic wished to set the great new Marian phenomenon in the wider context of Christian renewal through Mary and the Spirit: 'In a word, I would put all this into the framework of the spiritual renewal which Mary began at Lourdes and Fatima. Mary cannot do anything without the Holy Spirit. She was not able to conceive in her womb without the Holy Spirit in her heart. . . Today in the Church she cannot give Christ to the world without the Holy Spirit. Therefore, the Holy Spirit is leading the renewal of the Church through Mary. She is not a goddess, from whom we are expecting salvation, that comes from Christ through the Holy Spirit. She is only an intercessor, a mediatress between us and God and Christ. Her apparition and the signs of her motherly love come from the Holy Spirit, who together with Christ, takes care of the world. Under the direction of the Father she gives love to the world and is redeeming it.

Therefore, I see the work of the Holy Spirit especially in the charism of locutions, communications in words and inner speech. I am convinced that the same Spirit who is working in them is working in all the renewal movements in the Church, which we also have in our country, the focolarini, the neocatechumens, charismatic prayer groups, cursillos, volunteers in suffering. Such things come from abroad but they are growing here, as is Dom Gobbi's Marian movement for priests, as are our prayer groups which are increasing among young people in Zagreb, Split and other places. They arise spontaneously and independently. I would especially like to emphasise that young people, who are quite numerous in Split, say that they have adoration every Thursday in the church of St Philip. They also assist at Mass every Saturday, and they pray in their own way. They say that in Medjugorje they have received a call not only to come to religion classes but also to pray together and to assist at Mass.

This is something that has grown here from the grass roots. This is real faith, the real Church — Pentecost. This is a depoliticised Church, the Church which looks only for the glory of God, to give him thanks and praise, and which is endeavouring to save people. This is the Church which, through Christ's saving work, is bringing people to God, spreading his Kingdom and leading them to the eternal Kingdom.'

(iv)

Dr Franic admitted his surprise at the impact of the Medjugorje phenomenon: 'I absolutely never expected that the whole world would be attracted and touched by Medjugorje, which, to my great surprise has become the culmination of the working of the Holy Spirit. I see that Our Lady is calling all of us to come here from different countries to recognise that we are brothers and sisters. . . I especially see the importance of the role of Medjugorje in the ecumenical work of the Church where Our Lady is bringing us closer, uniting us with our brothers from the Orthodox Church, Moslems, and even our brothers who are Marxists. Our Lady spreads only love. She is the Mother of all and she is teaching us to love even at moments when we feel that our brothers do not understand us, that they interpret us falsely and think that this is a politicisation of the faith, without understanding us and Our Lady, and consider all this as an hallucination. One can conclude, according to what is happening there, what is being talked about there, and what the children say that one universal love is being born there through the gospel, which recommends that we love all men even when it seems that they are our enemies. Anxiety and divisions arise because of different opinions and convictions. Some think about Medjugorje and prayer groups in one way and some in another. . . I believe that we have to be ready for suffering and lack of understanding, to spread love even where we do not find it so that the message and victory of Our Lady is not defeated but becomes the salvation of everyone. Personally I return from Medjugorje with the firm conviction that I should never allow anxiety to arise in me about priests or the faithful who think differently. My desire is to retain the mental outlook which I had during these two days with you Franciscans who are working here day and night, hearing confessions, preaching, teaching people how to pray to God in meditation and in the liturgy.'

The Archbishop was insistent on the distinction between the question of the apparitions and the dispute between the secular clergy and the Franciscans. He advised the Franciscans in Medjugorje to follow his own practice of ignoring criticism except in cases where the faithful would be seriously misinformed. He appealed to the principle of information and communication accepted by the Church to justify diffusion of knowledge about Medjugorje: 'Therefore, there should be an information centre for events in Medjugorje so that people will know what is happening there. Things should be explained in a peaceful way, without attacking anyone, but aiming at sound information. This would help you, me and all those who have good will. We sometimes receive information which is in itself bad because it is false. We have to find the right solution for this.'

In passing it may be noted that such centres as the Archbishop desired do now exist in many countries. One of the best known is the Center for Peace in Boston, funded and directed by John Hill. It has helped disseminate a vast amount of primary documentation about Medjugorje; the English translation of the Archbishop's interview given to *Glas Koncila* and that given to the Franciscans have been distributed far and wide by the Centre.

(v)

Where Dr Franic differs entirely from Dr Zanic is in the context wherein Medjugorje should be judged. Dr Zanic locates it in an administrative setting, focusing attention on the conduct of the Franciscans, who are cast in the role almost of the villains in a detective story. Dr Franic widens the horizon to embrace the whole life of the post-conciliar Church, with its already dominant themes and its characteristic responses to the problems of the age. A theologian and a man of rare spiritual intuition, he does not overlook difficulties of men called to rule and to minister in the Church. But his wide sweep envelops such problems, reduces them to their true dimensions in the face of the almighty Spirit of God. He speaks no bad of anyone.

To appreciate Dr Franic's discernment of the Medjugorje

phenomenon itself we should read an earlier letter he sent to Fr Rastrelli.

Referring to your letter of 13 November 1984 may I say that I have followed very carefully the messages of Medjugorje. I have also followed the extraordinary cases of cures of various physical disabilities at Medjugorje, which have been reported to me by the pilgrims who go to and from Medjugorje. Among these pilgrims there have been several professors from Milan University, as well as theologians and Mariologists, for example Fr Laurentin.

I have written and said that there is need to examine every message separately and every extraordinary fact separately, because each message and each fact has its own degree of the supernatural or of what is not supernatural. In a word we must sift the wheat from the chaff.

But generally speaking I no longer have any doubt about the supernatural character of the religious phenomena in Medjugorje. God with his Spirit is present in that place. There is, however, need to avoid fanaticism, a too literal explanation of the messages and facts, as we need to avoid a rationalist approach which would dismiss the messages and facts at Medjugorje as not being supernatural and explain everything in terms of arrogance on the part of the children and material self-interest on the part of the Friars.

In my humble opinion, which I express privately, submitting to the definitive judgement of the Church, there is need to allow some time and not to rush to either positive or negative judgements. I do not deal with the case of the two Friars expelled from their order and I leave it to experts to find a just solution. In other messages I can see nothing against gospel teaching or the tradition of Holy Mother Church.

As you know, dear father, I am president of the commission for the doctrine of the faith of the Yugoslav episcopal conference, and I write this letter conscious of the responsibility of my office.

(vi)

On 18 February 1985 the Archbishop sent to Cardinal Ratzinger a report on the general situation in regard to Medjugorje and the Bishop's attitude:

I allow myself to refer to this Congregation about some difficulties over the facts of Medjugorje, which could prevent a serene and just view of these facts.

1. It is being said that the essence of these facts consists in disobedience to the diocesan Bishop; that is that the facts have been invented and orchestrated by the Friars on the spot, especially by the 'mystifier and charismatic magician' Fr Tomislav Vlasic (thus he is called by the Bishop of Mostar) against the diocesan Bishop to prove that the seven parishes which the Franciscans in Hercegovina should, by an order of the Holy See, many times repeated, hand over to the diocesan Bishop, ought on the contrary, to remain under their control.

The diocesan Bishop asserts that Our Lady of Medjugorje, who according to the Franciscans, defends their thesis, cannot teach disobedience to the Holy See, and therefore the apparition could not but be the work of Satan who takes on the appearance of Our Lady or else that it is a whole racket and a scheme of the Friars to defend their thesis, definitely a real fraud invented by Satan to destroy the Church in Hercegovina and gravely harm the Church in Yugoslavia and consequently the Church throughout the world.

To this objection one may reply:

For the last three and a half years over three million pilgrims have come to Medjugorje, from all five continents and all, after the pilgrimage, have returned home converted or brought back to the Christian life from religious indifference or from absolute atheism, renewing contact with prayer and religious practices like fasting, generally on Friday, and in some homes also on Wednesday, their food consisting of bread and water, in a word completely reconciled with God and men.

It is not therefore possible that the people of God in such a great number, could be deceived for so long by the Friars or by a Franciscan sorcerer who, besides, in my humble opinion and in the opinion of countless pilgrims, is recognised as a man of God as are all the other Franciscans of Medjugorje. To these remarks purely spiritual in character should be added as proof of the miraculous, the extraordinary healings verified by medical experts, set out in a book by Fr Laurentin, publication showing that outer signs prove the objectivity of the relevant facts, and that they have a true religious dimension.

The twenty-three page letter of the Bishop of Mostar, which contains grave calumnies against the Friars, against Fr Laurentin, and the visionaries, has already caused scandal, which will become more serious and known to all the world if the Bishop of Mostar also declares that all the facts of conversion and healing are false, alleging that they are a fabrication and mystification by the Franciscans and therefore, consequently, by Satan.

It is said that His Excellency the Bishop of Mostar is preparing to make this declaration very soon, before the feast of the Annunciation.

It is known that His Excellency the Bishop has transferred Tomislav Vlasic and Fr Slavko Barberic, only because they preached from the altar that the facts of Medjugorje are not bogus, and that he has threatened to transfer every Franciscan and every sister who does not preach that the said facts are bogus.

2. I have the feeling that the Yugoslav government is so opposed to the facts of Medjugorje that it considers them a counter-revolution and could cause a 'blood-bath' if the Church does not quickly pronounce on the non-supernatural character of these facts.

To this I reply that what is being taught in Medjugorje is the authentic doctrine of Vatican II on the Church as communion, that is on the Church as love towards God and all men, God as love, the Church as love, open to the other Christian churches, especially the Orthodox church which in Yugoslavia has about nine million faithful; towards the non-Christian religions, especially the Moslems, who in Yugoslavia number about four million, and towards distant atheists, just with the love of Christ dead and risen. Our Lady of Medjugorje teaches us expressly to love the Orthodox, marxists, Moslems, atheists and also those who persecute us.

This love for the dead and risen Christ is a specific message of Medjugorje, which enlarges the messages of Fatima by a new factor, giving thus a new and essential light on Our Lady of Fatima. And when this message is grasped by the Yugoslav Marxists it cannot but please the government since it tends to promote unity among peoples and religions in Yugoslavia and between atheist and theist. Already Medjugorje is tolerated by the political authority and in my humble opinion it will be ever more so.

The facts of Medjugorje have then a specific character which is truly important for the whole Church and not certainly directed against the authority of the diocesan bishop. I have never heard from the visionaries or the Franciscans a word against the authority of the diocesan bishop, always I have heard only words full of veneration and obedience towards their bishop and towards the Holy Father.

3. It is said that all the Yugoslav bishops have forbidden pilgrimages to Medjugorje:

I shall say humbly but firmly that this assertion is false. The Yugoslav bishops merely wished to say by this statement that they had not themselves initiated or organised pilgrimages to Medjugorje, as Fr Massimo Rastrelli, a Jesuit from Naples, can testify from the declaration given him by the Curia of Zagreb.

It is for all the reasons set forth above that I humbly beg the Holy See

*to deign to appoint as soon as possible an International Commission
dependent on the Holy See itself, to evaluate the difficulties raised by His
Excellency the Bishop of Mostar, especially on the disobedience of the
Franciscan Friars towards the diocesan bishop, in regard to the handing
over of the seven parishes, and, particularly the suspension* a divinis *of
the two young Franciscans who continue to celebrate Holy Mass, with
the tacit permission of their Provincial. With the certainty of course that
Our Lady has not advised the Friars to disobey the institutional Church.*

*I note that I have always advised the Franciscans of Hercegovina to
obey the Church, by handing over at once the seven parishes to the bishop,
taking account of the fact that the young Friars, who are suspended* a divinis
*are victms of the confused situation caused by conflicting claims between
the bishop and the province and that they are, nevertheless, in their hearts,
good priests and religious. They should, however, obey and submit to the
judgement of the Church and begin a stage of rehabilitation.*

*If all this can be settled, with patience and love, there will certainly
not be any further difficulties for the diocesan bishop, who will end by
recognising the presence of the Holy Spirit and Our Lady in Medjugorje,
although, in my humble opinion and in that of famous theologians like
Frs Laurentin and Urs von Balthasar, two things which have no
relationship with each other should be kept apart: the facts of Medjugorje
and the facts of the conflict between the diocesan bishop and the Franciscan
province of Hercegovina, which go back to Turkish times.*

*The Bishop of Mostar is, besides, so convinced that he is persecuted
by the Friars of Medjugorje as to behave accordingly: it is said, in fact,
in good and sure conscience that, driven by his persecution mania, he will
be satisfied only when he succeeds in declaring the facts of Medjugorje
unauthentic.*

*Therefore I humbly beg the Holy See to appoint at once an International
Commission to examine these difficulties before the Bishop succeeds in
banning pilgrimages to Medjugorje definitively.*

*Only thus can great scandal be avoided in the Church in Yugoslavia
and throughout the world.*

*The Bishop of Mostar, whom I appointed a Canon of Split and whom
I value highly for his positive qualities, has begun to speak against me,
saying that I have been converted to the charismatics; he also says that
because of old age, I have lost the proper exercise of my reason, etc.*

*I must say that I would never have believed that Bishop Zanic would
have reached this point, that his conscience would have sunk to the level
of wanting to destroy morally all those who hold different opinions from him.*

The facts of Medjugorje at this stage do not belong only to the Church of Mostar, they concern the whole Church. I insist, therefore once more, always humbly, on my request and that of the Yugoslav Bishops asking the Holy See to establish as soon as possible an International Commission which can examine, in veritate et caritate, *the difficulties which so seriously and dramatically upset the mind of His Excellency Bishop Zanic and of the diocesan priests, that the situation may be clarified definitively.*

I am, the most devoted child of this Congregation and of the Holy See, Frane Franic, Archbishop of Split.

P.S. The Archbishop makes a correction; he has checked the statement of the Yugoslav bishops at their meeting the previous October and found that they did not ask for an International Commission. But his own arguments, he contends, should stand.

(vii)

As a kind of reply to this letter the Bishop of Mostar sent a letter to the Secretariat of State — the Council for the Public Affairs of the Church; it is dated 29 January 1985:

The campaign for and against the apparitions of Medjugorje is assuming rather dramatic proportions.

Already in 1982, we in the Church of Yugoslavia were agreed that nothing should be written publicly either for or against the events of Medjugorje.

In 1983 Fr Ljudevit Rupcic, professor of Franciscan theology in Sarajevo, published a book in Croatian, The apparitions of Medjugorje, *without the knowledge or approval of his religious superiors.*

At Christmas time 1983 Fr René Laurentin came to Mostar, and despite the requests of the local bishop, he had this book translated into French.

In the year 1984 three articles by Fr Laurentin were published in Glas Koncila, *they had already been published in* France Catholique; *they were favourable to the apparitions. There followed some lesser articles and responses from readers, all in favour of Medjugorje.*

Though I thought this manner of acting extremely incorrect, I did not react against it.

Then Laurentin's book came out, in French and other languages.

In all this propaganda the attitude of his Exc. Most Rev. Frane Franic has appeared most improper and troublesome. His archiepiscopal Curia has become a kind of Medjugorje centre. He has, as he has publicly stated and as I am informed, been, up to now, three times in Medjugorje. He has preached there many times. He has given interviews to Glas Koncila *and to the Franciscans of Medjugorje. He has visited the homes of the visionaries without any notification to the local bishop or Fr Provincial, as if these did not exist.*

All this becomes a serious matter.

Therefore I beg the Holy See to be good enough to issue enlightened directives on the subject. With the deepest esteem, Monsignor Pavao Zanic.

(viii)

Two further letters will illustrate the apparently insoluble problem within the institutional Church in Yugoslavia on the issue of the tension surrounding Medjugorje — one illustrates Bishop Zanic's mode of action. On 25 March 1985 he wrote to Fr Tomislav Pervan, parish priest:

The latest development and event concerning the 'visionary' Ivan Dragicevic's letter about the sign, on 9 May 1982, written while he was still living in the seminary of Visoko, are certainly known to the personnel to whom is entrusted the pastoral care of the parish of Medjugorje.

Along with this letter we are sending you also the photocopy of the Minutes of the Commission set up to investigate the events of Medjugorje, those of the last session which took place at Mostar on 7 March this year, when the letter was opened which contained the description of the sign which will take place in confirmation of the 'apparitions' of Medjugorje.

Last year in conversation with Ivan Dragicevic, he declared before the Commission that the sign would be a shrine of Our Lady and that this sign will appear unexpectedly one morning.

Even before this the Episcopal Curia had reached the conclusion that there is no question of apparitions of Our Lady at Medjugorje. Nevertheless since, in 1982, a Commission for the investigation of these events was set up by this Episcopal Curia and since it wishes to and must, study each item in depth, the Episcopal Curia has not thus far issued an official declaration on the real state of affairs, but already many times by written documents has decided and asked that propaganda be stopped; all of which has been in vain by reason of the disobedience of the personnel in charge of pastoral care in Medjugorje and of the 'visionaries'.

I quote the documents which have been sent to you by means of which this stated request was made:

— *13.12.1981, No 977: Attitude in regard to the events in Medjugorje (Official bulletin, 4/81);*
— *12.4.1983, No 341: Letter to the Parish Priest with directive on his activity;*

Summons to discussion:
— *31.3.1983, No 297: Invitation to discussion;*
— *19.7.1984, No 777: Invitation to discussion;*
— *27.9.1984, No 982: Invitation to discussion;*

— *Public hand-out after the two day session of the Commission on Medjugorje, which says that the pastoral personnel and the visionaries of Medjugorje are asked not to make public statements not even for the press on the content of the visions and on claimed miraculous healings.*

In our meeting held at Mostar on 31 September 1984, in the Episcopal Curia I asked that the events in Medjugorje should 'be given low profile and very quietly extinguished'. Instead everything has remained as it was and we can expect great shame for the Church.

Now, after all this, I demand most pressingly of you that the 'visionaries' should not be allowed to come forward publicly in church and have 'visions' there as they have 'visions' in Mostar and in the past have had them in Sarajevo, in Visoko and in Dubrovnik, just as they have them also in their homes; they say they have had them towards the end of 1981.

Within about ten days — in the evening and without attracting notice — the new statue of Our Lady before the altar must be taken away and the one which was there previously must be put back.

Speaking about the apparitions must stop, no message must be published, there must be an end to devotions arising out of the 'apparitions', and from their messages, the sale of records and printed material which propagate the 'apparitions' must stop.

People can go to confession and Masses can be celebrated.

I do not allow the other priests, in particular Fr Jozo Zovko and Fr Tomislav Vlasic and Fr Ljudevit Rupcic, to celebrate Mass for the people or preach.

The 'visionaries' are to hand over to you everything they have written, in particular the so-called 'Life of Our Lady', since no excuse that there is question of a secret can justify them in not handing them over.

Since there has been talk in public of their Diaries and of other writings and since this has had a great influence on the events of Medjugorje, all these documents and materials are subject to the control of the Episcopal Curia and are a matter of investigation in regard to the phenomenon of Medjugorje.

I hope that you will carry out what I request you by the present letter. With greetings and wishing you God's blessing. (Signed and sealed).

The reader may recall what was said in the first chapter on the rights of those who receive visions or apparitions. They have the same right to their own property, writings included, as has everyone else. It is the Church which defends the right to private property. They could be invited to surrender these things: not ordered. It is particularly distasteful in this day and age to see young people the victims of such harshness. The reader will also recall the swingeing words of Hans Urs von Balthasar. The immediate effect of the Bishop's directive was that the visionaries had to meet Our Lady in the presbytery, as Dr Giorgio Sanguinetti has described. There was room at the inn!

(ix)

But what of Ivan's alleged revelation of the sign? A letter from Archbishop Franic will clear that up. On 28 June 1985 he sent the following letter to Bishop Zanic:

This morning I heard the tape recording of your conversation with Signora Diana Basile, and with others of our Italian brethren.

In this conversation you have given as probably the most convincing argument against the truth of the Medjugorje events the fact that you caught me in falsehood, in two matters precisely:

1. According to your assertion I have said that all the bishops of Yugoslavia support the authenticity of the events in Medjugorje, except the Bishop of Mostar.

2. According to you, moreover, I would have uttered another patent falsehood; though I had seen Ivan's written reply on the 'great sign', (I would have said) that he had said nothing about the 'great sign' in his written reply.

Your first assertion is completely false, the second is half false, because you passed over in silence the other part of my statement so that this half-truth is worse than your first entirely false statement.

1. Never, in presence of anyone or anywhere have I said or could I say that all the bishops of Yugoslavia support the authenticity of the facts of Medjugorje, since we are all aware, as an example, of the declaration made by Bishop Turk to the Italian public against the authenticity of these events; as we also know that the Bishop of Sibenick, Mgr Arneric, has several times expressed himself in public as against the authenticity of these events, which has not prevented us from remaining friends as before.

2. It is true that last spring (17 April 1985) during the session of the Yugoslav Episcopal Conference, I said that in the written reply of the visionary Ivan there is nothing written about the 'great sign', but I also added, in the same passage, that I was stating this on the basis of the declaration of Ivan himself and of all the other 'visionaries', who together, in agreement with Ivan assert that he lied when he said that he was writing about the great sign, for on the contrary he had written nothing about the great sign, as 'Our Lady had revealed it to him, for this for him was a secret he could not betray as in fact he had not betrayed it'; what he wrote was totally different. All this because he feared expulsion from the seminary if he wrote nothing. Behaving thus he evidently made a mistake; but he admits that he made his mistake, saying that for this happening he really deserved to be flogged.

That's what I said, Your Ecellency, within the Yugoslav Episcopal Conference. Your assertion on the other hand is a half-truth, which for me is worse than if there had been a total falsehood. And thus, along with the Franciscan priests of Medjugorje and along with the 'visionaries' I have been flung into the same cauldron of liars and falsifiers.

This wounds me, because I have always defended your prestige, while you have walked on my reputation before public opinion.

I hold you morally bound to restore my good name, by withdrawing your statement before the very people to whom you delivered it.

For my part from now on I forgive you everything, for to that we are bound in the power of the Gospel, which holds for me and for you, and also because Our Lady herself exhorts us to act thus.

1.   The point about the episcopal declaration was that it led to confusion worldwide. This was due to its appearance in the *Osservatore Romano* which, despite the fact that it was merely a news item, gave the impression that the Holy See was directly involved; the Vatican paper is now in many translations. All letters quoted here are from photocopies in my possession. I have said that Bishop Zanic is skilful in his use of the media; he has friends in many places.

8

SPIRITUALITY OF A PARISH

Have medieval historians given an exaggerated picture of community faith and practice? Were all deeply involved, entering into practices like the Way of the Cross as well as the great liturgical acts with the sentiment of life fulfilment? Were the great cathedrals mighty acts of communal faith, were the guilds and all the other legacies of those times just the expression of religious conviction so strong that it would not be denied an outlet?

Such questions may appear to be the result of fantasy or illusion to those whose social smugness cannot see beyond the spreading religious indifference of our time, who think that the spectacle of the non-practising masses, the sea of post-Christians for whom the gospel of Christ has little or no relevance to life, must be accepted, even taken for progress because it all has come with phenomenal advancement in science and technology. The consumer society and the permissive society seem indissolubly wedded in what we call the western world. What has come out of the alliance is not totally edifying unless we close our eyes to rising crime rates, spreading addiction to drugs, alcohol and gambling, suicide statistics which are a constant in countries with a high standard of living, broken homes, abortions on an irretrievable spiral, terrorism, abductions and the ineradicable mark of shame on the international community: while hundreds, perhaps a thousand million pounds, are spent daily in the arms race, millions suffer disease, ignorance and famine with no hope beyond the night that surrounds them.

What doom and gloom! Whoever protests should perhaps point out where the grim survey departs from fact. Nor is it helpful to believe that the worst evils of the world will not recur. Six million Jews were victims to Hitler, more than fifteen million people to Stalin; but we are moving out of such dark times. Yes?

What would the three million who died in Cambodia in quite recent memory say to that?

Our Lady's warnings in Medjugorje unquestionably have a relevance to the evils of our time and to the possible cosmic catastrophe which would both punish and totally dwarf them. The secrets are not all ominous and threatening. But some of them may be so interpreted and there are asides in the continuing dialogue with the visionaries which confirm this reading; as well as what may be deduced from the behaviour of one who has heard all the secrets.

So what to do? When the desert moves towards you, till your own garden. Our Lady has begun the reform which she would want to see worldwide, with the parish where the visionaries live. She has apparently echoed Old Testament times by making a covenant with the people of this community. She has chosen it and bestows her special favours on it. We are not in the realm of the pious invention here. This is a weekly occurrence, a series of communications which are documented.

They are set out here, down to the most recent communications. They are messages received each Thursday by the visionaries (mostly by Marija), for the parishioners. Our Lady had signified her wish to see the parishioners come to the church, dedicated to St James, on one day each week, to receive spiritual direction from her. The Franciscans chose Thursday in memory of the National Eucharistic Congress (NEK). It will be clear from the content that these communications have a wider relevance than the parish, or those who happen to spend some time there.

1 March 1984

'Dear children! I have chosen this parish in a special way and I wish to lead it. I am keeping it in love and I wish everyone to be mine.

Thank you for your response this evening. I wish that you will always be in greater numbers with me and my Son. Every Thursday I will speak a special message for you.'

8 March 1984

'Thank you for your response to my call. Dear children. In this parish start self-conversion. In that way all those who come here will be enabled to convert.'

15 March 1984

'This evening, dear children, in a special way I am grateful to you for being here. Continually adore the Most-holy Sacrament. I am always present when the faithful are in adoration. Special graces are then being received.' (Many men had remained in the church for adoration, despite a hard day's work in the fields.)

22 March 1984

'Dear children! This evening I am asking you in a special way during this Lent to honour the wounds of my Son, which he received from the sins of this parish. Unite with my prayers for this parish so that his sufferings may become bearable. Thank you for your response to my call. Make an effort to come in greater numbers.

29 March 1984

'Dear children! This evening in a special way I am asking for your perseverance in trials. Ponder how the Almighty is still suffering, because of your sins. So when sufferings come, offer them as your sacrifice to God. Thank you for your response to my call.'

5 April 1984

'Dear children! This evening I am especially asking you to venerate the Heart of my Son Jesus. Make atonement for the wounds inflicted on the Heart of my Son. That Heart has been offended by all kinds of sins. Thank you for coming this evening.'

12 April 1984

'Dear children! This evening I ask you to cease slander and to pray for the unity of the parish. For my Son and I have a special plan for this parish. Thank you for your response to my call.'

19 April 1984

'Dear children! Sympathise with me. Pray, pray, pray.'

26 April 1984

On this Thursday Our Lady gave no message. Marija thought that Our Lady had perhaps intended to give Thursday messages during Lent. On April 30 she spoke thus to Our Lady: 'Dear Lady, why have you not given me the message for the parish on Thursday?' Our Lady replied: 'Even though I had a special message for the parish to awaken the faith of every believer I do not wish to force anyone to anything he does not feel or does not want. Only a very small number have accepted the messages on Thursdays. At the beginning there were more, but now it seems as if it had become something ordinary to them. And some have been asking for the message recently only out of curiosity, not out of faith and devotion to my Son and to me.'

10 May 1984

'I am still speaking to you and I intend to continue. Just listen to my instructions.' This was Our Lady's response to the anxiety felt by many that she would not give any more messages to the parish, so affected were they by previous messages.

17 May 1984

'Dear children! Today I am very happy because there are many who desire to devote themselves to me. I thank you! You are not mistaken. My Son Jesus Christ wishes to bestow special graces on you through me. My Son is happy because of your dedication. Thank you because you have responded to my call.'

24 May 1984

'Dear children! I have already told you that I have chosen you in a special way just as you are. I, as your Mother, love you all. In your moments of difficulty do not be afraid. I love you even when you are far away from me and my Son. I ask you not to allow my heart to shed tears of blood because of the souls who are being lost through sin. Therefore dear children, pray, pray, pray! Thank you for your response to my call.'

31 May 1984

This was the feast of the Ascension. Our Lady told Marija that she would give the message on Saturday to be announced on Sunday.

2 June 1984

'Dear children! During the days of this novena (for Pentecost), pray for an outpouring of the Holy Spirit upon all your families and your parish. Pray, and you will not regret it. God will give you the gifts (of the Holy Spirit) and you will glorify him for them till the end of your life. Thank you for your response to my call.'

9 June 1984

On the previous Thursday (7 June) Our Lady did not give any message for the parish; she promised to give it this evening: 'Dear children! Tomorrow night (Pentecost Sunday), pray for the Spirit of truth, especially those of you from this parish. The Spirit of truth is necessary for you in order to convey the messages just as I give them to you, not adding anything or taking anything away. Pray that the Holy Spirit may inspire you with the spirit of prayer, that you pray more. I as your Mother say that you pray little.'

14 June 1984

No special message was given.

21 June 1984

'Pray, pray, pray! Thank you for your response to my call.'

5 July 1984

'Dear children! Today I wish to tell you: Always pray before your work and end your work with prayer. If you do that God will bless you and your work. These days you have been praying too little and working too much. Pray therefore. In prayer you will find rest. Thank you for your response to my call.'

12 July 1984

'Dear children! These days Satan is trying to thwart all my plans. Pray that his plan may not be fulfilled. I will pray to my Son Jesus that he may give you the grace to experience his victory in Satan's temptations. Thank you for your response to my call.'

19 July 1984

'Dear children! These days you have been experiencing how Satan is working. I am always with you and do not be afraid of temptations. God always watches over you. I have given myself to you and I sympathise with you even in the smallest temptations. Thank you for your response to my call.'

26 July 1984

'Dear children! Today also I would like to call you to persist in prayer and penance. Let the young people of the parish especially be more active in their prayer. Thank you for your response to my call.'

2 August 1984

'Dear children! Today I am happy and I thank you for your prayers. Pray more these days for the conversion of sinners. Thank you for your response to my call.'

11 August 1984

Our Lady did not give a message last Thursday. This is what she said to Marija this evening: 'Dear children! Pray, because Satan is continually trying to thwart my plans. Pray with your heart and in prayer give yourselves up to Jesus.'

14 August 1984

This apparition was unexpected. Ivan was praying in his home. After that he began to prepare to go to church for the evening service. Unexpectedly Our Lady appeared to him and asked him to report this message to the people: 'I am asking the people to pray with me these days. Pray all the more. Fast strictly on Wednesday and Friday; say at least one Rosary — joyful, sorrowful and glorious mysteries — every day.' Our Lady asked the people to accept this message with a firm will. She asked this especially from the parishioners and the faithful in places nearby.

16 August 1984

'Dear children! I beg all of you, especially those from this parish, to live my messages and report them to whoever you meet. Thank you for your response to my call.'

23 August 1984

'Pray, pray, pray!' Marija said that Our Lady had asked that people, especially the young, keep order in the church during Mass.

30 August 1984

'Dear children! The cross was in God's plan when you built it. Especially these days, go on the hill and pray at the foot of the cross. I need your prayers. Thank you for your response to my call.'

6 September 1984

'Dear children! Without prayer there is no peace. Therefore I say to you, dear children, pray at the foot of the cross for peace. Thank you for your response to my call.'

13 September 1984
'Dear children! I continually need your prayers. You wonder what all these prayers are for. Turn around, dear children and you will see how much ground sin has gained in this world. Therefore, pray that Jesus may conquer. Thank you for your response to my call.'

20 September 1984
'Dear children! Today I ask you to start fasting from your heart. There are many people who fast but only because everyone else is fasting. It has become a custom which no one wants to stop. I ask the parish to fast out of gratitude to God for allowing me to remain this long in this parish. Dear children, fast and pray with your heart. Thank you for your response to my call.'

27 September 1984
'Dear children! Your prayer has helped the fulfilment of my plans. Pray continually for their complete fulfilment. I beg the families of the parish to pray the family rosary. Thank you for your response to my call.'

4 October 1984
'Dear children! Today I would like to tell you that your prayers delight me, but there are those in the parish who do not pray and my heart is sad. Pray therefore, that I may bring all your sacrifices and prayers to the Lord. Thank you for your response to my call.'

Monday, 8 October 1984
(This message was given for the parish to Jakov in his home. He did not go to church that day because he was not well). 'Dear children! Let all the prayers you say in your homes in the evening be for the conversion of sinners because the world is in great sin. Pray the Rosary every evening.'

11 October 1984
'Dear children! Thank you for offering all your pains to God, even at this time when he is testing you through the crops which you are reaping. (Our Lady is alluding to prolonged rain which came in the middle of the harvest and caused great damage). Be aware, dear children, that he loves you and that it is for that reason that he tests you. Always present your burdens to God and do not worry.'

18 October 1984: Feast of St Luke, the Evangelist
'Dear children! Today I ask you to read the Bible in your homes every day. Place it in a visible place there, where it will always remind you to read it and pray. Thank you for your response to my call.'

25 October 1984
'Dear children! Pray during this month. God gave this month to me. I give it to you. Pray and ask God for graces. I will pray that he gives them to you. Thank you for your response to my call.'

1 November 1984
'Dear children! Today I call you to renew family prayer in your homes. The field work is over. Now, may all of you devote yourselves to prayer. Let prayer have first place in your families. Thank you for your response to my call.'

8 November 1984
'Dear children! You are not fully aware of the messages which God is sending to you through me. He is giving you great graces and you are not taking them. Pray to the Holy Spirit for enlightenment. If you only knew how great are the graces God is giving you, you would pray without ceasing. Thank you for your response to my call.'

15 November 1984
'You are chosen people and God has given you great graces. You are not aware of the importance of every message I am giving you. Now I only wish to say: Pray, pray, pray! I do not know what else to tell you because I love you and wish that in prayer you come to know my love and the love of God. Thank you for your response to my call.'

22 November 1984
'Dear children! These days, live all the main messages and continue to root them in your hearts this week (That week marked the end of one liturgical season and the beginning of Advent.) Thank you for your response to my call.'

29 November 1984
'Dear children! You do not know how to love and you do not know how to listen with love to the words I am giving you. Be

aware, my beloved ones, that I am your Mother and that I have come upon the earth to teach you how to listen out of love, how to pray out of love, and not out of compulsion because of the cross you are carrying. Through the cross, God is glorified in every person. Thank you for your response to my call.'

6 December 1984

'Dear children! These days, I am calling you to family prayer. Many times, I have given you messages in God's name, but you have not listened. This Christmas will be an unforgettable day for you, only if you accept the messages I am giving you. Dear children, do not allow that day of joy to be a day of deepest sorrow for me. Thank you for your response to my call.'

13 December 1984

'Dear children! You know that the day of joy is coming near, but without love you will obtain nothing. Therefore, first of all start loving your family and everyone in the parish. Then you will be able to love and accept all those who come here. Let this be the week of learning how to love. Thank you for your response to my call.'

20 December 1984

'Today I am asking you to do something concrete for Jesus Christ. On the day of joy, I want every family of the parish to bring a flower as a sign of abandonment to Jesus. I want every member of the family to have one flower next to the crib so that Jesus can come and see your devotion to him. Thank you for your response to my call.'

27 December 1984

'Dear children! This Christmas, Satan wanted in a special way to thwart God's plans. You, dear children, witnessed Satan even on Christmas day. But God conquered in your hearts. Let your hearts be continually joyful.'

3 January 1985

'Dear children! These days, the Lord granted you many graces. Let this be a week of thanksgiving for all the graces God has granted you. Thank you for your response to my call.'

10 January 1985

'Dear children! Today I want to thank you for all your sacrifices.

I thank especially those who come here gladly and have become dear to my heart. There are many parishioners who are not listening to my messages. It is because of those who are especially close to my heart that I give messages to the parish. And I will continue giving them for I love you and want you to spread them by your love. Thank you for your response to my call.'

Monday 14 January 1985
'Dear children! Satan is so strong. With all his power he wants to thwart the plans I have undertaken with you. You must only pray. Just pray and do not stop for a moment. I will pray to my Son that the plans I have started be fulfilled. Be patient and persevering in your prayers. Do not let Satan discourage you. He is working vigorously in the world. Be cautious.'

17 January 1985
'In these days, Satan is fighting deviously against this parish, and you, dear children, are asleep in (regard to) prayer. Only some of you are going to Mass. Persevere in these days of temptation. Thank you for your response to my call.'

24 January 1985
These days you have savoured the sweetness of God through the renewal in your parish. Satan is working even more violently to take the joy away from each of you. Through prayer you can totally disarm him and ensure your happiness. Thank you for your response to my call.'

31 January 1985
'Dear children! Today I want to tell you to open your hearts to God, like flowers in the spring yearning for the sun. I am your Mother and I always want you to be closer to the Father, that he may always pour abundant gifts into your hearts. Thank you for your response to my call.'

7 February 1985
'Dear children! Satan is manifesting himself in this parish in a particular way these days. Pray, dear children, that God's plan may be carried out, and that every work of Satan be turned to the glory of God. I have remained this long to help you in your great trials. Thank you for your response to my call.'

14 February 1985

'Dear children! Today is the day when I give you the message for the parish, but the whole parish is not accepting the messages and does not live them. I am sad and I want you, dear children, to listen to me and to live my messages. Every family must pray and read the Bible. Thank you for your response to my call.'

21 February 1985

'Dear children! From day to day I have been appealing to you for renewal and prayer in the parish. But you are not responding. Today I am appealing to you for the last time. This is the season of Lent, and you, as a parish in Lent, should be moved to love by my appeal. If you are not, I do not want to give you any more messages. Thank you for your response to my call.'

28 February 1985

'Dear children! Today I call you to live these words during this week: I love God. Dear children! With love, you can achieve everything, even what appears impossible. God wants this parish to belong to him completely. And I want that too. Thank you for your response to my call.'

7 March 1985

'Dear children! Today, I invite you to renew prayer in your families. Dear children, encourage the very young to pray and to go to holy Mass. Thank you for your response to my call.'

14 March 1985

'Dear children! In your life, you all experienced light and darkness. God gives every man the power to recognise good and evil. I am calling you to light, which you must carry to all those who are in darkness. From day to day, people come in your houses which are in darkness. You, dear children, give them light. Thank you for your response to my call.'

21 March 1985

'Dear children! I want to give you the messages. Therefore I ask you to accept these messages. Dear children, I love you in a special way. I have chosen this parish which is dearer to me than any other. . . .where I gladly came when the Almighty sent me. Therefore, dear children, I ask you to accept me for your well-being. Follow the messages. Thank you for your response to my call.'

28 March 1985
'Dear children! Today, I am asking you to pray, pray, pray. In prayer you will experience great joy and the solution to every helpless situation. Thank you for advancing in prayer. Each one of you belongs to my heart. I will be grateful to all who begin praying again in your families. Thank you for your response to my call.'

Wednesday 18 April 1985
'Dear children! Today I thank you for every opening of your hearts. Joy overwhelms me for every heart that opens to God, especially in the parish. Rejoice with me. Pray all the prayers for the opening of sinful hearts. I want this. God wants this through me. Thank you for your response to my call.'

Friday 25 April 1985
'Dear children! Today I want to tell you to begin to work in your hearts as you work in the fields. Work and change your hearts so that the Spirit of God may move in your hearts. Thank you for your response to my call.'

2 May 1985
'Dear children! Today I invite you to pray with your heart and not only through habit. Some are coming but they do not pray with their hearts. Therefore, as a mother, I beg you to pray that prayer may prevail in your hearts at every moment. Thank you for your response to my call.'

9 May 1985
'Dear children! You do not know how many graces God is bestowing upon you these days when the Holy Spirit is working in a special way. You do not want to advance. Your hearts are turned to earthly things and you are occupied by them. Turn your hearts to prayer and ask that the Holy Spirit be poured upon you. Thank you for your response to my call.'

16 May 1985
'Dear children! I am calling you to more attentive prayer and to participation in the Mass. I want you to experience God within yourselves at Mass. I want to tell the young people especially to be open to the Holy Spirit because God desires to draw you to himself during these days when Satan is active. Thank you for your response to my call.'

23 May 1985

'Dear children! These days, I am calling you especially to open your hearts to the Holy Spirit. These days, the Holy Spirit is acting through you in a particular way. So, open your hearts and surrender your lives to Jesus so that he may work through them and make you stronger in faith. Thank you for your response to my call.'

30 May 1985

'Dear children! I am calling you again to prayer of the heart. Let prayer, dear children, be your everyday food. In a special way now when work in the fields is exhausting you, you cannot pray with your heart. Pray and then you will overcome every tiredness. Prayer will be your happiness and rest. Thank you for your response to my call.'

6 June 1985

'Dear children! These days many people of all nationalities will come to the parish, and now I am calling you to love. Love first of all the members of your own families, and then you will be able to accept and love all who are coming. Thank you for your response to my call.'

13 June 1985

'Dear children! Until the anniversary day of the apparition I am calling you in the parish to pray more and to let your prayer be an act of devotion and surrender to God. Dear children! I know about your tiredness but you don't know how to surrender yourselves to me. These days, I beg you, make an act of total surrender to me. Thank you for your response to my call.'

20 June 1985

'Dear children! For the coming feast I want to say to you: Open your heart to the Lord of all hearts. Give me all your feeling and all your problems. I want to console you in all your temptations. My wish is to fill you completely with God's peace, joy and love. Thank you for your response to my call.'

27 June 1985

'Dear children! Today I give you the messages through which I am calling you to humility. These days you have felt great joy because of all the people who were coming and you have spoken about your experiences with love. Now I call you to continue with humility and an open heart to speak to all those who are coming. Thank you for your response to my call.'

4 July 1985
'Dear children! I thank you for every sacrifice you have made or offered. Now I urge you to offer every sacrifice with love. I desire that you who are helpless begin to help with trust and the Lord will give you always in trust. Thank you for your response to my call.'

11 July 1985
'Dear children! I love the parish and with my mantle I protect it from every work of Satan. Pray that Satan may flee from the parish and from every individual who comes to the parish. In that way you will be able to hear every call of God and answer it with your life. Thank you for your response to my call.'

18 July 1985
'Dear children! Today I beg you to put more blessed objects in your homes, and that everyone carry blessed objects. Let everything be blessed so that Satan will tempt you less because you are armed against him. Thank you for your response to my call.'

25 July 1985
'Dear children! I want to shepherd you but you do not want to obey my messages. Today I ask you to obey my messages so that you will be able to live everything that God tells me to tell you. Open yourselves to God and God will work through you and give you everything you need. Thank you for your response to my call.'

1 August 1985
'Dear children! I wish to tell you that I have chosen this parish. I protect it, holding it in my hands like a fragile little flower that struggles for life. I beg you to give yourselves to me so that I can offer you clean and without sin as a gift to God. Satan has taken one part of the plan, and he wants to have it all. Pray that he does not succeed, because I desire to have you for myself to offer you to God. Thank you for your response to my call.'

8 August 1985

'Dear children! Today I call you to pray against Satan in a special way. Satan wishes to work more now that you know that he is active. Dear children, arm yourselves against Satan; with the Rosary in your hands you will conquer. Thank you for your response to my call.'

15 August 1985

'Dear children! Today I bless you, and I want to tell you that I love you. I appeal to you at this moment to live my messages. Today I bless you with a solemn blessing that the Almighty grants me to give. Thank you for your response to my call.'

22 August 1985

Our Lady gave no message.

24 August 1985

'Dear children! Today I wish to inform you that God wishes to send you trials: you will be able to overcome them with prayer. God tries you in your daily occupations. Pray, therefore, so as to be able to overcome every trial in peace. In all the situations through which God tries you, open yourselves to God and come near to him with love. Thank you for your response to my call.'

29 August 1985

'Dear children! I call you to prayer especially now when Satan wishes to make use of the grapes of your vineyards. Pray that he does not succeed. Thank you for your response to my call.'

5 September 1985

'Dear children! Today I thank you for all your prayers. Continue praying all the more, so that Satan will be further from this place. Dear children, Satan's plan has failed. Pray for the fulfilment of what God plans for this parish. I thank the young people in a special way for the sacrifices they have offered. Thank you for your response to my call.'

12 September 1985

'Dear children! I wish to tell you that the cross is central these days. Pray especially before the cross from which many graces are coming. Make a special consecration to the cross in your homes. Promise that you will not offend or abuse Jesus and his cross. Thank you for your response to my call.'

19 September 1985
'Dear children! Today I am calling you to live the messages I am giving you in humility. Dear children, do not become proud living the message and saying, 'I am living the message.' If you bear the messages in your heart and live them, everyone will feel it. So the words will not be necessary which are being used by those who do not listen. You do not have to speak with words. You, dear children, have to live and witness with your lives. Thank you for your response to my call.'

26 September 1985
'Dear children! I thank you for all your prayers. I thank you for all your sacrifices. I wish to tell you, dear chldren, to renew the messages I am giving you. Especially live the fasting, because with fasting you will give me joy for the fulfilment of all God's plans here in Medjugorje. Thank you for your response to my call.'

3 October 1985
'Dear children! I want to tell you to thank God for all the graces he has given you. Thank God and give him glory for all the fruits. Dear children, learn to give thanks in little things and then you will be able to thank God for big things. Thank you for your response to my call.'

10 October 1985
'Dear children! Today, also, I want to call you to live the messages in this parish. Especially I want to call the young people of the parish which is dear to me. Dear children, if you live the messages, you live the seed of holiness. I, as the Mother, want to call all of you to holiness, so that you can give it to others. You are a mirror to others. Thank you for your response to my call.'

17 October 1985
'Dear children! Everything has its own time. Today I am calling you to start working on your hearts. Now that work in the fields has ended, you find time for cleaning the most neglectd areas, and you leave your hearts aside. Work more and clean every part of your heart with love. Thank you for your response to my call.'

24 October 1985

'Dear children! From day to day I wish to dress you in holiness, goodness, obedience and love of God, so that from day to day you become more beautiful and ready for your Lord. Dear children, listen and live my messages. I want to lead you. Thank you for your response to my call.'

31 October 1985

'Dear children! Today I want to call you to work in the Church. I love all equally and I want everyone to work as much as he can. I know, dear children, you are able, but you are not willing because you feel lowly and humble in these things. You should be courageous and with little flowers, contribute to the Church and Jesus so that all might be pleased. Thank you for your response to my call.'

7 November 1985

'Dear children! I am calling you to love of your fellowmen, love of those from whom evil comes to you. In that way you will be able to discern the intentions of hearts with love. Pray and love, dear children. With love you can do even what you think is impossible. Thank you for your response to my call.'

14 November 1985

'Dear children! I, your Mother love you and wish to urge you to prayer. Dear children, I am tireless, I am calling you even when you are far from my heart. I am the Mother, and though I feel pain for everyone who goes astray, I forgive easily and I rejoice for every child who comes to me. Thank you for your response to my call.'

21 November 1985

'Dear children! This is a special time for you who are in the parish. You say that you have a lot of work when it is Summer. Now there is no work in the fields, work on yourselves personally. Come to Mass, because this time is given to you. Dear children, there are many who come regularly in spite of the weather, because they love me and want to show their love in a special way. I beg you to show me your love by coming to Mass and the Lord will reward you abundantly. Thank you for your response to my call.'

28 November 1985
'Dear children! I want to thank everyone for all they have done for me. Especially the young people. I beg you, dear children, come to prayer with awareness. You will realise the majesty of God in prayer. Thank you for your response to my call.'

5 December 1985
'Dear children! I call you to prepare yourselves for Christmas through penance, prayer and works of charity. Dear children, do not look at the material things because you will not experience Christmas through them. Thank you for your response to my call.'

12 December 1985
'Dear children! This Christmas I invite you to give glory to Jesus with me. I offer him to you especially on that day. I invite you with me to praise Jesus and his birth. Dear children, pray more and think more about Jesus on that day. Thank you for your response to my call.'

19 December 1985
'Dear children! Today I want to invite you to love your neighbour. If you love your neighbour you will experience Jesus more, especially on Christmas day. God will bestow great gifts on you if you surrender yourselves to him. Particularly at Christmas, I want to give mothers my own special motherly blessing. And Jesus will bless the others with his blessing. Thank you for your response to my call.'

26 December 1985
'Dear children! I want to thank all of you who have listened to my messages, and have lived as I asked you on Christmas day. Cleansed from your sins I want to lead you further in love. Surrender your hearts to me. Thank you for your response to my call.'

2 January 1986
'Dear children! I invite you to decide completely for God. I beg you, dear children, surrender yourselves completely and you will be able to live everything I am telling you. It will not be difficult for you to surrender yourselves completely to God. Thank you for your response to my call.'

9 January 1986
'Dear children! I invite you to help Jesus through prayer to fulfil all the plans he is forming here. Offer your sacrifices to Jesus in order that all he has planned may be fulfilled and that Satan can do nothing. Thank you for your response to my call.'

16 January 1986
'Dear children! Today also I am calling you to prayer. I need your prayer so that God may be glorified through all of you. Dear children, I beg you, listen and live your Mother's call, because I call you only out of love so that I may help you. Thank you for your response to my call.'

23 January 1986
'Dear children! I invite you again to prayer of the heart. If you pray from your heart, dear children, the ice-cold hearts of your brothers will be melted and every barrier will disappear. Conversion will be easy for those who want it. You must beg for this gift for your neighbour. Thank you for your response to my call.'

30 January 1986
'Dear children! Today I call you to pray so that God's plans for you may be realised, and that everything God wants through you may be fulfilled. Help in order that others may be converted, especially those coming to Medjugorje. Dear children, do not allow Satan to take possession of your hearts, and do not allow yourselves to be Satan's image, but my image. I am calling you to prayer, so that you may be witnesses of my presence. Without you God cannot realise what he wants. God gave everyone free will and you have it in your hands. Thank you for your response to my call.'

6 February 1986
'Dear children! This parish which I have chosen is different from others, and I am giving great graces to all those who are praying from their hearts. Dear children, I am giving the graces first of all to the parishioners and then to the others. You must receive the messages first, then the others. You will be answerable to me and to my Son Jesus. Thank you for your response to my call.'

13 February 1986
'Dear children! This Lent is a special incentive for you to change. Start from this moment. Turn off the television and renounce other things which are useless. Dear children, I am calling you individually to conversion. This time is for you. Thank you for your response to my call.'

20 February 1986
'Dear children! The second message of these Lenten days is that you renew your prayer before the cross. Dear children, I am giving you special graces and Jesus is giving you special gifts from the cross. Accept them and live them. Reflect on the Passion of Jesus and unite yourselves with Jesus in life. Thank you for your response to my call.'

27 February 1986
'Dear children! Live the messages I am giving you in humility. Thank you for your response to my call.'

6 March 1986
'Dear children! Today I am calling you to open yourselves more to God, so that he can work through you. For as much as you open yourselves, you will receive the fruits of it. I wish to call you again to prayer. Thank you for your response to my call.'

13 March 1986
'Dear children! Today I am calling you to live this Lent with your little sacrifices. Thank you for every sacrifice you have brought me. Dear children, live in such a way, continuously, and with love, help me to bring the offering. For that God will reward you. Thank you for your response to my call.'

20 March 1986
'Dear children! I am calling you to an active approach to prayer. You wish to live everything I am telling you, but do not have results from your efforts because you do not pray. Dear children, I beg you, open yourselves and begin to pray. Prayer will be a joy. If you begin, it will not be boring because you will pray out of pure joy. Thank you for your response to my call.'

27 March 1986
'Dear children! I wish to thank you for your sacrifices and I invite you to the greatest sacrifice, the sacrifice of love. Without love

you cannot accept me or my Son. Without love, you cannot speak of your experiences to others. That is why I invite you, dear children, to begin to live the love within yourselves. Thank you for your response to my call.'

3 April 1986
'Dear children! I wish to call you to live the Holy Mass. There are many of you who have experienced the beauty of the Holy Mass, but there are some who come unwillingly. I have chosen you, dear children, and Jesus is giving you his graces in the Holy Mass. Therefore, live consciously the Holy Mass. Let every time you come to Holy Mass be joyful. With love, come and accept Holy Mass. Thank you for your response to my call.'

10 April 1986
'Dear children! I wish to call you to grow in love. A flower cannot grow normally without water. Neither can you grow, dear children, without God's blessing. You should seek God's blessing from day to day so that you may grow normally and do everything with God. Thank you for your response to my call.'

17 April 1986
'Dear children! You are preoccupied with material things, and in the material you lose everything that God wants to give you. I am inviting you, dear children, to pray for the gifts of the Holy Spirit which you need so as to witness to my presence and all that I am giving you. Dear children! Surrender yourselves to me so that I can lead you completely. Do not preoccupy yourselves with material things. Thank you for your response to my call.'

24 April 1986
'Dear children! Today I am calling you to pray. Dear children, you are forgetting that you are all important. The elderly are especially important in the family. Urge them to pray. Let the young people be an example to others, let them witness to Jesus by their lives. Dear children, I beg you, start changing yourselves through prayer and you will know what you have to do. Thank you for your response to my call.'

1 May 1986
'Dear children! I beg you to start changing your life in the family. Let the family be a united flower that I wish to give to Jesus.

Dear children, let the family be active in prayer. I wish that the fruits should be seen in the family one day. Only in that way as petals will I give you to Jesus, in fulfilment of God's plan. Thank you for your response to my call.'

8 May 1986

'Dear children! You are responsible for the messages. The source of grace is here, but you, dear children, are the vessels transmitting the gifts. Therefore dear children, I am calling you to work with responsibility. Everyone will be responsible according to his own measure. Dear children, I am calling you to give the gift to others with love and not to keep it for yourselves. Thank you for your response to my call.'

15 May 1986

'Dear children! Today I am calling you to give me your heart that I may change it and make it like mine. You ask yourselves, dear children, why you cannot respond to what I seek from you. You cannot because you have not given me your heart, that I may change it. You speak, but you do not act. I call you to do everything I tell you. In that way I will be with you. Thank you for your response to my call.'

22 May 1986

'Dear children! Today I am calling you to a life of love towards God and your neighbour. Without love, dear children, you cannot do anything. Therefore, dear children, I am calling you to live in mutual love. Only in that way can you love me and accept everyone around you. Through coming to your parish, everyone will feel my love through you. Therefore, today I beg you to start loving with the burning love with which I love you. Thank you for your response to my call.'

29 May 1986

'Dear children! Today I will give you my love. You don't know, dear children, how great is my love and you don't know how to accept it. In many ways I wish to express it, but you, dear children, do not recognise it. You don't comprehend my words with your hearts; so you are unable to comprehend my love. Dear children, accept me in your lives and so you will be able to accept all I am calling you to. Thank you for your response to my call.'

5 June 1986

'Dear children! Today I am calling you to decide if you wish
to live the messages I am giving you. I wish you to be active
in living and transmitting the messages; especially, dear children,
I desire you to be reflections of Jesus, who enlightens this
unfaithful world, which is walking in darkness. I wish that all
of you may be a light to all and witness to the light. Dear children,
you are not called to darkness; you are called to light. Therefore,
live the light in your lives. Thank you for your response to my
call.'

12 June 1986

'Dear children! Today I invite you to start to pray the rosary
with a deep faith. I will then be able to help you. Dear children,
you wish to receive graces but without praying. I cannot help
you if you do not start on your way. Dear children, I invite you
to pray the rosary. May the rosary be your engagement that
you will accept with joy. Like this you will know why I am staying
so long with you. I want to teach you to pray. Thank you for
your response to my call.'

19 June 1986

'Dear children! In these present days, Our Lord has permitted
me to intercede for extra graces for you. For this reason I again
wish to invite you to pray. Pray without ceasing. In this way
I can give you the joy that Our Lord gives me. With these graces,
dear children, I wish that your sufferings may be transformed
into joy. I am your Mother and I want to help you. Thank you
for your response to my call.'

26 June 1986

'Dear children! You must strive to realise with Him this oasis
of peace. My desire is to call you to take care of this oasis so
that it remains always pure. There are some who, through their
thoughtlessness, ravage peace and prayer. So I want to call you
to testify and to help, by your own life, to see that peace is
preserved. Thank you for your response to my call.'

3 July 1986

'Dear children! Today I call on all of you to pray. Without
prayer, dear children, you cannot be aware of God or of me or
of the grace that I give you. For this reason, so that the beginning

and end of your day may always be a prayer, dear children, I wish to guide you more and more, as much as possible, in prayer. But you cannot grow because you do not wish to. I appeal to you, dear children, that prayer may come first for you. Thank you for your response to my call.'

10 July 1986
'Dear children! Today I call you to sanctity. You cannot live without sanctity. So, overcome every sin with love. And again, with love overcome all the difficulties that come to you. Dear children, I beg you to live love within you. Thank you for your response to my call.'

17 July 1986
'Dear children! Today I invite you to reflect on why I am so long with you. I am a Mediatress between you and God. That is why I wish to invite you to live at all times with love what God expects of you. Then, dear children, in all humility, live all the messages I give you. Thank you for your response to my call.'

24 July 1986
'Dear children! I rejoice because of all of you who are on the way of holiness. I beg of you to help by your witness, those who do not know how to live holily. Dear children, let your family be the place where holiness is born. Help everyone to live holily, but very particularly the members of your own family. Thank you for your response to my call.'

31 July 1986
'Dear children! Hatred engenders discord and sees neither persons nor things. I invite you to bear always concord and peace. Especially, dear children, act always with love in the place where you live. Let your only means be love. By love change into good all that Satan wishes to destroy and take to himself. Only thus will you belong to me and will I be able to help you. Thank you for your response to my call.'

7 August 1986
'Dear children! You know that I have promised you an oasis of peace. But do you not know that beside the oasis is a desert where Satan is spying, desirous to cause each of you suffering. Dear children, only by prayer can you triumph over every

influence of Satan. I am with you, but I cannot deprive you of
your freedom. Thank you for response to my call.'

14 August 1986
'Dear children! I invite you to make your prayer joyful in the
encounter with the Lord. I cannot lead you that far so long as
you do not feel joy in prayer of yourselves. I wish to lead you
more profoundly to prayer from day to day. But I do not wish
to force you. Thank you for your response to my call.'

21 August 1986
'Dear children! I thank you for the love you show me. You know
that I love you infinitely, and from day to day I pray to the Lord
to help you to understand the love that I show you. That is why,
dear children, you must pray, pray, pray. Thank you for your
response to my call.'

9

THEOLOGY

(i)

There are three possible approaches to the theology implicit in Medjugorje word and deed. Preliminary to these approaches is the question of overall validity of the alleged supernatural communications. If this is accepted, if we have reasonable certainty that we have messages from the powers above, from Our Lady as God's special messenger, we are in a position to consider these three questions:

— What do they tell us about God?
— What do they tell us about Our Lady?
— What is the spiritual and moral programme suggested and how are its particulars related to the Church and the lives of the faithful at the present time?

The first thing we learn about God from the apparitions at Medjugorje is that in a critical moment in world and Church history he does not intervene personally with the offer and promise of special help to stricken or tempted humankind, but chooses, by an exercise of his omnipotence, to entrust his mission of mercy and renewal to the Blessed Virgin Mary. It was not God the Father, nor God the Son incarnate, nor God the Holy Spirit who took the initiative in Medjugorje. It was Our Lady.

It is pointless trying to attenuate this fact. It is tempting to do so at the present time when for ecumenical reasons, some, perhaps many, Catholics do not wish to see Our Lady so prominent. These Catholics echo the sentiments — for it was sentiment more than sound theology — of the Council Fathers who, in September 1964, during the debate on the Marian conciliar text, chapter VIII of the *Constitution on the Church*, argued strenuously against the title Mediatress as appropriate to Our Lady; they would not for a moment consider Mediatress of all graces as justifiable. They were mostly representatives of the Church in western countries and they were preoccupied, if obsessed is too strong a word, with the difficulties of western Protestants in what concerns teaching and practice about Our Lady. The attitude, sincere no doubt, was understandable within a limited context and with mental categories bound by a rigid stereotype.

The context did not allow for reflection on the Orthodox who have just as strong a claim on our ecumenical aspirations. They are often geographically heirs to the Christians of the first centuries. These eastern Christians gave Marian doctrine and devotion to the west. The essential dogmas concerning Mary were thought out and formulated in the east, principally at Ephesus in 431 AD. The seeds of thought which would grow and flower in later dogmas, the Immaculate Conception and the Assumption, were sown then.

The creative intuition of Mary as the New Eve came from the east; the great titles, *Theotokos, Panagia, Aeiparthenos* are first found in eastern texts. The first feasts of Our Lady and the most popular prayer to her, 'We fly to thy patronage' were brought to us from the Orient. The debt was to remain constant. As to the controversial doctrine of mediation, contrary to a widely held assumption that its exponents are predominantly western — St Louis Marie Grignion de Montfort and St Alphonsus Liguori foremost among them — these and similar writers pale into insignificance beside a great fourteenth century trio, Gregory Palamas, Nicolas Cabasilas and Theophanes of Nicaea: never has Mary's mediation been so fully and so thoroughly established as by Theophanes. Note that these writers came after the break with Rome in 1054.

It is not only that Our Lady is seen to take the initiative. She speaks words like these: 'I have chosen this parish in a special way and I wish to lead it. I am keeping it in love and I wish everyone to be mine. . .' 'My son and I have a special plan for this parish. . .' 'My Son Jesus Christ wishes to bestow special graces on you through me. . .' 'I beg all of you, especially those from this parish, to live my messages and relate them to whoever you meet. . .' 'Your prayer has helped my plans to be fulfilled. . .' 'Pray to the Holy Spirit for enlightenment. If you only knew the greatness of the graces God was giving you, you would pray without ceasing. . .' 'You are a chosen people and God gave you great graces (it must be recalled that she made the choice).. . .' 'Pray and ask for the graces of God. I will pray that he gives them to you. . .' 'You are not aware of the messages which God is sending to you through me. He is giving you great graces and you are not grasping them. . .' 'I love you and in a special way I have chosen this parish, which is more dear to me than others where I have gladly gone when the Almighty has sent me. . .' 'This parish which I have chosen is different to others and I am giving great graces to all those who are praying with their hearts. Dear children, I am giving the graces first to all the parishioners and then to the others. . .' 'Dear children, I am giving you special gifts from the Cross. Accept them and live them. . .' 'Thank you for every sacrifice you have brought me. Dear children, live in such a way, continuously, and with love, help me to bring the offering. For that God will reward you. . .' 'I have chosen you, dear children, and Jesus is giving you his graces in the holy Mass.' I am a Mediatress between you and God.'

These texts are not selected to establish Our Lady's mediation so much as to show that intrinsic to the Medjugorje phenomenon is the fact that this is God's choice. We are witnessing a manifestation of the supernatural, which is God's entirely privileged domain, a chain of events either totally spurious or directly attributable to God, a divine intervention, with as its salient feature, a dominant, continuing, utterly self-assured role given to Our Lady.

God is then one who uses his creatures, especially his most perfect creature, to accomplish his objectives. And in the accomplishment of his plan he allows Mary to speak from a central position. To the brief extracts from the Thursday messages could be added those received by the cross on the hill on Monday evenings. There more than once Our Lady has thanked those who, by their prayer, had helped her to 'accomplish her project.'

(ii)

Is God then displaced? Is there an implicit Mariolatry in the message of Medjugorje? Not for those who read and ponder the words and watch the course of events. When Our Lady appears to the children her greeting is always 'Praised be Jesus.' When she prays with them she says the 'Our Father' and the 'Glory', and she recommends the 'Our Father', the 'Hail Mary' and the 'Glory' as prayers to be repeated.

It is not only that the whole programme of life outlined by Our Lady is in strict conformity with the Gospel of Christ, her divine Son, as we shall see. It is especially the implicit Trinitarian framework within which her thought is cast: 'During the days of this novena (for Pentecost) pray for an outpouring of the Holy Spirit upon all your families and your parish. Pray, and you shall not regret it. God will give you the gifts (of the Holy Spirit) and you will glorify him for them till the end of your life. . .' 'Always start your work and end your work with prayer. If you do that God will bless you and your work. . .' 'I will pray to my Son, Jesus, that he give you the grace to experience his victory over Satan's temptations. . .' 'Pray to the Holy Spirit for enlightenment. If you only knew how great are the graces God is giving you, you would pray without ceasing. . .' 'I am your Mother and I always want you to be closer to the Father, that he may always pour abundant gifts into your hearts. . .' 'Joy overwhelms me for every heart that opens to God, especially in the parish. . .' 'You do not know how many graces God is bestowing upon you these days when the Holy Spirit is working in a special way. . .' 'Turn your hearts to prayer and ask that the Holy Spirit be poured upon you. . .' 'These days, I am calling you especially to open your hearts to the Holy Spirit. These days the Holy Spirit is acting through you in a particular way.'

The recurring mention of the Holy Spirit is notable and accords so well with the revival, within the last lifetime, of doctrine and devotion about him: he was always part of the Christian creed, accepted by believers, honoured in certain common prayers. But it is not so long since a spiritual work about him appeared with the title *The Forgotten Paraclete*, or since a great master of the spiritual life, Dom Columba Marmion, could assert that for some the attitude would be that expressed in an important text in Acts: 'We have not even heard if there be a Holy Spirit.'

The visionaries have made it clear that the Mass and Holy Communion are, by Our Lady's wish, central to all their prayer.

That is a fact which seizes the attention of every visitor to Medjugorje. They are drawn there by Our Lady and led by her to the centre of the Christian life, the Eucharist. If any parish in the world may be taken to illustrate the teaching of Vatican II, it is Medjugorje. These words could have been written with the parishioners in mind: 'But the other sacraments, and indeed all ecclesiastical ministries and works of the apostolate are bound up with the Eucharist and are directed towards it. For in the most blessed Eucharist is contained the whole spiritual good of the Church, namely Christ himself, our Pasch and the living Bread which gives life to men through his flesh — that flesh which is given life and gives life through the Holy Spirit. Thus men are invited and led to offer themselves, their works and all creation with Christ. For this reason the Eucharist appears as the source and summit of all preaching of the Gospel; catechumens are gradually led up to participation in the Eucharist, while the faithful who have already been consecrated in baptism and confirmation are fully incorporated in the Body of Christ by the reception of the Eucharist. Therefore the Eucharistic celebration is the centre of the assembly of the faithful over which the priest presides.' (*Decree on the Ministry and Life of Priests, art. 5*)

This sublime reality is witnessed in a most striking way daily in Medjugorje.

(iii)

What does Medjugorje tell us about Our Lady?

First, that she cares immensely for those caught in the tragedy of our time. She has a mission from Almighty God to help suffering and threatened humanity. But with what devotion, delicacy, perseverance she fulfils it. She constantly appeals to men to allow her to help them. There is throughout the story and in the mentality of the children an astonishing certainty of Our Lady's knowledge of all things, of her power in grasping a whole comprehensive plan and of entering into every detail which its accomplishment will entail. This knowledge is so necessary to what she says, how she rebukes the villagers, what she promises, the kind of encouragement she constantly gives, that it is easily taken for granted. This should not be.

Our Lady is maternal which accords with the Catholic tradition. She is emphatically a loving person. The love recurs so often that it might not be fully appreciated.

Mary is a person very conscious of the principal danger threatening those she loves: Satan. The Catholic journalists who almost staged an intellectual sit-down strike when Pope Paul VI mentioned Satan, should read these passages, especially the messages to the parish, in which the Woman of the Apocalypse speaks of her unrelenting, desperate, ever-conquered foe, the great dragon. She follows his every move, knows his design, shows how to defeat him. For her there is no 'death of Satan.'

Overall is the magnetic idea of Mary's choice. Like her divine Son she chooses some for special favours, not because of who they are, but because of who she is. One cannot and should not make any apology for this fact. It goes deep into the unknown and unknowable recesses of the divine mind. This is the mystery of predestination. Men have been baffled by it, frightened, rebellious, despairing. It remains. Only one comes really into close proximity with it, shares its working, can announce its decrees, Mary still a creature, but one in the confines of the deity.

The Madonna of Medjugorje presents another face. She is one who shows a most sensitive respect for those she is dealing with. This is revealed in her touching habit of excluding the others when she has a rebuke to make to one of the visionaries. They do not hear. It is manifest too in her wit, just like that of happy people who do not hurt others: 'Are you tired of me already?' Or again when asked her age the reply that she would soon be 2,000 years!

But one of the really surprising things is the freedom she allows her children. She tells them she would like them to be priests and nuns, but they are free to choose. Her thoughtful answers to those who inquire about their departed friends or relatives are also truly touching.

A most consoling aspect of the whole Medjugorje phenomenon is the special session which Our Lady gives the prayer group on the hill of Cricevac on certain late evenings, as late as eleven o'clock. As they pray and sing she appears and Ivan generally is given a message for those present. So often Our Lady thanks those present for helping in the accomplishment of her plan; and she blesses them.

(iv)

Can we, without impertinence, evaluate the programme proposed by Mary? Before entering into any particulars, what of the secrets? Is it not strange that, with the whole apparatus of Church government publicised as it has never been before, with all the public relations, successful or a failure, of Vatican II, with incessant assemblies, meetings, seminars, renewal courses, committees, commissions, the Mother of the Church should pick out some unsophisticated children in a remote Yugoslav village to talk to them about matters affecting the future of the whole human race? There is no time, in passing, to delay over the psychological aspect of this hidden dialogue. In every intelligent plan the parts cohere to produce a final result intended. A singular aspect of the Medjugorje phenomenon is the very normal — natural in a good sense — lifestyle of the visionaries. How is it attained and retained? With the support of the whole parish. If these children were singled out for a mission, onerous and dramatic, they were planted within a community which is called to the heights of holiness, which, through the wisdom, activity and constant watchfulness of the central directing figure, Our Lady herself, has solidarity with them, identifies with them without encroaching on their vocation, protects them in countless ways.

Their secrets are their destiny. Character is destiny and so they are being fashioned day by day for the moment of destiny's fulfilment. They have been faithful thus far to the duty of secrecy. One did divulge something to a medical practitioner who took advantage of her hypnotic state but he feels bound by professional secrecy. The reply given by Marija to an interviewer from the Canadian paper, *L'Informateur,* may be looked at carefully. Asked if there would be a nuclear war she replied that this was part of the secrets. Something unconsciously given away?

The secrets are a personal matter of conscience for the visionaries. They are also bound by the whole moral programme which they teach others in Our Lady's name. Opinions will differ here in the matter of interpretation and scale. But unquestionably the question of prayer is one of primary importance. The Thursday messages should be read through to note the recurrence of the idea, the simple direct call to prayer, the call to whole-hearted prayer, the exhortation to pray for a certain time, especially the need of prayer for sinners. In the Thursday messages recorded, prayer is mentioned in one way or another very, very often. Sometimes it is a cry from Mary: Pray, pray, pray.

One form of prayer is preferred by Mary — that is as a personal form, for of course she insists on the Mass, as we have seen, and urges that the Mass be prayed. But the Rosary has priority in the brief homiletic moments when she communicates with her children. So insistent is she on the great traditional prayer that she holds out the hope that if it were widely and fervently used, the troubles of the Church would wither away.

With prayer, if we still remain on the level of practice, she associates fasting. Its origin is in the Scriptures, it has been sanctioned by usage in the Church from ancient times; its corrective, as well as its meritorious aspect needs to be recalled in the permissive age.

If we rise above particular points of religious practice to consider ideals we meet two in some prominence: conversion and reconciliation. There must be conversion from sin. Our Lady of Medjugorje does not minimise the meaning of sin. She points the way to freedom and proclaims the importance of the Church's remedy for sin: sacramental confession.

Reconciliation between individuals and families leads to peace. The ideal of peace is the summary of Our Lady's programme as taught in Medjugorje. Significantly the Yugoslav word for peace, which in this instance is a Croatian word, MIR, was seen written in the sky over the blessed spot.

Peace and joy are the fruits of love and love is the essential practice which Our Lady urges on her faithful children.

10

THE PEOPLE OF GOD

We have allegedly left the age when the role of the laity was to 'pray, and keep quiet.' Vatican II in one substantial document and in passages elsewhere, taught the importance of the laity in the Church and issued directives on how this should be exercised practically.

That is in the sphere of action and historians of our age will judge the degree of success in achievement, whether practice matched theory. But the Council pointed to a power vested in the laity which is beyond the realm of mere action. They contribute to the teaching of the Church that it may remain orthodox. They help ensure the transmission of divine truth of which the Church is the custodian.

Consider such a passage as this:

> The Tradition that comes from the apostles makes progress in the Church with the help of the Holy Spirit. There is a growth in insight into the realities and words that are being passed on. This comes about in various ways. It comes through the contemplation and study of believers who ponder these things in their hearts (cf. Lk 2:19, 51). It comes from the intimate sense of spiritual realities which they experience.[1]

This is from the *Constitution on Divine Revelation* and these words come before the statement that the Tradition grows through the preaching of those who have received, along with the right of succession in the episcopate, the sure charism of truth.

Or take this from the Decree of the Lay Apostolate:

> From the reception of these charisms, even the most ordinary ones, there arises for each of the faithful the right

191

and duty of exercising them in the Church and in the world for the good of men and the development of the Church, of exercising them in the freedom of the Holy Spirit who 'breathes where he wills' (*Jn 3:8*), and at the same time in communion with his brothers in Christ, and with his pastors especially. It is for the pastors to pass judgement on the authenticity and good of these gifts, not certainly with a view to quenching the Spirit, but to testing everything and keeping what is good. (cf. 1 Th 5:12, 19, 21).[2]

This passage touches individuals only, for charisms are given to individuals. But the strongest words of the Council are in regard to the sentiment of the whole body of the faithful:

The holy People of God shares also in Christ's prophetic office; it spreads abroad a living witness to him, especially by a life of faith and love and by offering to God a sacrifice of praise, the fruits of lips praising his name (cf. Heb 13:15). The whole body of the faithful who have an anointing that comes from the holy one (cf. 2 Jn 2:20, 27) cannot err in matters of belief. The characteristic is shown in the supernatural appreciation of the faith (*sensus fidei*) of the whole people when 'from the bishops to the last of the faithful' they manifest a universal consensus in matters of faith and morals. By this appreciation of the faith, aroused and sustained by the Spirit of truth, the People of God, guided by the sacred teaching authority (*magisterium*), and obeying it, receives not the mere word of men, but truly the Word of God (cf. 1 Th 2:13), the faith once for all delivered to the saints (cf. Jude 3). The People unfailingly adheres to this faith, penetrates it more deeply with right judgement, and applies it more fully in daily life.[3]

Here then we have a Council endorsing the teaching of a nineteenth century Catholic. Who was he, a frustrated layman, a pragmatist or activist looking for some justification for his personal innovations or experiments in the life of the Church? Nothing of the kind. It was the great intellectual recruit to the Church, the 'imperial intellect', John Henry Newman, who publicly defended the idea. It was boldly expressed in the very title of his essay: *On Consulting the Faithful in Matters of Doctrine*, a contribution to the *Rambler* in 1859, later reprinted with some alteration as an appendix to the third edition of *The Arians of the Fourth Century*.

What accolade did the writer receive for this superb piece of theological exposition? A recent commentator scarcely exaggerates:

> His publication of this essay was an act of political suicide from which his career within the Church was never fully to recover; at one stroke he, whose reputation as the one honest broker between the extremes of English Catholic opinion had hitherto stood untarnished, gained the Pope's personal displeasure, the reputation at Rome of being the most dangerous man in England, and a formal accusation of heresy preferred against him by the Bishop of Newport.[4]

A cloud descended on the giant of his age.

Newman has been vindicated. During his life Leo XIII made an *amende honorable* by naming him Cardinal; he even pointed to the Englishman as a symbol of his whole papal programme. The happy ending does not, however, obliterate a sad, painful phase in Catholic intellectual history.

It is not history that interests us here but the lessons Newman may have for our subject. He had come to the conclusion that in the face of the worst heresy in history it was the faithful who were steadfast in orthodoxy, not the episcopate:

> It is not a little remarkable, that, though, historically speaking, the fourth century is the age of doctors, illustrated, as it was, by the saints Athanasius, Hilary, the two Gregories, Basil, Chrysostom, Ambrose, Jerome, and Augustine, and all of these saints bishops also, except one, nevertheless in that very day the divine tradition committed to the infallible Church was proclaimed and maintained far more by the faithful than by the Episcopate.[5]

Newman knew that the 'great body of the bishops were in their internal belief orthodox', that there were 'numbers of clergy who stood by the laity' and that 'the laity actually received their faith, in the first instance, from the bishops and clergy.' He still contended that 'in that time of immense confusion the divine dogma of Our Lord's divinity was proclaimed, enforced, maintained, and (humbly speaking) preserved far more by the *Ecclesia docta* than by the *Ecclesia docens*: that the body of the episcopate was unfaithful to its commission, while the body of the laity was faithful to its baptism; that at one time the Pope, at other times the patriarchal, metropolitan, and other great sees, at other times general councils, said what they should not have said, or did what obscured and compromised revealed truth; while, on the other hand, it was Christian people who, under Providence, were the ecclesiastical strength of Athanasius, Hilary, Eusebius of Vercellae and other great solitary confessors, who would have failed without them.'[6]

Newman was greatly cheered by the fact that, as in ancient times the faithful had powerfully influenced the promulgation of the dogma of the divine maternity at Ephesus in 431, so they would also have some merit in the final triumph of the dogma of the Immaculate Conception.

> The history of the definition of the Immaculate Conception shows us this; and it will be among the blessings which the Holy Mother, who is the subject of it, will gain for us, in repayment of the definition, that by that very definition we are all reminded of the part which the laity have had in the preliminaries of its promulgation. Pope Pius has given us a pattern, in his manner of defining, of the duty of considering the sentiments of the laity upon a point of tradition, in spite of whatever fullness of evidence the bishops had already thrown upon it.[7]

If Newman had lived in the days of Pius XII he would have rejoiced that this Pope too required from his bishops in the consultation prior to the dogma of the Assumption that they take account of 'the devotion of your clergy and people (taking into account their faith and piety) toward the Assumption of the most Blessed Virgin Mary.' Here too was recognition of the role of the laity in the area of doctrine.

Has this truth then relevance to the happenings at Medjugorje over the last five years? Significantly it is the person of Our Lady that is in question, as Newman had noted in regard to the dogma of the Immaculate Conception — he had in an earlier theological work *The Essay on the Development of Doctrine* noted a similar factor in the dogma of the divine motherhood proclaimed at Ephesus in 431.

It is a question, nonetheless, to be approached delicately. There is no question of withdrawing the problem of authenticity of an apparition of Our Lady from the competence of a bishop. It is the bishop who really has the problem: How is he, in a case like Medjugorje, to assess the importance of worldwide opinion?

It is clear from the documents presented in this book that the Bishop of Mostar has chosen to ignore this factor in his judgement of the reported visions. He appears totally indifferent to the universal response from the Catholic Church to the events taking place in his diocese. He also chooses to ignore enlightened disinterested theological opinion and apparently dismisses altogether the valuable contribution made by scientists of the highest competence and integrity to investigation of the psychic phenomena involved. In view of these facts now known through the Bishop's own mode of procedure, what value, if any, would attach to any judgement he chooses to publish?

The commission established by Bishop Zanic has sunk to the level of a charade. One session was given up to the presentation of papers on different rather abstract subjects: not to scientific (that is totally competent and objective) examination of the witnesses, with a view to evaluation of their testimony.

Any Catholic now seeking information and a value judgement on Medjugorje must look elsewhere. The question is now beyond the scope of the local bishop. He is, in a way, saved from the onerous task of decision. Perhaps through all this we are entering a new phase in the assimilation by the Church of the fruits of such a divine intervention.

In conversation and in his letter to the Cardinal Secretary of the Congregation for the Doctrine of the Faith, Dr Franic proposed the establishment of an international commission. The Roman authorities hesitate to interfere in the affairs of a diocesan bishop. But are these events any longer to be so considered? Certainly the geographical location of Medjugorje is in the diocese of Mostar. But the repercussion of the events covers the

entire world. It has proved quite impossible to prevent people
going there, as it has proved impossible to prevent the publication
of essays, articles, books, the making of films, videos sound
cassettes. What a futile gesture it was to forbid or seek to
discourage such things. To have accepted such a suggestion
Catholic authors and technicians would, in effect, have been
abandoning the field to the secular media. These have certainly
moved in, generally to their credit. World famous periodicals
like the *New York Times*, the *Sunday Times* — with Gitta Sereny
as the contributor — the *Reader's Digest*, the *Corriere della Sera*,
Il Tempo, have all been impartial in their presentation of the
unusual story. So have Italian and Bavarian television,
Independent Television and the BBC from London and, greatest
surprise of all, Lubljana and Belgrade television services — it
was an Orthodox priest on Belgrade television who defended the
authenticity of the phenomena.

Yet it would have been very strange then if Catholics and the
Catholic media refrained from reporting or comment on
Medjugorje — doubly strange in this age when the Church
proclaims the right to information. It is unthinkable that an event
attracting Catholics from all over the world should be taboo to
Catholic writers and broadcasters trained to appraise this very
kind of event. No one has a monopoly on supernatural things;
no one has the right to exclude Catholic research workers from
things affecting millions of Catholics. The Church was losing
the battle of public relations in the early days of the Council,
almost all through the first session. Action was taken in time
during the second session and it was found that 'truth is the better
friend.'

In the evolution of events with a core of exceptional
supernatural power it is sometimes vaguely believed that the
principals must suffer — from which a facile conclusion follows
that they must be made to suffer. A little searching analysis will
reveal the error and the danger of such a view. It would easily
justify cruelty, even sadism. Those who easily cast themselves
in the role of inquisitor, judge and minister of punishment in
such cases will generally be found highly indignant at any
suffering inflicted on themselves. It is the human condition,
riddled with paradox, self-contradiction, illogicality and self-
righteousness. How good of God to trust his saving mysteries
to such creatures.

Reference to God must be the absolute criterion. With that norm in mind I have no hesitation, at the end of this review of different, disparate, complex and complicated evidence in asserting that the apparitions at Medjugorje are authentic divine signs. I have weighed the arguments against, admirably stated by Fr Laurentin. I do not find that they prevail.

Are there too many apparitions? Who is to decide on number but the Almighty? In what way could repetition undermine reality? The apparitions do not last long. Their frequency could be a concession to the repetitive age in which we live. It could, as Laurentin suggests, be specially designed to offset the incessant, prolonged repetition of marxist propaganda.

Such considerations too may be apposite to the multiplicity of words. One cannot expect total verbal consistency here. It does not exist in the gospels. And we must not forget that God in such communications leaves a margin for error. It would be angelic to receive and transmit everything heard in moments of ecstasy with total accuracy.

The objection based on politics is scarcely pressed any longer. There may be moments of sporadic change but the regime seems to have come to terms with things beyond its mental categories, in which it can discern no threat to its institutions.

Catholics, on their side, seem to have come to terms with certain rules of conduct which seemed a threat to the post-consiliar ethos and mores. If the directives are radical, traditional, far-reaching, it is because they are consonant with the gospel: a demanding code of conduct, if ever there was one. It must be remembered also that certain demands made by Our Lady are addressed to the privileged ones who are already living in an exalted spiritual world: not a world that makes its inhabitants abnormal, but one which fosters heroism.

The thirst for heroism is unquenchable in the human spirit. There will always be those who choose the heroic way. More readily if they have every reason to rely on exceptional help.

We have had to deal at length with the tension between Medjugorje and the local bishop. It has been fully illustrated in the foregoing chapters. The question of the diary which almost induced paranoia in the Bishop is thus explained: a) there is a pocket notebook of July 1981; b) there is a dairy kept from 12 October to 13 December 1981 (a half page each day); c) there is a notebook given by Fr Yanko Bubalo to Vicka during her questioning of her so that she could note each apparition; d) there are three large notebooks in which Vicka writes down the life of Our Lady as she reveals it each day since the end of 1982. In none of these writing materials is there anything about the Bishop.[8]

Against these objections one must align so many reasons for accepting authenticity. Some are mentioned and developed at length by Laurentin, others by Dr Franic. In summary it may be urged that:

a)   the visionaries have survived a systematic drive to nullify their testimony, to subvert their so edifying way of life, to pervert their witness; their tenacity is awe-inspiring;

b)   they have, day after day, during five years, spoken of spiritual realities with entire orthodoxy;

c)   thrown suddenly into an existence so different from what they knew and lived with, they show no signs of abnormality. They have, on the contrary, impressed experts by their normal behaviour and sincerity;

d)   they live exemplary lives of prayer, fasting, detachment from the evils of their age and peers, materialism, pleasure-seeking, waste of time in entertainment — pop music and so on, not to mention the terrible addictions which plague their contemporaries;

e)   they manifest respect and obedience, true love towards the Church at a time when so many, even Catholics, adopt a critical, irreverent attitude towards it; with which goes their love for the Pope and their fidelity to him. He in turn (and it is noteworthy) has sent them tokens of his favour, autographed photographs with the message *Pax Vobis*.

In *fine* let us adapt the biblical advice: *Judge the tree by its fruits*. The fruits here have been so overwhelmingly good, in the parish which is transformed, in the lives of countless people who admit that they have been brought back to the practice of their religion or to more serious commitment through contact with this holy place and the prayer movement which is daily in it. The fruits have been miraculous in some cases. These alleged miracles I have not described or discussed in detail, as it would take too much space. I accept the records in a number of cases as reliable.

There are, finally, the luminous signs. The photograph of a woman's figure near where the cross should be, but without the cross, has been widely circulated. Photographers cannot explain how a woman should appear where none was visible at the time of the photograph.

The sun dance has been seen by many. Probably the most striking instance was on 29 May 1985, when it was witnessed by Fr Rupcic and others. The Franciscan included an account of the phenomenon in a report which he sent to Rome for the attention of the Holy Father.

1. Art. 8; *Vatican Council II, The Conciliar and Post-Conciliar Documents*, 754;

2. Art. 3, op.cit., 769;

3. *Constitution on the Church*, art. 12, *op.cit.*, 363;

4. *On Consulting the Faithful in Matters of Doctrine*, ed. John Coulson, London, 1961, Introduction, 2;

5. *Op.cit.*, 75;

6. *Op.cit.*, 76;

7. *Op.cit.*, 104;

8. *Is the Virgin Mary Appearing at Medjugorje?* Boston, 1983, 115.

THE COMMISSION

Bishop Zanic, in his statement of December 1984 gave the history of the diocesan commission down to October 1984. On 25 April 1986 the Bishop was in Rome. Shortly after his return to Yugoslavia he summoned a meeting of the commission, which took place on 2 May. The Bishop took a vote on the events in Medjugorje and then announced that the commission was dissolved. The entire matter has been transferred to Rome.

Some members of the commission have visited Medjugorje. It cannot be said that the entire body has conducted an inquiry on the spot into the ecstasies, or summoned all the visionaries to an investigation such as has taken place in other such cases — there have been alleged apparitions where very little has been done by way of investigation.

Meetings took place in the episcopal residence in Mostar and explanatory statements were generally issued. The Bishop has been criticised for packing the commission with members known to be critical of the Medjugorje phenomenon. He has defended himself against this charge, protesting that the choice was made after consultation with ecclesiastical superiors of those appointed. It did not inspire confidence in the deliberations of the commission that the Bishop himself was a member, nor that he announced beforehand what the findings would be — this is known from a letter quoted in this book. Though the Bishop generally presided at the opening of meetings, he would leave soon after and give the body time to proceed independently.

We have no minutes of the meetings and must be content with approximate views. One or two unfortunate incidents did occur: the pricking of Vicka while in ecstasy is on videotape and has been widely shown. On another occasion a commission member asked one of the visionaries: 'Well, what has Tomislav Vlasic told you to say that Our Lady told you?' And a commission member during the ecstasy was heard saying 'Ode', which is what the visionaries themselves exclaim: a piece of mockery, less than edifying.

We now await a decision from Rome, whether as the result of an international commission such as Archbishop Franic suggested, or after evaluation from within one of the Roman Congregations. Meanwhile there will be speculation about the immediate background to the Roman decision. It is known that Signor Flamirio Piccoli, president of the Italian Christian Democrat Party, intervened at the Vatican and protested against the fact that good priests were being slandered. Fr Massimo Rastrelli's brother, who is also interested in Medjugorje, is an Italian Senator and may have added his voice to such an initiative.

What will be the reaction of the visionaries? Will they rejoice at what could be taken as a rebuff to the Bishop of Mostar? Such behaviour would be completely out of character. They have always spoken of him with respect, and insisted that they prayed and fasted for him. Fr Henri Joyeux will be similarly respectful. In a recent interview with *Paris Match* (23 May 1986) the illustrious specialist has reaffirmed, in the light of subsequent research and examination of scores of videotapes, the scientific conclusions which he published in a June 1985 issue of the weekly; these are reproduced in this book. He has made a decisive contribution to the history of Medjugorje. But there is no note of triumphalism in his latest replies to the questions put him by *Paris Match*.

Much was made in the media of the request sent to the Italian episcopal conference by Mgr Bovone on 23 May 1985, asking that the advisability of pilgrimages to Medjugorje be examined. Mgr Bovone is an official of the Sacred Congregation for the Doctrine of the Faith. He was clearly influenced by the Bishop of Mostar for his communication began: 'From many places and especially from the competent authority in Mostar a vast propaganda for the ''facts'' linked with the alleged apparitions in Medjugorje is being noted and deplored. . .' The matter is now with a higher authority.

The Cardinal Archbishop of Zagreb, Franjo Kuharic, gave an interview on 15 February 1985 to Fr Massimo Rastrelli. He did not commit himself on the subject of Medjugorje. He was willing to await the decision of the Commission: 'Medjugorje is an important phenomenon. But I cannot give a properly based or definitive judgement. . . I am waiting for serious study by the Commission established by Bishop Zanic. I had for a long time advised him to set up a Commission which should look at, hear everything, then question the seers, each separately and under oath, collect everything, then to put it up to the Bishop to make the analysis and judge the character of the event (supernatural or not): the reasons for, the reasons against, to resolve problems: theologically, psychologically, and from every scientific aspect, and eventually to give judgement on this basis. There is no hurry.' His Eminence was closely interrogated by the Jesuit on the behaviour of Bishop Zanic, what he said and did. He did his best in difficult matters. He concluded: 'Let us pray. I reflect seriously on this problem, but I have no clear and definitive judgement for or against. I await the Commission. I get prayers: monasteries and contemplative nuns have prayed, for a whole month, before the Blessed Sacrament exposed for an hour, for Medjugorje, so that judgement may be given according to the Spirit.'

   Many will welcome the Roman decision, scarcely foreseen by the Cardinal, as the answer to these and so many other prayers. In that all can join, together with the suffering Vicka, asked once again to forego her daily apparition — this time for forty days — with all the family of Our Lady of Medjugorje in Croatia and the Croatian settlements, throughout the whole world.

STATEMENT OF ARCHBISHOP FRANIC
AT THE MEETING OF THE YUGOSLAV
EPISCOPAL CONFERENCE, ON 17 APRIL 1985[1]

I declare that I have always from the outset defended the good name of His Excellency the Bishop of Mostar (Hercegovina), especially since I have been interested in the events of Medjugorje. I have taken it on myself to convince the Franciscans to hand over the seven parishes to the bishopric and I have advised the two Friars who are suspended to submit to their Master General and to their bishop, unconditionally. This has been reported in a well-known issue of *Glas Koncila* last year.

This programme of obedience began, in my opinion, in February this year, when the two Franciscans, invited by me with Fr Pejic as intermediary to have lunch at Split and to a discussion together with Frs Rupcic and Barberic, declared that they were wholly disposed to unconditional obedience. Besides, Frs Zovko, Tomislav Vlasic and Slavko told me that they wished that the seven parishes would be handed over as soon as possible and that in this way the Hercegovina question could be settled. The matter is proceeding, but what is now awaited is love and mercy from the bishop, as well as from the head of the Franciscan Order and the Holy See itself. For their part they have been moved to write to their General and to Cardinal Ratzinger, asking how they should proceed. This, I submit, is the true miracle of Medjugorje.

Our Lady of Medjugorje has never urged disobedience to the Church, but her messages reach us through the children and there can be misunderstandings, for they are not clearly transmitted through human imperfection; that is why these messages should be studied by theologians so that the Church could render judgement. The messages are addressed to the Church and therefore the Church is expected to interpret them. The Church in Medjugorje is the Bishop of Mostar, with his priests and his faithful, with his Commission, and finally the Holy Father with his Congregations.

Seeing that the events in Medjugorje have become the problem not only of the Church in Mostar, but of the Church generally, because these events draw the attention of theologians in the whole Church, as well as of doctors and scientists, particularly in Italy and France, I think that their opinion should be taken into account. Groups of theologians and of doctors are set up to keep the Holy See and the Episcopal Curia of Mostar informed. Their scientific contribution is precious because we are dealing with theologians of world reputation such as R. Laurentin, M. Scanlan, TOR, President of the Franciscan University of Steubenville in the United States.

I began to take an interest in these facts, because of the proximity of our archdiocese to Medjugorje, and because of so many pilgrims, young people especially, who have learned profound prayer there. The are some thousand people in Split and its neighbourhood who persevere in prayer because of Medjugorje.

That is why I maintain that it was my duty to go to Medjugorje in a private capacity. I wanted to be able to say to my faithful whether they were right or not in going to Medjugorje on private pilgrimage.

I noted that in Medjugorje the true Catholic faith is taught, that people pray well, that God is given glory in extended prayers, that people do penance and frequent the sacraments. I saw young people who pray and go to confession in crowds, every day. I saw Franciscans, who are men of God. I spoke to the visionaries. I noted their spiritual growth and progress in holiness. I saw pilgrims who come from the five continents; three millions have gone there up to now. Among them were famous people like, for example, Signore Piccoli, President of the Christian Democrat Party in Italy, many Italian theologians, for example Fr Sgreva, Professor of Theology in Verona, Fr Cristiano, Professor of Theology in Genoa, Fr Scanlan, already mentioned, so many doctors and professors from the Faculty of Medicine in Milan University, who have studied the visionaries with the most modern electronic apparatus; Professor Spaziante, for example, whose book, written with scientific method, is currently printing. He describes the case of Signora Basile, healed suddenly in

Medjugorje of disseminated sclerosis; she was also completely blind in the right eye and has recovered one hundred per cent vision. This lady lives happily, is cured and able to work. She has been thanking and glorifying God for a year. If we must wait four years for the miracle to be recognised officially by the Church, we should not be in a hurry to approve or disapprove. We must delay for the required time to clarify everything.

Professor Henri Joyeux of Montpelier took encephalograms during the ecstasy of the visionaries and showed scientifically that there is no sign of hallucination, of epileptic manifestation, of hysteria or dream state. These young people are normal.

Doctor Frigerio has proved by applying an electronic instrument to the eyes, ears and mouths of the visionaries during the ecstasy, that they have no cornea reaction and their eyes do not see objects put before them while the ecstasy lasts. This proves that there is no question of play acting as in a theatre where the actors would be attentive to their public, and would not be able to repress spontaneous cornea reaction.

There is talk of a young Frenchman, who, we are told, put his two fingers in front of the visionaries' eyes and they reacted. This led to disillusion on his part and he left Medjugorje. I met this Frenchman in Medjugorje. He invited me to his lodgings to let me see some video-cassettes, but I had not the time to delay. But now this Frenchman is given attention because he was not 'converted', while millions of converts do not count and are not believed; they are taken for victims of collective hallucination, even though science rules out the possibility of this diagnosis. . . What else is there to say; I could show you 141 documents in my possession on the cure of Signora Basile.

My contribution in *Glas Koncila* was fortuitous. I answered a particular invitation of the editor, Doctor Kustic, and without any preparation I told him of my experience and personal observation; this was in the course of a brief interview which would fit on one typed page. That is very little indeed in comparison with the 23 typewritten pages by the honoured Bishop of Mostar on the subject. I have always held, in regard to the facts of Medjugorje, that they can be freely discussed, that we are free to accept them or not, because these facts are not indispensable to salvation. Accordingly I have never said that all are obliged to believe in these events. For my own part, I hold that, allowing for human factors, these events are of themselves supernatural.

In Rome, during the pilgrimage of youth (30 March 1985), I met the honoured Bishop of Mostar and I told him my opinion, quoting to him St Augustine's word: '*In dubiis libertas, in omnibus caritas.*' (In matters doubtful freedom, in all things charity).

He answered me that the facts of Medjugorje are not in the class of doubtful matters, but that to believe in these events means that you are a victim of a fraud, sprung from fanaticism. I invited the Bishop of Mostar, orally and in writing, to come to Split for the feast of St Duje (7 May), to strengthen and display publicly the brotherhood and love which should exist between two bishops despite the difference of opinion on Medjugorje. But you have heard here the conditions he lays down before accepting my fraternal invitation: I must publicly withdraw my pronouncements on Medjugorje, and I must beg forgiveness for holding this opinion and for expressing it.

The case of Ivan Dragicevic is held by certain members of the Commission to be proof positive that everything that happens in Medjugorje is pure fantasy. We must distinguish Ivan the seer from Ivan the human being. Ivan the human being can fall into error, as the patriarch Abraham was mistaken when he asked his fair wife Sara to tell the Egyptians that she was his sister, not his wife, to avoid being killed by the Egyptians, or when the patriarch Jacob misled his father to take the place of the elder brother (instead of Esau). Ivan the human being was under duress from authority. As a seminarist he had a reverential fear of his superiors and of the Bishop, while on the other hand he knew that he could say nothing about the great sign, as Our Lady had forbidden him to do so. He deceived, because he wrote a lie, through fear of being expelled from the seminary if he wrote nothing. That was a mistake on his part, but he wrote nothing about the secret. With this proviso he could say that he had written nothing, that there was nothing on the paper, that he had written nothing on it, all the time in the context of the secret. The other seers testify that Ivan wrote nothing on the secret of the great sign.

Ivan admitted his fault to me on 11 April 1985, and told me that he should be punished for it.

I have always said that each message should be examined

separately, because all the messages have not the same superhuman quality, to be so understood. Human suggestion or the evil spirit can easily infiltrate the messages.

Conclusion

Medjugorje gives great and manifest fruits of prayer, of fasting and of conversion. The devil could not have produced such fruits in four years; it would have destroyed his kingdom.

What is taught in Medjugorje is love for the Orthodox; the ecumenism of Vatican II is thus confirmed. Love for Moslems is taught there, and for marxists, which confirms equally what Vatican II has required. This attitude enriches the fruits of Medjugorje, Lourdes and Fatima. The Church can only gain from that.

Our Cardinal has just now said that we cannot forbid private pilgrimages. I meant to say nothing else in the interview in *Glas Koncila*.

In his directive of 25 March 1985, the Bishop of Mostar ordered the Franciscans to phase out the pilgrimages and other facts of Medjugorje gradually, and that the seers should give him all their writings, whether they contained the 'secrets' or the 'messages' of Medjugorje.

The Bishop has no right to make such a request; he cannot enter the secrets of conscience. I can say that Vicka has completed her *Life of the Virgin*. She will publish the text at the right time. Ivanka is writing what Our Lady has told her on the problem of the Church and the world. I have not seen, even slightly, these writings. One may well ask what purpose the diocesan Commission of Medjugorje serves, after the directive of the Bishop on 25 March 1985.

I wish to state that the Franciscans and the visionaries have done everything that this directive asks of them, everything it was possible to accomplish: the young visionaries no longer go to the chapel of apparitions, the new statue has been replaced by the old one, the young people no longer come to recite publicly the seven Paters etc.

The great misfortune lies in the fact that the Bishop of Mostar has assigned elsewhere the Franciscans who speak foreign languages. Who will now hear the confessions of foreigners and preach to them? The Bishop of Mostar has told us here that the

Franciscans as monks, have no right of recourse to the protection of the Holy See, as seculars have, that they come under his orders and consequently must do always, without objection, what the Bishop orders them. In my opinion, such behaviour, *salva reverentia*, is not the most efficacious.

To conclude I beg his Excellency the Bishop of Mostar to verify the facts of Medjugorje with his Commission, accepting the help also of people of competence from abroad, so as to act in conformity with the maxim: *Cum Petro et sub Petro* (With Peter and under Peter's authority). The facts of Medjugorje concern not only the Church of Mostar, but the Church of the whole world.

Father Bishop, I beg you, despite our differences (on points which are not necessary to the faith), to be my guest for the feast of St Duje in Split, because for us, bishops also, Christ prayed thus: *That they may be one so that the world should believe in you.* Thank you.'

This surely is one of the great documents of the Medjugorje file. It is the product of a lucid mind, a great heart and a courageous spirit. It will survive the vicissitudes of human frailty, misery, malice.

1. Text released by the Archbishop.

REPORT SENT TO ROME BY
FR TOMISLAV VLASIC OFM[1]

After the apparition of the Blessed Virgin on 30 November 1983 Marija Pavlovic came to me and said, 'Our Lady says that the Supreme Pontiff and the Bishop must be informed immediately of the urgency and great importance of the message of Medjugorje.'

This letter seeks to fulfil that duty.

1. Five young people (Vicka Ivankovic, Marija Pavlovic, Ivanka Ivankovic, Ivan Dragicevic and Jakov Colo) see an apparition of the Blessed Virgin every day. The experience in which they see her is a fact that can be checked by direct observation. It has been filmed. During the apparitions the young people do not react to light, they do not hear sounds, they do not react if someone touches them, they feel that they are beyond time and space.

All the young people agree basically that:

*'We see the Blessed Virgin just as we see anyone else. We pray with her, we speak to her, and we can touch her.'

*'The Blessed Virgin says that world peace is at a critical stage. She repeatedly calls for reconciliation and conversion.'

*'She has promised to leave a visible sign for all humanity at the site of the apparitions at Medjugorje.'

*'The period preceding this visible sign is a time of grace for conversion and deepening of the faith.'

*'The Blessed Virgin has promised to disclose ten secrets to us. So far Vicka Ivankovic has received eight. Marija Pavlovic received the ninth one on 8 December 1983. Jakov Colo, Ivan Dragicevic and Ivanka Ivankovic have each

received nine. Only Mirjana Dragicevic has received all ten.'

*'These apparitions are the last apparitions of the Blessed Virgin on earth. That is why they are lasting so long and occurring so frequently.'

2. The Blessed Virgin no longer appears to Mirjana Dragicevic. The last time she saw one of the daily apparitions was Christmas 1982. Since then, the apparitions have ceased for her, except on her birthday (18 March 1983). Mirjana knew that this latter would occur.

According to Mirjana Our Lady confided the tenth and last secret to her during the apparition of 23 December 1982. She also disclosed the dates on which the different secrets will come to pass. The Blessed Virgin has revealed to Mirjana many things about the future, more than to any of the other young people so far. For that reason I am reporting below what Mirjana told me during our conversation on 5 November 1983. I am summarising the substance of her account, without word-for-word quotations. Mirjana said:

'Before the visible sign is given to humanity, there will be three warnings to the world. The warnings will be in the form of events on earth. Mirjana will be a witness to them. Three days before one of the admonitions, Mirjana will notify a priest of her choice. The witness of Mirjana will be a confirmation of the apparitions and a stimulus for the conversion of the world.

After the admonitions, the visible sign will appear on the site of the apparitions in Medjugorje for all the world to see. The sign will be given as a testimony to the apparitions and in order to call people back to faith. The ninth and tenth secrets are serious. They concern.chastisement for the sins of the world. Punishment is inevitable, for we cannot expect the whole world to be converted. The punishment can be diminished by prayer and penance, but it cannot be eliminated. Mirjana says that one of the evils that threatened the world, the one contained in the seventh secret, has been averted thanks to prayer and fasting. That is why the Blessed Virgin continues to encourage prayer and fasting: 'You have forgotten that through prayer and fasting you can avert war and suspend the laws of nature.' After the first admonition, the others will follow in a rather short time. Thus, people will have some time for conversion.

That interval will be a period of grace and conversion. After the visible sign appears, those who are still alive will have little time for conversion. For that reason, the Blessed Virgin invites us to urgent conversion and reconciliation. The invitation to prayer and penance is meant to avert evil and war, but most of all to save souls.'

According to Mirjana, the events predicted by the Blessed Virgin are near. By virtue of this experience, Mirjana proclaims to the world: 'Hurry, be converted; open your hearts to God.'

In addition to this basic message, Mirjana related an apparition she had in 1982 which we believe sheds some light on some aspects of Church history. She spoke of an apparition in which Satan appeared to her disguised as the Blessed Virgin. Satan asked Mirjana to renounce Our Lady and follow him. That way she could be happy in love and in life. He said that following the Virgin, on the contrary, would only lead to suffering. Mirjana rejected him, and immediately the Virgin arrived and Satan disappeared. Then the Blessed Virgin gave her the following message, in substance:

'Excuse me for this, but you must realise that Satan exists. One day he appeared before the throne of God and asked permission to submit the Church to a period of trial. God gave him permission to try the Church for one century. This century is under the power of the Devil, but when the secrets confided to you come to pass, his power will be destroyed. Even now he is beginning to lose his power and has become aggressive. He is destroying marriages, creating division among priests and is responsible for obsessions and murder. You must protect yourselves against these things through fasting and prayer, especially community prayer. Carry blessed objects with you. Put them in your house and restore the use of holy water.'

According to certain Catholic experts who have studied these apparitions, this message of Mirjana may shed light on the vision Pope Leo XIII had. According to them, it was after having had an apocalyptic vision of the future of the Church that Leo XIII introduced the prayer to St Michael, which priests used to recite after Mass up to the time of Vatican II. These experts say that the century of trials foreseen by Leo XIII is about to end.

Holy Father, I do not want to be responsible for the ruin of anyone. I am doing my best. The world is being called to conversion and reconciliation. In writing to you, Holy Father, I am only doing my duty. After drafting this letter I showed it to the young people so that they might ask the Blessed Virgin whether its contents are accurate. . . Ivan Dragicevic relayed the following answer: 'Yes, the contents of the letter are the truth. You must notify first of all the Supreme Pontiff and then the Bishop.'

This letter is accompanied by fasting and prayers that the Holy Spirit will guide your mind and your heart during this important moment in history.

Yours in the Sacred Hearts of Jesus and Mary,

Medjugorje, 2 December 1983   Tomislav Vlasic

---

1. Others have sent letters to the Holy Father or to the Head of the Congregation for the Doctrine of the Faith, Cardinal Joseph Ratzinger. It is known that the Pope received a Rosary blessed for him by Our Lady at Medjugorje; Vicka has also received a Rosary from Our Lady personally.

RECENT MESSAGES FROM OUR LADY

28 August 1986
'Dear children! I want you to be an example to everyone in everything, especially in prayer and witnessing. I cannot help the world without you. I want you to cooperate with me in everything, even in the smallest things. Therefore, dear children, help me by your prayer from the heart, and by surrendering completely to me. In that way I shall be able to teach you and lead you along the road which I began with you. Thank you for your response to my call.'

4 September 1986
'Dear children! Today I am again calling you to prayer and fasting. You know, dear children, that I can do everything with your help: I can force Satan not to seduce people to evil and I can remove him from this place. Dear children, Satan keeps watch over every individual; he particularly wants to bring confusion to every one of you in everyday things. So, dear children, I ask that every day in your life may become filled with prayer and complete surrender to God. Thank you for your response to my call.'

11 September 1986
'Dear children! During these days when you are joyfully celebrating the cross, I desire that your own cross may also become a source of joy for you. Pray especially, dear children, that you may be able to accept illness and suffering with love, as Jesus accepted pain. Only when you accept them in that way with joy will I be able to give you the graces and healings which Jesus allows me. Thank you for your response to my call.'

18 September 1986
'Dear children! Today as well I thank you for everything you

have done on my behalf recently. In particular, dear children, I thank you, in the name of Jesus, for the sacrifices you have offered these past few weeks. You forget, dear children, that I desire sacrifices from you in order that I may help you and drive Satan away from you. That is the reason why I appeal to you once again to offer sacrifices to God with special reverence. Thank you for your response to my call.'

2 October 1986
'Dear children! Once again today I invite you to prayer. Dear children, you cannot know how great the value of prayer is so long as you do not say for yourself: now it is time to pray, now nothing else is important, now no one is more important to me than God. Dear children, devote yourselves to prayer with a special love, so that God will be able to reward you with his graces. Thank you for your response to my call.'

9 October 1986
'Dear children! You know that I want to guide you along the road of holiness, but I do not wish to force you to become holy. It is my desire that each of you, through your little acts of self-denial, should be of help to yourselves as well as to me, so that I can better guide you, and that from day to day you may come closer to holiness. This long while that I have been with you is a sign that I love you beyond measure, and that I wish for each of you that you become holy. Thank you for your response to my call.'

16 October 1986
'Dear children! Today again I want to show you how much I love you; therefore it saddens me not to be able to help each of you to understand my love. For this reason, dear children, I invite you to prayer and to total abandonment to God, because Satan desires to conquer you in everyday affairs and to take first place in your lives. Because of this, dear children, pray constantly. Thank you for your response to my call.'

23 October 1986
'Dear children! Today again I invite you to pray; in particular, dear children, I invite you to pray for peace. Without your

prayers, dear children, I cannot help you to realise the message given to me by the Lord for you. Therefore, dear children, pray; because in prayer you know the peace which the Lord is giving you. Thank you for your response to my call.'

30 October 1986
'Dear children! Today also I want to call you to take seriously the messages which I give you. Dear children, for you I have stayed so long, to help you to put into practice the messages which I give you. Therefore, dear children, live with love for me, the messages I give you. Thank you for your response to my call.'

6 November 1986
'Dear children! Today I want to invite you to pray daily for the holy souls in Purgatory. Prayer and grace are necessary to every soul to attain the love of God. In so doing dear children, you also acquire new intercessors, who will help you in life to understand that all earthly things are unimportant for you; that you should aim only at heaven. Therefore, dear children, pray without ceasing. In that way you will help yourselves and also the others to whom your prayer will bring joy. Thank you for your response to my call.'

13 November 1986
'Dear children! Today I ask you to pray with your whole heart and to change your life day by day. I especially ask you, dear children, to begin to live in a holy way, with prayers and sacrifices. Because I desire that every one of you who has been in this fountain or near to this fountain of grace, may reach heaven by the special gift which has been given to me, that is holiness. Therefore, dear children, pray and change your life that you may become holy. I shall always be close to you. Thank you for your response to my call.'

20 November 1986
'Dear children! Today I invite you to live, and to follow with special love, all the messages I give you. Dear children, God does not want you to be lukewarm and indecisive, but to be completely abandoned to him. You know that I love you and that I am ardent with love for you. Therefore, dear children,

decide to make love your life and day by day to know the love of God. Dear children, decide for love that love may reign in all; not human love, however, but divine. Thank you for your response to my call.'

27 November 1986

'Dear children! Today I invite you to consecrate your life to me, with love, in such a way that I can guide you with love. I love you, dear children, with a special love, and I want to lead all of you to God in heaven. I want you to understand that this life lasts a little while compared to that in heaven; therefore, dear children, today decide anew for God; only thus can I show you how dear you are to me, and how much I desire all of you to be saved and to be with me in heaven. Thank you for your response to my call.'

4 December 1986

'Dear children! Today I ask you to prepare your hearts for these days in which the Lord desires in a particular way to cleanse all the sins of your past. Dear children, you cannot do it alone; therefore, I am here to help you. Pray, dear children, only thus can you know all the evil that is in you and surrender it to the Lord in such wise that the Lord may purify your hearts completely. Therefore, dear children, pray without ceasing, and prepare your hearts by penance and fasting. Thank you for your response to my call.'

11 December 1986

'Dear children! I call you to pray especially at this time that you may succeed in experiencing the joy of encounter with Jesus who is born. I desire, dear children, that you live these days as I live them, in joy. I wish to guide you, and to show you the joy to which I wish to lead each one of you. Therefore, dear children, pray and abandon yourselves totally to me. Thank you for your response to my call.'

18 December 1986

'Dear children! Today again I want to invite you to prayer. When you pray, you are so much more beautiful; like flowers which after snow show all their beauty, and their colours are beyond description. So also you, dear children, after prayer, show, in the sight of God, all the beauty which makes you more dear to him. For this reason, dear children, pray and offer your inmost being to the Lord, because he makes of you a harmonious and heavenly flower. Thank you for your response to my call.'

25 December 1986

'Dear children! Today again I bless the Lord for all that he is doing for me, in particular for the gift of being able to be with you today. Dear children, in these days the Father offers special graces to all those who open their hearts to him. I bless you and I desire that you too, dear children, may know these graces and entrust everything to God so that God may be glorified through you. My heart is most attentive to your progress. Thank you for your response to my call.'

1 January 1987

'Dear children! Today I want to invite all of you to live, in the new year, all the messages I give you — to be able to teach you how to advance on the road of holiness. Therefore, dear children, pray unceasingly, and live all the messages which I give you, because I do all this with great love towards God and towards you. Thank you for your response to my call.'

8 January 1987

'Dear children! I would like to thank you for all the times you have responded to my messages, and especially, dear children, to thank you for all the sacrifices and prayers you have offered to me. I wish to continue giving you messages — not any more, however, every Thursday, but rather on the 25th of each month. I have now accomplished the mission of my Lord, so from this time on I shall be giving you fewer messages. But I shall still be with you. Therefore, dear children, listen to my messages and live them, and in that way I will be your guide. Dear children, thank you for your response to my call.'

THE MONTHLY MESSAGES

25 January 1987

'Dear children! I now wish to call all of you, from today, to begin to live a new life. Dear children, I wish you to understand that God has chosen each of you so that he could use each one for his great plan of salvation for mankind. You cannot understand how great your role is in the design of God. That is why you must pray, dear children, so that you may know in prayer God's plan through you. I am with you so that you may realise it in its fullness. Thank you for your response to my call.'

25 February 1987

'Dear children! Today I want to wrap my mantle around you, and lead you all along the road to conversion. I ask you, dear children, to offer to the Lord your whole past and all the evil which has accumulated in your hearts. I desire each one of you to be happy, but sin prevents that. For this reason, dear children, you must pray and in prayer you will find a new way to happiness. Joy will reveal itself in your heart and you will become happy witnesses which is what my Son and I await from each one of you. I bless you all. Thank you for your response to my call.'

25 March 1987

'Dear children! Today I thank you for your presence in this place where I give you special graces. I call each of you to begin from today to live the life which God wants from you, and to begin doing good works of love and mercy. I do not want you, dear children, to live the messages and commit sin; this displeases me. That is why, dear children, I want each one of you to live a new life without destroying all that God does in you, and what he gives you. I give you my special blessing and I remain with you on your way to conversion. Thank you for your response to my call.'

25 April 1987

'Dear children! Today again I am inviting you to pray. You know that God grants special graces in prayer. Therefore, dear children, seek and pray in order that you may understand everything I give you here. I call you, dear children, to prayer of the heart. You know that without prayer you cannot comprehend everything God plans through each one of you, so pray. I desire that through each one of you God's plan may be fulfilled and that all God has given you in the heart may increase. Therefore, dear children, pray that you may have God's blessing to protect you from the evil which threatens you. I bless you, dear children. Thank you for your response to my call.'

25 May 1987

'Dear children! I call each one of you to begin to live in the love of God. Dear children, you are ready to commit sin and to place yourselves in Satan's hands unthinkingly. I call on you so that each one should knowingly decide for God against Satan. I am your Mother and for this reason I wish to lead all of you to complete holiness. I wish each one of you to be happy here on earth, and that each one should be with me in heaven. This, 'Dear children! is the purpose of my coming here, and my wish. Thank you for your response to my call.'

25 June 1987

'Dear children! Today I thank you all and I desire to call you all to the peace of God. I wish each of you to know in his heart this peace which God gives. Today I want to bless all of you, and I bless you with the blessing of God; I beg you, dear children, to follow and to live my way. I love you, dear children; that is why I have called you, how many times, and I thank you for all you do for my intentions. Help me, I beg you, so that I may be able to offer you to God, to save you and to guide you on the way of salvation. Thank you for your response to my call.'

25 July 1987

'Dear Children! I ask you to accept from today the way of holiness. I love you and that is why I wish you to become holy. I do not want Satan to stop you on this way. Dear children, pray and accept everything that God offers you on this bitter way, because to everyone who begins to walk on this way God reveals joys that are felt and each one will respond still more to every call from God. Pay no attention to things without importance, but reach towards heaven. Thank you for your response to my call.

25 August 1987

'Dear children! Today again I renew my call to all of you that each one of you decide to live the messages. God has allowed me again, during this year, which the Church has consecrated to me, to speak to you and to encourage you to holiness. Dear children, ask from God the graces which he gives so that your sanctity may be complete. For this reason, dear children, do not forget to ask, because God has promised me that I may obtain graces for you. Thank you for your response to my call.'

25 September 1987

'Dear children! I wish again today to invite all of you to pray. Let prayer become your life. Dear children, consecrate your time to Jesus himself and he will give you all that you ask. He will reveal himself to you fully. Dear children, Satan is strong; he lies in wait to tempt each one of you. Pray: in this way he will be powerless to harm you or block you on the road to holiness. Dear children, make progress as much as possible from day to day through prayer towards God. Thank you for your response to my call.'

25 October 1987

'Dear children! Today I invite each of you to aim at paradise. The road is difficult to those who have not decided in favour of God. Dear children, make up your minds and believe that God is offering himself to you in all his fullness. You are invited and you need to answer the call of the Father, who is calling you through me. Pray, for it is in prayer that each one of you can reach perfect love. I bless you and I wish to gather each one of you under my maternal mantle. Thank you for your response to my call.'

25 November 1987

'Dear children! I invite each of you to decide again to abandon yourselves completely to me. Only in that way can I present each one of you to God. Dear children, you know that I love you immensely, and that I want each one of you to belong to me. But God has given to each of you freedom, which I respect with all my love. And I bow, in humility, to your free choice. I desire, dear children, that you act in such wise that all that God has planned for this parish may be realised. If you do not pray you will not be able to discern my love and the plans God has for this parish and for each one of you. Pray that Satan does not attract you through his pride and his power to deceive. I am with you and I want you to believe that I love you. Thank you for your response to my call.'

25 December 1987

'Dear children! Rejoice with me. My heart rejoices because of Jesus. Today I wish to give him to you. I want each one of you, dear children, to open your hearts to Jesus. I will give him to you lovingly. It is my wish that he will change you, teach you and protect you. Today I am praying in a special way for each one of you and presenting you to God. Thus he will reveal himself to you. I am calling you to sincere prayer of the heart, so that your every prayer may be an encounter with God. Every single day let him take first place in your work and in your life. Today I appeal to you in all seriousness to obey me and to do as I ask. Thank you for your response to my call.'

25 January 1988

'Dear children! Today I again call you to complete conversion to God, which is difficult for those who have not chosen God. I call you, dear children, to complete conversion to God. He has it in his power to grant everything you seek from him. However, you seek God only when there is illness or problems, or in difficult moments. You think that God is far from you, that he does not listen to you, and that he does not accept your prayers. No, dear children, that is not the truth. When you are far from God you cannot receive graces because you do not seek them with a firm faith. I am praying for you, dear children, and I desire to draw you ever closer to God. But I cannot do this if your will is lacking. Therefore, dear children, put your life in God's hands. I bless you all. Thank you for your response to my call.'

25 February 1988

'Dear children! Today I want to call you to prayer and total abandonment to God. You know that I love you and it is on account of this love that I come here to show you the road to peace and the salvation of your souls. I wish you to heed me and not to allow Satan to seduce you. He is powerful enough, dear children. I seek your prayers, that you may offer them to me for those who are under Satan's influence, that they may be saved. Be a witness through your life. Sacrifice your lives for the salvation of the world. I am with you and wish to thank you. In heaven you will receive from the Father the reward he has promised you. Therefore, little children, have no fear. If you pray, Satan can do you no harm, because you are God's children and he watches over you. Pray and may the Rosary be ever in your hands as a sign to Satan that you belong to me. Thank you for your response to my call.'

25 March 1988
'Dear children! Today again I am calling you to complete abandonment to God. Dear children, you are not aware of the love with which God loves you. That is why he allows me to be with you, to teach you, to help you to find the way of peace. But you cannot discover this way if you do not pray. For this reason, dear children, leave everything and consecrate time to God; and then he will give you gifts and he will bless you. Little children, do not forget that your life is passing like flowers of the spring, which today are wonderful, but which tomorrow no one thinks of. For this reason pray, so that your prayer and your abandonment to God may serve as a guide along your way. Thus your witness will have value not only for you but for eternity. Thank you for your response to my call.'

25 April 1988
'Dear children! God wishes to make you holy. Therefore through me he is inviting you to complete surrender. Let Holy Mass be your very life. Understand that the Church is God's palace, the palace in which I gather you and wish to show you the way to God. Come and pray. Neither look to others nor slander them, but rather let your life be a testimony to the way of holiness. Churches deserve respect and are set apart as holy because God, who became man, dwells in them day and night. Therefore, little children, believe and pray that the Father increase your faith, and then ask for whatever you need. I am with you and I rejoice

because of your conversion, and I protect you with my motherly
mantle. Thank you for your response to my call.'

25 May 1988

'Dear children! I am inviting you to complete surrender to God.
Pray, little children, that Satan may not carry you about like
the wind in the branches. Be strong in God. I desire that through
you the whole world may get to know the God of joy. By your
life bear witness to God's joy. Do not be anxious or worried.
God himself will help you and show you the way. I wish you
to love all men with my love. Only in such a way can love reign
over the whole world. Little children, you are mine. I love you
and I wish you to surrender to me so that I can lead you to God.
Never cease praying so that Satan cannot take advantage of you.
Pray for knowledge that you are mine. I bless you with the
blessing of joy. Thank you for your response to my call.'

25 June 1988

'Dear children! Today I am calling you to love which is loyal
and pleasing to God. Little children, love means everything that
is bitter and difficult for the sake of Jesus, who is love. Therefore,
dear children, pray God to come to your aid and not, however,
according to your desires but according to his love. Surrender
yourselves to God so that he may heal you, console you, and
forgive you everything within you which is a hindrance on the
way of love. In this way God can mould your life and you will
grow in love. Dear children, glorify God with a canticle of love
so that God's love may be able to grow in fullness in you day
by day. Thank you for your response to my call.'

25 July 1988

'Dear children! Today I am calling you to complete surrender
to God. Give everything you do and everything you possess to
God so that he can take control of your life, as King of all you
possess. That way, through me, God can lead you into depths
of the spiritual life. Little children, do not be afraid because I
am with you even when you think there is no way out and that
Satan is in control. I am bringing peace to you. I am your Mother
and the Queen of Peace. I bless you with the blessing of joy so
that God may be everything for you in life. Thank you for your
response to my call.'

25 August 1988

'Dear children! Today I invite you to rejoice in the life which God gives you. Little children, rejoice in God the Creator because he has created you so wonderfully. Pray that your life be joyful thanksgiving which flows out of your heart like a river of joy. Little children, give thanks unceasingly for all that you possess, for each little gift which God has given you, so that a joyful blessing may always come down from God on your life. Thank you for your response to my call.'

25 September 1988

'Dear children! Today I am inviting all of you without difference to the way of holiness in your life. God gave you the grace, the gift of holiness. Pray that you comprehend it more and more in such a way that you may, by your life, be able to bear witness for God. Dear children, I bless you and I intercede for you to God, that your way and your witness may be complete and a joy for God. Thank you for your response to my call.'

25 October 1988

'Dear children! My call to you to live the messages which I give you is a daily one. Especially, little children, because I wish to draw you near to the Heart of Jesus. Little children, to this end I invite you today to consecrate yourselves to Jesus, my beloved Son, so that each of you should belong to him in your heart, and then I invite you to consecrate yourselves to my Immaculate Heart. I desire you to consecrate yourselves personally, in families and in parishes, so that everything should belong to God through my hands. So, my dear little children, pray to understand the greatness of these messages which I give you. I want nothing for myself, but everything for the salvation of your souls. Satan is strong and for this reason, little children, entrust yourselves to my maternal heart through continuous prayer. Thank you for your response to my call.'

25 November 1988

'Dear children! I invite you to prayer so that you may meet God. In prayer God gives himself to you, but he wishes you to answer his call in all freedom. For this reason, little children, set aside a time during the day to pray in peace and humility, to have this encounter with God the Creator. I am with you and I intercede greatly before God. Be watchful so that every encounter in prayer be a joyful contact with God. Thank you for your response to my call.'

25 December 1988
'Dear children! I call you to peace. Live it in your heart and around you that all may know that this peace does not come from you, but from God. Little children, today is a great day. Rejoice with me. Celebrate the Nativity of Jesus in the peace which I give you. It is for this peace that I have come, as your Mother and as Queen of Peace. Today I give you my special blessing. Bear it to all creation that it may know peace. Thank you for your response to my call.' *

---

* This message was sent to us by Marija Pavlovic from Birmingham, Alabama in the United States where she had travelled to offer one of her kidneys to her brother who was seriously ill with a kidney disease. As a result of her generosity, the transplant operation has been successfully carried out.

RECENT HAPPENINGS

To give the reader an idea of the history of Medjugorje since this book was first published it may be appropriate to take aspects which suggest themselves naturally.

World reaction: This increases continually. The numbers of pilgrims are increasing. For the fifth anniversary of the first apparition, 24 June 1986, an estimated 200,000 pilgrims were assembled in Medjugorje. At an evening prayer meeting at Krizevac Our Lady was reported to have expressed her gratitude that all five continents were represented — a matter of intense joy to the two Australians present. Increasing attention is being given to the problems of transport.

It would require a detailed, carefully researched study to list and analyse the books, pamphlets and articles which have appeared on Medjugorje over the last year. Inevitably the quality is uneven — I speak of those I have seen. But some maintain a high standard: such a judgement would be valid about Fr René Laurentin's continuing series on the subject.

Rather exceptional in all this flow of print is the writing of Wayne Weible, an American Lutheran. He was a newspaper columnist and the publisher of four weekly community newspapers. He knew nothing about Our Lady beyond the Bible passages. But at a Sunday school class he heard about the apparitions at Medjugorje and was later given a video. Here is his account of what happened:

'About midway through watching the film, I suddenly "felt" a strong message within myself. I really don't know how to explain it. I heard no audible voice, but the message was there just as clear as though I had actually heard it. In essence it said: "You are my son, and you are to do my Son's work. Write about the events in Medjugorje. Afterwards you will no longer be in this work (newspapers), for your life will be devoted to the spreading of the message".'

When Wayne Weible had recovered from this shock he decided to do as he had been told. He went to Medjugorje twice and wrote columns in his paper describing and explaining what had taken place there since 1981. He soon found that his papers had changed ownership so that he was free to work at spreading the message. To satisfy many requests he composed eight pages in tabloid form recounting his experience and reprinting his columns. In September 1986 he ordered a print-run of 3,000, sufficient for a year. By May 1987 three million copies had gone and three printing plants were working to meet the demand. With the Boston Center for Peace, this is one of the effective means for the diffusion of the Medjugorje message. The man behind it remains a Lutheran.

Other means are the answerphones where one can receive the monthly (formerly weekly), messages. By dialling 3335981084 in France with the appropriate international prefix (16 in Ireland) you can get the message with, occasionally, items of useful information. A number of radio and television programmes have been made about Medjugorje. Channel 4 was one of the first to see the potential: this is unique television material, striking landscape, sparkling personalities, religious enthusiasm shared by crowds — and mystery. Italian, Bavarian and Yugoslav (twice) companies have seized the opportunity, as have makers of videos like the Boston Center. Last February the BBC put John Bird's fine documentary on the *Everyman* Sunday night programme. It was shown on Irish television on Good Friday and is due to appear frequently in other countries.

Church authority: Many people will be curious about the attitude of Pope John Paul II to the events at Medjugorje. The Pope has made visits to Marian shrines a feature of his world-wide pastoral activity. He said, characteristically of so many similar episodes, at Knock: 'Today I have reached the goal of my pilgrimge to Ireland, Our Lady's shrine at Knock.' His many pronouncements on Our Lady, his emphasis in recent years on the Immaculate Heart of Mary, which he associates with the Sacred Heart of Jesus, have raised hopes of a revival of Papal teaching on Our Lady similar to that of Pius XII; one must not overlook the splendid treatise of Paul VI, *Marialis Cultus*, 2 February 1974. A high point has been the Encyclical *Redemptoris*

Mater, 25 March 1987 and the proclamation of a Marian Year, to run from 7 June 1987 to 15 August 1988; we must not forget the Pope's keen interest in Russia which in 1988 celebrates the Millennium of its Christianity. On 13 May 1988 he will travel to Fatima to close the seventieth anniversary year of the apparitions there.

It is unthinkable that the Pope does not reflect on Medjugorje. Letters, articles and oral reports have been sent to him, as have copies of René Laurentin's works and of this book. He has been receiving reports of Marian apparitions from all over the world. What does he think?

On 24 January 1987 the Pope received in audience the bishops of Triveneto in Italy; it was their *ad limina* visit. The Pope showed knowledge of Medjugorje; there was nothing but good there, he thought, but seeing the differences of theologians and bishops one had to be careful.[1]

It is now known that several bishops have visited Medjugorje in a private capacity, one of them three times, another twice. As reported in this book, Mgr Frane Franic, Archbishop of Split, has gone there and publicly expressed his conviction of the authenticity of the reported apparitions. At the end of July 1987 the Papal Nuncio to Ireland, Monsignor Gaetano Alibrandi, went with an Irish group to Medjugorje, in a personal capacity.

The reader will know of the commissions set up by the Bishop of Mostar and of the Roman decision to end the working of the diocescan body. *Glas Koncila*, the Zagreb Catholic paper, in its issue of 18 January 1987, gave the text of a communique issued by the national episcopal conference, dated 9 January 1987. I am using the Italian translation of this text made by Fr Barnaba Hechich OFM, of the Antonianum University in Rome, thanking him for this and many similar kindnesses.

Signatories of the document are Cardinal Franjo Kuharic, president of the conference, and Pavao Zanic, as Bishop of the diocese. The first three paragraphs summarise the commission's history thus far, and relate the suggestion made by the Congregation for the Doctrine of the Faith that the inquiry should be continued at national level. The text continues thus:

'Accordingly the Episcopal Conference of Yugoslavia is establishing a commission with the duty of continuing the inquiry into the events of Medjugorje. While awaiting the results of the commission's work and the judgement of the Church, pastors and faithful are to maintain the position of prudence customary in such cases. Accordingly the organisation of pilgrimages or of other manifestations which would be motivated by the supernatural character attributed to the phenomena of Medjugorje is not permitted. Marian devotion, lawful and recommended by the Church, must be in harmony with the directives of the Magisterium (Teaching Authority), and in particular with the directives of the Apostolic Exhortation, *Marialis Cultus* of 2 February, 1974 (cf. AAS 66(1974), 113-168).'

At once there was a press campaign against Medjugorje, allegedly based on this ruling. In fact, there was evidence of anxiety among Catholics: Were all pilgrimages to Medjugorje forbidden? In places press headlines gave an affirmative answer. I follow the opinion of Mgr Francic, Archbishop of Split. He is president of the Yugoslav Episcopal Conference's Commission for the Doctrine of the Faith. He was interviewed in Milan by the ARPA agency, which issued the following communiqué on 13 February 1987.[2]

'Having been present at the meeting of the Episcopal Conference of Yugoslavia, in early October last year, my opinion is that the Yugoslav bishops did not want to prohibit all pilgrimages unconditionally, but to ensure that the final judgement of the Church on the supernatural character of the facts in question was not pre-empted; to this end the declaration speaks clearly and prohibits in fact all pilgrimages "motivated" by the supernatural character attributed to the phenomena at Medjugorje. This means, in my opinion, that the only pilgrimages not allowed are those arranged by pastors and faithful who would wish to usurp the role of the competent authority and/or to forestall and force its categorical and legal judgement.'[3]

Pressed further on the question of pilgrims going individually or in privately organised groups Mgr Franic had this to say:

'It is my profound conviction that pilgrims going to Medjugorje to pray, go to confession and fast, if they do so in a spirit of submission to the definitive judgement of the competent ecclesiastical authority, can do so with a clear conscience, according to the norms of Urban VIII, confirmed by Paul VI, for manifestations of this kind (*New Code of Canon Law*, 822,823ff);

actually pilgrimages to Medjugorje from my own and other Yugoslav dioceses continue without any difficulty on the part of the Ecclesiastical authorities.'

It is my personal view that the statement by Mgr Franic not only allays anxiety felt by those going or intending to go to Medjugorje; it also saves the honour of the Yugoslav hierarchy. It is very doubtful if bishops can prevent people going anywhere to pray, confess their sins and fast. This is said with complete respect for Church authority within its domain. If history tells us anything, it is that all authority is strengthened by scrupulous regard for the limits of its sphere of action.

There is another important point. If everyone stayed away, the apparitions would only concern the visionaries themselves, like all private apparitions through the ages: there would be no need for a Church statement. It is fairly certain that the strong hand of Bishop Zanic has been felt in the hierarchy's decision and statement. I have the text of a letter he wrote, on 19 December 1986, to Mgr Franic, which I am not publishing; it shows little change of mind, which I find infinitely sad.[4] In effect, what further proof of authenticity can there now be? The Medjugorje events have been witnessed by thousands, examined by experts in science, psychology, psychiatry, assessed by historians and theologians. What else can be sought or found?

The visionaries: These young people, at the focus of world interest, continue to live exemplary lives. Ivan, 22 on 25 June, completed his military service on 16 June; he was in a tank regiment stationed near Ljubljana in Slovenia. Jakov is attending a technical school in Citluk. It is believed that Our Lady visits him at home when he is alone in his room. Vicka has to endure illness when she is asked to forgo her apparitions. Ivanka was married on 28 December 1986, Feast of the Holy Family, to Rojko Elez, from the locality. He graduated in Economics at Sarajevo University, but is part of the unemployed masses, obliged to take work in restaurants. Ivanka told René Laurentin that she would have become a religious if Our Lady asked her. Our Lady's word was 'You are free; it's for you to choose'. Rojko is five years older than her. The marriage was blessed by Fr Pero (Petar) Ljubicic, the priest chosen by Mirjana to receive the secret ten days before the decisive event foretold by Our Lady. Mirjana had an extraordinary apparition on 28 January 1987 with a special message; this is reproduced separately below.

Marija is the one seen regularly at Medjugorje. She sees Our Lady at the evening apparitions and when Our Lady appears on the mountain of Krizevac or Podbrdo. On 24 June 1986, the fifth anniversary, she saw Our Lady at Podbrdo accompanied, as usual on these occasions, by five angels. She told Marija that it was like the Transfiguration on Mount Tabor. She was happy that so many people were there and she would give them all the graces they needed. She blessed all those present, even the curious, and said: 'Now go down from Tabor and take the blessing to each family, to the children, to parents and to the beloved sick.'

Message to Mirjana: 'My dear children! I have come to lead you to purity of soul, and through this to God. How have you received me? At the beginning without believing and in fear and with distrust towards the children whom I chose. Then most of you welcomed me in your hearts and began to put into practice my maternal requests. Unfortunately, however, this did not last very long. Wherever I come, my Son is with me, but Satan comes also. You have allowed him unwittingly to take the upper hand in you and to rule over you. At times you have understood that what you do is not allowed by God, but you quickly smother this feeling.

Do not give in, dear children! Dry the tears on my face which I pour down as I observe what you do. Look around you. Take time to come to God in the church. Come to your Father's house. Take time to get together in your family to implore grace from God. Remember your dead. Give them joy with the celebration of Mass.

Do not look with scorn at the poor man who begs for a little crust of bread. Do not chase him from your plentiful table. Help him and God will help you. The blessing he gives in place of thanks may be fulfilled; God may listen to him. You, my children, have forgotten all this. Satan has had his part in it. Do not give in. Pray with me. Do not fool yourselves, thinking, 'I am good, but my brother here next to me is useless'. This is not right.

I, your Mother, love you and therefore I warn you. There

are secrets, my children, which remain unknown; but when you know them it will be too late. Return to prayer. Nothing is more important. I would like the Lord to allow me to explain the secrets to you, even in part. But already the graces which he offers you are too much.

Think of what you have offered to him. When did you last give up something for the Lord?

I do not wish to reproach you further. I wish instead to invite you once again to prayer, to fasting, to penance. If with fasting you wish to obtain God's grace, let no one know that you are fasting. If, with the gift to a poor man, you wish to obtain grace from God, let no one know it, but yourself and the Lord. Listen to me, my children. Reflect in prayer on my messages.'

1.   *La Vita del Popolo,* 1 February 1987.

2.   ARPA Agency is of a high cultural-scientific character.

3.   Text of the message in *I Messagi della Madonna all communità di Medjugorje* ed. Barnaba Hechich OFM, p. 69f; in German in *Medjugorje Gebetsaktion,* Vienna, no. 5, 1987, p. 62; Fr. Hechich is Croatian and translates directly from the language. It is of interest to note that centres for distribution of material relevant to Medjugorje exist in many countries in Europe and other continents notably in North and South America. A review of popular religious interest launched with the collaboration of René Laurentin, now the most valuable crusader for the triumph of truth in the affair of Medjugorje, *Chrétiens Magazine,* has gone from success to success. René Laurentin, who has certainly suffered for his fearless testimony, will be honoured by an international symposium of essays for his seventieth birthday this year. The committee sponsoring this tribute to one of the greatest Mariologists of modern times includes Cardinals Poupard and Léger, Fr Carré OP and Jean Guitton, both of the French Academy, the world-famous biblical scholar, Fr Henri Cazelles PSS and the eminent medical scientist, Dr Henri Joyeux. I hope I may say without exhibitionism that I am proud to represent Ireland in this tribute. I took part with René Laurentin in the Fatima symposium on the Hearts of Jesus and Mary, September, 1986. It was sponsored by Cardinal Sin and the Philippine Hierarchy and strongly supported by Pope John Paul II.

4.   It is still sadder to read the lengthy declaration made by the Bishop of Mostar on 19 May 1986. For the present, I am not publishing this as the matter was taken out of the Bishop's hands and is now to be decided by the National Episcopal Conference. The Bishop, not surprisingly, declared that the apparitions were not supernatural in origin; all the good fruits were due to prayer and faith, he thought!

GEOMETRICAL PROGRESSION

Continuing expansion: The world movement inspired by the events in Medjugorje has two aspects. Quantitatively it increases in every dimension. Pilgrims increase in numbers. After the canonisation of St Lorenzo Ruiz, the Filipino martyr, in Rome last autumn, one thousand Filipinos went from the Rome ceremonies to Medjugorje; there will be a regular flow of travellers directly from the Catholic Republic, all imbued with gratitude to Our Lady for her miraculous intervention in their country's very recent history; in February 1986, she assured the avoidance of civil war and the revival of democracy. Already arrangements are being made for pilgrimages from all over the world during this Marian Year: a multitude is expected for the seventh anniversary of the first apparition, 24 June 1988.

The figure given in the last edition of this book for the distribution of Wayne Weible's pamphlet must now be revised. Last September it had passed seven million. In the United States John Hill maintains publishing and other means of communication with the same generosity which has marked his work since he founded the Boston Center for Peace; this initiative followed his encounter with the Medjugorje phenomenon. Anne de Baets, who resigned from the American Navy to collaborate in this work, has undertaken special studies to equip her for greater proficiency; she still serves the work. Stan Karminski, Wayne, Pennsylvania and his wife Margie, carry on an intensive programme of instruction on Medjugorje; they distribute a thousand videotapes a month to those interested.

Interest in the movement is manifest in Brazil and elsewhere in Latin America. In faraway Australia the apostolate of Leon Legrand, a Melbourne millionaire, has caused excited comment. He speaks on the subject of Medjugorje on television; like John Hill he is generous in supporting the necessary pedagogy. This work too is undertaken by Bernadette Harris in a newsletter issued from New York. Phenomena like metal in Rosary beads and crosses changing colour have been reported. I checked two cases, a Rosary beads in Dublin, a little cross in Manila.

In a different world we hear a story, apparently well founded, of direct interest in Medjugorje on the part of President Reagan. Maria Pavlovic is said to have written to Mikhail Gorbachev and Ronald Reagan. A response came from the latter, prior to the signing, on 8 December, feast of the Immaculate Conception, 1987, of the agreement on weapons restriction. We await more precise information.

Information in European countries is now being published regularly by *Nouvelles de Medjugorje* (Belgium), Peter Batty's *Mirecorder* and *Medjugorje Information Service*, and *Medjugorje Messenger* (England), *Echo of Medjugorje* (Italy, appearing in many languages), *Messages de Notre Dame* (Rouen), *Medjugorje Gebetsaktion* (Vienna), *Medjugorje Herald* (Galway, Ireland). The list is by way of illustration and does not claim to be exhaustive. Certain periodicals carry news items on Medjugorje. Such is *Stella Maris* (France) and from the same country the periodical launched by René Laurentin and his friends, *Chrétiens Magazine*, a mine of information on things Marian throughout the world. René Laurentin has now published ten books on Medjugorje — he has written sixteen on Lourdes.

Over a million copies have been distributed free, in many languages, from Milan, of two books in which Fr Tomislav Vlasic and Fr Slavko Barbaric expound in meditative manner, with quotations, the messages received from Our Lady in their country. The titles of these are *Open your Hearts to Mary, Queen of Peace* and *Abandon Yourselves Totally to Me*. The authors provide formulae of consecration to the Sacred Heart of Jesus and the Immaculate Heart of Mary, dictated by Our Lady to Jelena.

All this is a quantitative estimate of the world influence of a new spiritual phenomenon. Within it there has grown up a global fraternity, made up of new relationships, friendships, cooperative works, all nourished and fostered by Medjugorje. Hundreds of thousands of people have been brought into this spontaneous, beneficent movement through their commitment to the message, their desire to live it and to bear witness to its authenticity. Such things are now entering the fabric of the Catholic ecclesial communion and must have vast effects as time unfolds and God's purpose becomes more manifest. It would take volumes to narrate, describe, analyse the stories of lives transformed, hope recovered, new zest for Christ, enrichment of service to the Church, all now forming part of a mighty new Christian legend. There are moments of splendour and of the poignancy which, at times, is another face of Christian splendour. Such is the death in Medjugorje of a gracious, valiant Armenian woman, an exile in Belgium, partly handicapped, known to the present writer. She loved Our Lady of Banneux, whom she visited annually, manifesting a sensitive faith and piety. Desiring to honour Our Lady she went to Medjugorje and there her body awaits the resurrection.

Medjugorje is a very prominent instance, at the present time, of a worldwide return to Our Lady. Why there should be need for this change is beyond the limits of this work to examine. But the facts are patent. Pilgrimages to all the Marian shrines increase in number: for example in 1987 four and a half million people went to Lourdes compared with three million some years ago. Publications on Marian subjects are increasing in number: even in the lean years after the Council — hopefully *post hoc* and not *propter hoc* — quality was improving steadily, sharpened no doubt by the realisation that very considerable manuscript materials, especially in the Byzantine world, await study and publication.

Our age especially is marked by a whole series of reported apparitions of Our Lady. Some, like Akita in Japan and Zeitoun in Egypt (within the Coptic jurisdiction), are approved. Others, like Kibeho in Rwanda, receive sympathetic consideration from the local Church authorities. The whole list of countries, and one cannot claim certainty on the number, is impressive: Argentina, Nicaragua, Venezuela, Korea, the Ukraine, Hungary, Belgium, Spain, Italy, Ireland, Holland; some cases are outstanding for years, still await judgement. This is rendered by the competent Church authority.

An *a priori* approach to such phenomena at times blandly denies the possibility of their happening. At the other extreme is the naive credulity which accepts and looks for any preternatural manifestation. A scientific approach demands investigation of the facts. The *a priori* approach which rejects, if it does not scoff at, a multiplicity of such happenings, is akin to that which condemns Lourdes or any of the accepted European apparitions on the grounds that they were unnecessary; they should have taken place in missionary lands! Performers on the media sometimes make 'witty', caustic remarks about persons brought to prominence by such alleged happenings. There is a lesson of history that serious problems have rarely been solved by 'witty', caustic comments.

Are the apparitions of Our Lady caused by the anxiety of the times? Do people think she can save the world and project their psychic state on to a concrete image of her, adding appropriate words from the visual creation? It is a big claim by an interpreter and, in some cases reported, he would have the greatest difficulty in carrying it beyond the hypothesis stage. For surprisingly, the apparitions are not all reported from crisis areas. It is in Syria, not the Lebanon, that experts have been drawn by strange, inexplicable phenomena. Akita and Kibeho are not the tormented areas of their region. Until quite recently it was from places in the Irish Republic, not from the suffering North, that we had reports.

CONFRONTATION

I withheld the texts of Bishop Zanic's letter to Archbishop Franic, 19 December 1986, and the declaration which he had drawn up on 19 May 1986. The second document was composed in his capacity as local ordinary of Mostar. Both had lost their relevance to Medjugorje with the decision by the Roman authorities to refer the matter to the national episcopal conference. In any complete documentation on Medjugorje, which I or someone else may publish, these items will appear integrally.

I thought that I should do likewise with the statement made by the Bishop on 25 July 1987; it is also void of legal value for the same reason as the other episcopal texts. It has, however, been given wide publicity and it has evoked a reply which has likewise been widely read, from Fr Ivan Dugandzic, OFM. It seems proper then, and fair to both men, to reproduce their words.

I have not met Bishop Zanic, but I have read enough by him and heard enough about him from truthful people to know what he thinks about the apparitions, the Franciscans and Canon René Laurentin. In an interview given for publication to Fr Ruben E. Rios, who reproduced it in *Sacerdos*, religious organ of the diocese of Leon, Mexico, 29 September 1986, the Bishop was at his most condemnatory:

Q. **Are the Christian people right in thinking that the Virgin speaks at Medjugorje?**

A. She does not speak. It's all an invention of Fr Tomislav Vlasic and Fr Barbaric. Their attitude towards the Provincial is one of open hostility.... It is something terrible. One could die of it. Three times I have suggested to the Fr Provincial that he should remove Fr Barbaric from Medjugorje, because he says a lot of things which are inexact. He persists, for example in saying that the so-called

237

seers are healthy persons. That is not so. The seers are sick. A commission of doctors invited by defenders of Medjugorje stated that Vicka was hysterical. So, as soon as Fr Barbaric knew of this diagnosis, he flew off to Vienna and spoke to a psychiatric doctor to extract a favourable diagnosis from him. Without delay he convened many journalists and organised a press conference during which he said: 'All the seers are healthy.' I have informed the Holy Father and Cardinal Ratzinger that these fathers are deceiving people.

Q.　**Are there miracles?**

A.　There has not been a single miracle. Lamentably, these gentlemen invent miracles. It's all a question of money. They are collecting enormous sums of money and they buy journalists, they buy theologians, they buy propaganda, they buy everything.

Q.　**Is there punishment for those who visit Medjugorje? Can Mass be said there?**

A.　There is no punishment. All can celebrate if they wish to do so. . . . But I am entirely, one hundred per cent, sure that all these stories of apparitions are a pure lie, a swindle (*estafa*), a falsehood and I cannot speak against my conscience; I would prefer death. You can say in Mexico that you spoke with me and that I state: there are no apparitions, there are no miracles. It is all the result of enormous propaganda which has attacked me from the beginning.

Q.　**Your Excellency, what do you say about the conversions, the spirit of penance and of prayer which are reported from Medjugorje?**

A.　In the Middle Ages heretics did great and terrible acts of penance. That did not prove them right. In my opinion Medjugorje is the greatest deceit and swindle in the history of the Church.

Q.　**Why does the Provincial of the Franciscans not punish the inventors of this lie?**

A.　Because he fears the opposition of the whole Province. This Province has given many vocations to the priestly and

religious life. In addition the people are pious and
traditionalist, and a punishment meted out to the Province
would have fatal results.

Q. **Excellency, have you in mind to publish a document
which will show up this falsehood?**

A. Yes, certainly.

Q. **When?**

A. I don't know.

The Bishop had given interviews of this kind previously. But
this one constitutes a kind of peak. He really soared to heights
he had not hitherto scaled. In his previous interviews it was
common currency to hear of the Franciscans in the parish as
money-grabbing, unscrupulous to the point of hiring the great
French Mariologist, René Laurentin, to boost their case. But
he has left such accusation behind and is now ready to talk of
a 'swindle', the greatest in the history of the Church!

This would be amusing in a macabre sense, were we not
dealing with living persons — the Franciscans and the visionaries
— whose rights are violated, primarily the right to their
reputation; and with a spiritual reality which is having worldwide
repercussions. A very grave question arises: To whom is a bishop
accountable, and who can innocent people, so subject to
denigration, summon to defend them? Do Catholics forfeit their
right to a reputation by claiming to have seen an apparition?
No one surely believes that visionaries automatically merit
punishment! How, by divine or ecclesiastical law, is such
punishment justified?

Bishop Zanic has created a problem for the Yugoslav
hierarchy, irrespective of the authenticity of the apparitions: Do
they condone the use of such language about the faithful in their
jurisdiction? A serious question, but in the general climate of
the Church's public stand on behalf of human rights, a
compelling one. It is one of the many ironies of the Medjugorje
phenomenon that the man who defended the visionaries against
unjust charges by the civil officials now brands them as
accomplices in the greatest swindle of the Church's history.

The Bishop raises a question which has been answered more
than once: What does the prohibition on organised pilgrimages

mean? I refer the reader to the explanation given by Archbishop
Franic. But we must turn to another episcopal statement. I give
it in the text he personally issued, making the linguistic alterations
he desired. The heading and introductory works are his.

Declaration of the Bishop of Mostar about Medjugorje

Note: The Bishop spoke at Medjugorje on 25 July 1987, about
Saint James and the Sacrament of Confirmation. Then he said:

My brothers and sisters,
    On this occasion perhaps you expect me to say a few
words on those events all the world is talking about. The
Church must take this into consideration with her mission
as she entrusts this to certain persons and commissions.
You know that this matter is now to be discussed at the
level of a special commission recently established by the
Bishops' Conference of Yugoslavia. It is not so easy for
the Church to manifest her credibility to the people of this
century, who are suspicious, critical.
    I can say that I have spent six years praying, studying,
keeping silence. Others too have prayed and I thank them
very much. In every Mass of mine Medjugorje was included
as an intention. In every Rosary, every day, I prayed to
Our Lady to beg light from God for me, the Holy Spirit
too. That helped me very much to reach a strong and sure
conviction about everything I had heard, read,
experienced. . . .
    Over here many people are praying and fasting very
much, but in the belief that all these events are supernatural.
To preach to the faithful an untruth about God, Jesus, Our
Lady, deserves the pit of hell.
    In all my work, prayer, study, I had in mind only one
subject: to reach the truth. For that reason I created the
commission of four members in 1982. Subsequently I
expanded it, with the help of some bishops, and fathers
provincial — 15 members from 9 theological faculties, 7
dioceses, 4 provinces, with 2 first-class psychiatrists, who

could, of course, consult others among their colleagues.

The work took three years. About that work, and the events, the Holy See was informed from time to time. Now the commission of the Bishops' Conference is working on the matter.

However, there were some who went hastily ahead of the Church's judgement. They proclaimed 'miracles and supernatural events' and from the altar preached about private revelations, which it is prohibited to do, until the Church authenticates those revelations. That is why different authorities ordered that pilgrimages should not be organised, but the Church's judgement should be awaited. First of all the Commission for Medjugorje issued a warning on 24 March 1984. Regretfully this had no effect. Then the Bishops' Conference, in October of the same year, decided that official pilgrimages should not be organised ('official' means a gathering and association in common). But it was useless. Afterwards in Rome, the Congregation for the Doctrine of the Faith, on 23 May 1985, sent to the Italian Bishops' Conference a letter asking that bishops make efforts to reduce organised pilgrimages from Italy to Medjugorje.... and every form of propaganda. It was useless again.

Finally, when this last commission was formed, his Excellency Cardinal Franjo Kuharic and myself, in the name of the Bishops' Conference of Yugoslavia, on 9 January 1987, declared to the public: 'It is not allowed to organise pilgrimages or any manifestations motivated by the supernatural character which would be attributed to the events of Medjugorje.' That was declared from the highest forum in the Church and should be respected.

From the first news which announced extraordinary events in this parish, the Bishop's office carefully followed and picked up everything which would be a help in searching for the truth. To the visionaries and parish personnel the Bishop gave full freedom. He even defended them from the attacks of newspapers and politicians.

For three years the aforementioned fifteen-member commission went through recorded dialogues, much written material, chronicles, diaries, letters, documents... And the result: two voted for the supernatural character of the apparitions; one abstained; another one remarked: 'At the start there was something, then...'. The other eleven members voted against (*'non constat de supernaturalitate'* — no apparitions).

I am profoundly aware that all the members worked according to their conscience and examined everything which could help in seeking the truth. The Church cannot risk her credibility. We know that, in similar cases, she carefully examined such events and dismissed crowds if they assembled at the places where the events were not found to be supernatural. Let us call to mind Garabandal in Spain, San Damiano in Italy and many other places in our time. At Garabandal visionaries said that Our Lady had promised a great sign for all the world. Twenty-five years passed without a sign. If Our Lady left a sign here, everything would be clear.

Our Lady, according to the visionaries, began to appear on the mountain Crnica, then after the police stopped people going there, she descended into houses, fences, fields, vineyards, tobacco plantations; she was seen in the church, on the altar, in the sacristy, on the roof, the belfry, in roads, in schools, many times in Mostar, Sarajevo, Zagreb, Varazdin, Switzerland; in motorcars, on buses, and again in Krizevac, in the presbytery, etc., everywhere.

A sensible man should say: 'Our Lady, what they do to you!'

In this diocese I am pastor, teacher and judge by divine law in matters of faith. Because the events of Medjugorje create tension and division within the Church — some believe, some do not — and escape the Church's control, and because all the recommendations and decisions of the above-mentioned authorities — the Commission for Medjugorje, the Congregation (for the Doctrine of the Faith), the Bishops' Conference — failed, I, Bishop of Mostar, before the Lord responsible for discipline in this diocese, repeat and approve the previous decisions of the Church authorities, and I forbid all priests organising pilgrimages, who come here and attribute a supernatural character to these events, before the Commission of the

Bishops' Conference finishes its work, to say Mass in my diocese.

I appeal to you, Immaculate Virgin and Mother, Mother of God and Mother of the Church, Mother of this people who seek you, pray to you and love you. I appeal to you as your servant, and before all the world I express my profound and firm faith in all the privileges which the Lord bestowed on you, first and most favoured of creatures. I express my profound and firm faith in your prayer for all your children in this valley of tears. I express my profound and firm faith in your love for us sinners. That love you manifested also by your apparitions and sustaining help. I have myself conducted pilgrimages to Lourdes. With the strength of that faith I, Bishop of Mostar, before the multitude of your admirers throughout the world, discern and accept your great sign, which becomes certain and clear after these six years. It is your SILENCE. I did not need any special sign... But those who believed falsehood, certainly needed one. You persistently kept silence despite all the announcements about the sign: 'Be patient... it's very near... it's going to be on (the feast of) the Immaculate Conception (1981)... then at Christmas time... before the New Year etc.'

I thank you, my Lady, because of your silence for six years. That is the way you show us whether you really spoke here, whether you appeared, spread messages, whether you promised a special sign....

Holy Virgin, Mother of Christ and our Mother, may you intervene on behalf of peace in this restless province of the Church, the diocese of Mostar, especially may you intervene on behalf of this place, this parish, where your name has been spoken many times in sermons you would not want. May you put an end to invention of spurious messages from you. May you accept, Holy Virgin, as reparation, the sincere prayers of devout souls who remain far from fanaticism and disobedience towards the Church. May you obtain that all of us reach the truth. Dear Lady, humble and obedient Handmaid of the Lord, grant to us that Medjugorje, with strength, keeps step with the Pastor of this local Church, and may all of us, together, be able to glorify and praise you in truth and love. Amen.

Pavao Zanic
Bishop of Mostar

This statement provoked a number of comments, the latter only too easy. Fr T. Pervan wrote a dignified letter to Cardinal Zuharic, by way of protest. It seems, however, that the document which best meets the episcopal statement is the one that follows, from Fr Ivan Dugandzic. It is reproduced integrally.

Open Letter from the Franciscan Friars of Medjugorje to the Bishop of Mostar

(Transcribed from the *Echo of Medjugorje* No. 46, 1 November 1987)

'Father Bishop,

Almost two months have passed since, in the presence of a shocked crowd of thousands, you raised Hell and consigned us, the friars of Medjugorje, to its depths. At the time, we thought you had allowed yourself to be carried away by some irresistible impulse but the past two months have shown otherwise. You have continued, in your meetings with people, to feed these fires; our only consolation is the certainty that it is not you who will decide what place is reserved for us.

During this period, you have endevoured to demonstrate that Satan, in person, is acting here (in Medjugorje) and that what is happening here is his greatest deception since the time of Christ (see the Bishop's talk with Father Viktor Kosir). How can we begin to comment on this? Is it possible that, now, what Jesus said was impossible has become possible? Is it possible that Satan can be divided against himself and not fall? Has he come to the conclusion that his usual schemes to bring man to damnation are not working so that he has to fall back on the extreme resorts of prayer and fasting?

You, Father Bishop, persistently take every opportunity

to slander and morally destroy everyone connected with Medjugorje, with the intention of thereby destroying Medjugorje itself. These tactics provoke great anxiety and scandal in many souls. The American journalist, Jacqueline Srouji, who spent some time here in prayer, asked for an interview with you before she returned to America, which you granted her on 18 September 1987. After two hours spent with you, which were recorded on film and tape, she returned here in tears, saying; "If someone had tried to persuade me that the Bishop hated you, I would not have believed it; after this interview, I know he hates you."

When you spoke on the day of Confirmation in Medjugorje (26 July 1987) and especially when it was published by the press, many rubbed their hands in satisfaction, others expressed consternation and yet others asked us why we still remain silent. After much reflection, I have decided to draw people's attention to some of your statements.

You affirm; "I can say that for six years I have prayed, studied and remained silent." I accept that you have prayed, although you have, more than once, refused the prayers offered to God for you in Medjugorje. I also accept that you have studied, but I know how much more you, and the Commission you appointed, have studied the problems which you have raised rather than the phenomenon of the apparitions. Your "silence" is a chapter in itself. If you had remained silent, you would have given evidence of your prudence and wisdom. Instead, you chose to speak openly for quite some time now, casting doubts in the minds of the public, accusing and passing judgements upon both visionaries and priests in Medjugorje, and even upon those who come here as pilgrims. The climax came with your famous circular letter of 30 October 1984 which you broadcast throughout the world. This letter clearly let it be known that you had pre-judged the findings of the Commission and I informed you that the Commission had nothing further to do with the case.

Your conception of the role of the Commission was confused; you used it to suit your own pre-conceived ideas. This became obvious when you wished to use it to issue an ordinance or prohibition. Whenever the Commission looked like coming to a conclusion which was not to your liking, it suddenly became unimportant; then you knew how to say; "I am the Commission".

It is clear from your initiative on the day of Confirmation in Medjugorje that you continue to hold the same views. You do not recognise even the authority vested in the third Commission, established by the Episcopal Conference of Yugoslavia, and have not the patience to wait for the results of its work. In the beginning, you went around saying how great the responsibility was, yet showed yourself unwilling to share it with the other Bishops, as had been suggested for some time. Now that the Congregation for the Doctrine of the Faith has transferred this responsibility to the Episcopal Conference, you seem unable to accept it as a matter of fact and persist in doing all you can to bedevil the phenomenon of Medjugorje.

You, Father Bishop, asked us members of the preceding Commission to take an oath of secrecy on the deliberations of the Commission; you did not consider yourself bound by this oath: I cite two cases:

a) When the envelope given us by Ivan Dragicevic was discussed, the Commission agreed with you that the matter should not be disclosed outside the Commission. Only a few days later, you spoke publicly of the matter to a group of priests gathered in the cathedral for a spiritual retreat.

b) When the Commission, on your orders, ceased its function in May 1986, we submitted to you our individual, written, considered opinions. You then asked us to vote on the matter, emphasising that this would be a secret vote. I made a point of asking whether this vote would really remain secret; you, expressing surprise, said that that question should not even be asked. I reminded you of the violation of the secret set out in (1) above, but it was clear you were not pleased by this. You convinced us that this vote would, indeed, be secret; you did not even tell us the result but collected the papers and dissolved the Commission. Only a few days later, a number of foreign priests having had talks with you, spoke of the negative results of the vote, giving various proportions of the vote, but all agreeing that the overwhelming majority had voted against the probability of the apparitions being authentic.

The voting papers, themselves, could be the subject of a separate chapter. You offered us just the two options; a) *constat de supernaturalitate*; b) *non constat de supernaturalitate*. Two psychiatrists sustained that the phenomenon had to be studied further and pointed out that, since they were not theologians, they were not qualified to give an opinion on these options; they, therefore, abstained from the voting. We four theologians maintained, similarly, that the Commission had not finished its work but since we were in a minority the vote went ahead. In the manner in which you continue to allude to the results of the vote, two things are particularly disconcerting. You always give the result as though all fifteen members had voted when only thirteen took part. Even worse, option b) *non constat de supernaturalitate*, is transformed by yourself into *"constat de non-supernaturalitate"* ("there have been no apparitions"). The option (b) that is found in the directive of the Congregation for the Doctrine of the Faith signifies that the actual phase of research in the matter is not complete and that it is still open to investigation. Your presentation of the results of the vote give a false impression and distort them before public opinion.

Father Bishop, you state that 'the happenings in Medjugorje have created tension and division in the Church — some believe us, others do not'. What shall we take these words to mean? Perhaps you wish to say that, before Medjugorje happened, peace and unity reigned throughout the Church in Hercegovina and that this has been disrupted because some accept the apparitions as authentic and others do not? By the same logic, it could be said that Lourdes and Fatima have also divided the Church since, even after their approval by the Church, some people go on pilgrimage there while others are indifferent to such places.

Such a notion has never carried credence up to now since

everyone is free to go to those places or not to go as they will. Here things are different; those who do not accept Medjugorje cannot allow this freedom to those who do accept it, cannot remain calm; they become aggressive towards them, just wanting Medjugorje to disappear.

You must recall that stormy meeting of the episcopal curia which took place in Mostar in November 1985. You summoned the parish priest, Father Tomislav Pervan, Father Peter Ljubicic, me (Father Ivan Dugandzic), Sister Janja Boras and three of the visionaries, Marija Pavlovic, Ivan Dragicevic and Jakov Colo to this meeting. In front of us all you placed this ultimatum; "Someone has to disappear; you of Medjugorje or myself. I have no wish to disappear and to that end I will use all means at my disposal." You have been true to your word; since then you have been indiscriminate in the use of any way, time or place to achieve this end.

I must touch, briefly, on the case of the two curates of Mostar whom you frequently and readily introduce into this subject. During the course of the work of the first two Commissions, many members — encouraged by you — raised the question of these two priests during the sessions as if it were the 'philosopher's stone'. Because of this, I repeatedly asked, during the sessions, that a sub-committee of three be formed to study the question independently of the events in Medjugorje and thus eliminate it from the main agenda of the Commission. You opposed this suggestion with the result that this 'stone' continued to dominate the deliberations. Most people are unaware that these two Franciscans have taken their case to the Segnatura, the highest ecclesiastical court in Rome; that omissions and defects have been found in the procedure used to punish them and they have been advised to appoint counsel to bring the matter before the court. The case was proceeding but has now been blocked by your powerful 'friends at court'. Why do you fear the result of this case if you are sure that all is as it should be? You complain to the world at large about the dissension which exists between you and the Franciscans in Hercegovina, blaming it all on the friars of Medjugorje. During the whole of your episcopate of Mostar, you have done everything you can in Rome to make normal life impossible for the Franciscan Community. The most recent example is only two months old; you put every obstacle in the way of the regular and democratic mission of three visitors, invited by the General Curia of the Order last May, so that the object of their visit was rendered impossible.

Father Bishop, all obedience in the Church is rooted in obedience in that Faith which we hold in common. He who is in authority should strive, in charity, to create conditions which are conducive to obedience in charity; but he can transform obedience into a dangerous weapon; he can create conditions in which obedience becomes difficult or even impossible without betraying one's own conscience and the teachings of the Gospel.

I cannot but mention something about which you spoke to the Italian magazine *Jesus*. With what hypocrisy you spoke of the dignified behaviour of the parishioners confronted by your provocative words (during the Confirmation Day sermon): you interpreted their silence as assent to what you had to say, letting you know that they were tired of the whole business. What would you have had to say if they had reacted in the same way as the faithful did in the Franciscan Church in Mostar in 1980? You would have announcd, triumphantly, to the whole world that the very parish which had preached peace is, in fact, a rebellious parish. It is difficult for us to dismiss the notion that it may well have been your intention to provoke such a rebellion. But, during these six years, we have learnt to prize peace above all else. Witnesses of this event from other parishes have told how painful it was for them to see our parishioners' grief and how they admired their dignified behaviour. If, indeed, you were sure of the parishioners' approval of what you had to say, how is it that you had not one word to offer them, as a good father would, after Holy Mass.

Father Bishop, these words of mine do not constitute an attack, accusation or some political move; they are spoken in self-defence. I firmly believe in the final victory of Truth, even though this may always take much time. However, in this case, it must be obvious to the people at large who is being aggressive and who is being attacked. Although we, here, are at the service of the message of peace, we cannot renounce our love of truth, nor accept, against our personal convictions, the dictates of power; this would not be in the interests of the Church, nor of the Gospel.

Expressing my dutiful respect, I remain in Jesus and Mary, yours faithfully,

Father Ivan Dugandzic,
Medjugorje, 22 September 1987'

The Franciscans, in sending this document, have assumed the defence of the visionaries, who have been exposed to so much misrepresentation. They continue their lives of prayer and fasting faithfully. Vicka has had another period of forty days without apparitions. Maria and some of her friends from her prayer group have withdrawn from the village to give themselves to prayer in a contemplative centre. Fr Tomislav Vlasic had already taken the same decision, returning to Medjugorje for a few days to explain his position.

JELENA VASILJ AND MARIJANA VASILJ

Along with the reported apparitions discussed in the present work there is another phenomenon in Medjugorje which has attracted the attention of the Franciscans and of others who know and appreciate the local scene. This is the development, with a remarkable charismatic dimension, of a prayer group, in which the leading members are Jelena Vasilj and Marijana Vasilj, principally the former. They were in the initial stages under the direction of Fr Tomislav Vlasic. An assessment of the events was made by Fr Slavko Barbaric in October 1985; concentrating mostly on Jelena, who will be sixteen next May. His general descriptive statement was: 'Jelena Vasilj and Mirjana Vasilj claim that they hear the voice of Our Lady, that she teaches them and leads through prayer, that she gives messages for them personally, for the prayer group, for the whole parish and the entire world. The two of them claim that they at the same time see Our Lady, but in a different way from the first group of visionaries.'[1]

Fr Slavko reproduces interviews and messages to afford evidence for his evaluation of the phenomena. On 3 August 1987 Sean Conroy interviewed Jelena for the Galway *Medjugorje Herald*. The text is reproduced with grateful acknowledgement:

Q. Did Our Lady ask you to lead a prayer group?

A. No, a priest leads the prayer group. Our Lady gives them messages, and they all pray together. The usual prayer is the Rosary. They pray from the heart.

Q. Tell us about your Inner Locutions.

A. Our Lady is always with me in prayer. I do not feel the Madonna like a person. It is hard to explain, her voice is like a human voice. She comes almost every day.

Q. How do you know the Inner Locutions are from God?

A. I always pray to God and follow his way. The Madonna and I share a happiness. I have no special spiritual director. All the priests help me.

Q. How do you know you are praying from the heart and not from the head?

A. I feel Jesus like a brother, like a friend. When I pray I feel Jesus is love. I feel he is total security when I pray from the heart rather than from my head.

Q. When you pray do you ask for favours?

A. I pray for God's will, so that I will be able to carry out his will in my everyday life. I do not ask for favours.

Q. Is Our Lady sad as well as happy when she comes to you?

A. It depends. Sometimes sad, perhaps we are not good enough, sometimes happy. She thanks everyone, for she is Mother of us all. She wants to help everyone and we should pray and feel her help for us.

Q. Any advice on how to pray?

A. Everyone who knows Our Lady's messages given in Medjugorje should understand about praying. If we live with Jesus, we will understand every cross we have to carry. The more we open our hearts the greater is the experience of joy we will have in carrying our crosses.

Q. How strong was your faith before the Inner Locutions?

A. I did go to church, but it was not the same as going since Our Lady started coming to me. I did not feel God as close as I do now.

Q. What message would you like to give us?

A. In the main it's an invitation to pray for conversion. Gospa (Our Lady) tells people to believe in Jesus. She sees Jesus in everybody, and whenever we feel difficulties we should pray to God and feel love for everybody.

Q. Do you plan to enter a convent after Our Lady stops coming to you?

A. I am only fifteen years old, so I have plenty of time to think about that.

1. p.3; the typescript runs to 86 pages.

ECUMENISM

Some people may have got the idea that the message of
Medjugorje implies a form of religious indifference.[1] The fact
is that Our Lady taught the children to respect all religions; she
asked them to avoid the conflicts which arose from religious
animosity. She stated that in God there were no divisions, no
'religions'. We have made the divisions. 'The only Mediator
is Jesus Christ. The fact that you belong to one or another religion
is not without importance. The Spirit is not the same in each
Church.' Thus Mirjana, who also said: 'The Madonna has often
said that believers, for example here in Medjugorje, are too
opposed to the Orthodox and Muslims. This is not good. She
also said that there is but one God, that men have become
separated. You are not Christian if you do not respect the other
religions, Muslims and Serbs (i.e. Orthodox). You are not
Christian if you do not respect them. Often you make fun of
one another.'

Asked a somewhat similar question by Fr Svetsovar, Ivanka
Ivankovic replied: 'Keep the faith, persevere in it. Help your
friends. Do not be snobbish towards other religions but respect
them in so far as they praise God.' The interview continued:

Q. **It is important that people of good faith regardless of
denomination, not be turned against each other. But
tell me more about this. What did the Madonna say
about this?**

A. The Madonna said that religions are separated on earth,
but the people of all religions are accepted by her Son.

Q. **Does that mean that all people go to heaven?**

A. That depends on what they deserve.

Q. **Yes, but many have never heard about Jesus.**

A. Jesus knows all about that. I don't. The Madonna said basically religions are similar, but many people have become separated.

On another occasion also the Madonna insisted that the 'power of the Holy Spirit is not equally strong in all the Churches, and the power of the Holy Spirit acting in the priests leading these communities is not the same.'

All things considered, one may accept René Laurentin's judgement: 'In a word, if one compares these messages the teaching in them is clear: they refer to a very concrete reality: the atmosphere of hostility, contempt, religious war, which dominates in many Croatian villages. The Virgin asks them to overcome these quarrels, through an ecumenism of charity, which is made admirably clear by this message received by Archbishop Franic from the visionaries — the Madonna speaks thus to Croatian Catholics: ''Love your Serb Muslim brothers. Love your Serb Orthodox brothers. Love those who govern you.'' '

1.   R. Laurentin, *Dernières Nouvelles, Juin 1987*, no. 6, pp. 23-27. The author notes some concern in Rome on this whole matter, which he clarifies.

UPDATE, JANUARY 1989

Peter Batty: One event stands out since the publication of the last edition of this book. Peter Batty died on 24 June 1988, the seventh anniversary of the first apparition. This man was a truly great apostle of Our Lady of Medjugorje. He came to know of the events in Medjugorje in 1983, when he called on a friend on his way back from Walsingham. He went there on pilgrimage, a birthday gift from his wife Marie. He found his role in the periodical very aptly entitled *Mirecorder,* which was to spread the message and the events far and wide from his home in Sussex. His publication set the model and style for many others. But it was distinctive, marked by Peter's own personality: lively, well-informed, always up to date. The writer was clear-headed, industrious, staunch, persevering, a true knight of Mary Immaculate. His correspondence reached forty-four countries and in his last months of illness he was surely sustained by an immense volume of prayer. Many messages were received by his devoted wife Marie during this ordeal. Many prayed for him on news of his death. With characteristic courage he let us know in his last bulletin that it was imminent. Blessed are they who die in the Lord with Mary waiting eagerly to lead them home.

President Reagan: I take the following from the excellent Galway *Medjugorje Herald,* June 1988, just adding that I have a photocopy of the letter from Ambassador Kingon to Marija Pavlovic, to which reference is made. (See Appendix XI, p. 264 for full text).

'The following was translated from the Croatian newspaper, *Sveta Pastina,* February 1988 issue: "Last year the American Ambassador to the European Community, Alfred H. Kingon, stayed in Medjugorje for two weeks. The reason for his coming to Medjugorje was to pray for his sick son and give thanks for receiving God's graces. He accepted the messages of Medjugorje, so he regularly fasts and prays a lot. During his stay he had a meeting with the visionary, Marija Pavlovic. Just before he returned to America in a special spiritual atmosphere there was an opinion that it would be very convenient to send over with him a spiritual peace message for President Reagan. Being sincerely delighted Kingon, Reagan's ambassador, said that he would deliver the message to the President as soon as he returned to the White House.

This message was written by Marija Pavlovic and translated into English by Kathleen Parisod. The message was given to President Reagan just before his meeting with the Russian leader Mikhail Gorbachev, when the very well-known contract about destroying intermediate missiles was signed.

On 8 December 1987, there was a phone call to Marija from Brussels at 7.00 p.m. Parisod translated the conversation. Ambassador Kingon was the one who called and at the very beginning of the conversation he said that President Reagan himself wanted to talk to Marija, but it was impossible because the meeting with Gorbachev was still going on. During the conversation Kingon confirmed that he himself gave Marija's message to the president and that Reagan was delighted with the message. Kingon emphasised that after the President read the message he cried out:

'Now, with a new spirit I am going to the meeting with Gorbachev.'

The same night the White House tried to call Marija, but could not get through. On 14 December 1987 Kingon sent Marija a letter in which he encouraged her to send a peace message to Gorbachev. He assured her that American Ambassador, Jack Matlock, would give it to the secretary of the Russian leader. He also added that it would be beautiful if two great leaders and the two greatest countries would learn about her prayer and Our Lady's messages.

Finally, on Christmas Day Marija received a picture of Ronald Reagan under which was written:

To Marija Pavlovic. With my heartfelt thanks and every good wish. God bless you. Sincerely. Ronald Reagan.'' '

To this account from the Herald I add the text of Marija's letter to the American President:

'Dear President Reagan,
    God's Holy Mother is appearing each day in this small
village of Medjugorje, Yugoslavia. She is giving us a
message of peace. We know your concern for world peace
and are remembering you in our prayers each day. You
are very close to our hearts and we want you to know that
you can count on our prayers and sacrifices to help you
in your great task.
    Our Holy Mother has said that with prayer and fasting
even wars can be avoided. May her message help you and
her daily visits be a sign to you of God's loving concern
for his people.
    United in prayer and in the Hearts of Jesus and Mary
we send our love and greet you with the peace of the Queen
of Peace. Marija Pavlovic.'''

Church authority: People are naturally curious about the attitude
of Pope John Paul II to events in Medjugorje. The Pope cannot
commit himself while the matter is under investigation by a
commission named by the national episcopal conference, to which
Rome has transferred responsibility. On 23 July this year a very
large group was received by the Pope at Castelgandolfo. Among
those present was Mirjana. Archbishop Franic introduced her
to the Pope, who said: 'I pray every day for a good solution in
regard to Medjugorje.' Those officially in attendance on the Pope
forbade release of the photograph taken. They are under
instructions to prevent anything which could be imprudently
exploited.
    Archbishop Philip Hannan of New Orleans wrote the *Mir
Group* an account of his meeting with the Pope on 31 May and
the detailed report he gave the Holy Father of the thousands
of Catholics — and some non-Catholics — who had gone to
Medjugorje from his area; the American prelate emphasised that
many of these were young people and signs of true conversion
were evident in their lives. The Pope said that he knew the
difference of attitude between Dr Zanic and Dr Franic. He
seemed to welcome what was said, at any rate he gave no
'warnings or caveats', as Archbishop Hannan concluded. In mid-
July the youngest bishop in the United States, Dr Carl A. Fisher,
Auxiliary Bishop of Los Angeles, went to Medjugorje. He let

it be known that when he informed the Pope that he was going, the Holy Father said 'Go with my blessing'.

At another level, the Bishops of Croatia met in Zagreb on 16 September to consider Dr Zanic's sermon of 25 July. They reproached him with disobedience to the Roman authorities who have taken the matter out of his hands, and refused to print the text in the semi-official periodical, *Glaz Koncila*. They allowed his request that organised pilgrimage would also mean one organised by a priest, as well as by a bishop. But Dr Franic immediately explained that this did not exclude the presence of priests, who would say Mass, preach, give advice to pilgrims.

In January this year one of the strong men of central Europe, Cardinal Tomashek, known as the 'Iron Cardinal' gave an interview to *Sveta Pastina*. He gave thanks for the apparitions which he called 'important events'. 'We have received much from Mary through Medjugorje.'

The visionaries: One item of news will surprise readers. Both Marija and Ivan are in the United States at the time of this writing. The message for 25 November was received by Marija and sent out from her American address. Marija is with her brother who is very ill and Ivan is with his uncle. They are besieged with calls.

On 26 November Marija received this additional message: 'Dear children! I ask you once more to pray especially for my intentions. If you pray for my intentions I will be glorified through you. All your prayers are going to help you through my hands. Thank you for your response to my call.' Marija had spent five months on retreat in Italy up to 13 August.

Noteworthy, I think, are the messages given to Ivan on Podbrdo, on 4 July 1988 and subsequently. Our Lady appeared with three angels at 10.50 p.m. In July Ivan said that she was very happy because there were so many pilgrims present. 'She was most beautiful. She blessed everyone with her hands over us, and she said that we should pray with our hearts, not only with our lips. Because Satan has a great deal of power, we should use our Rosary. Our Rosary is a powerful weapon against Satan. If we pray to her, she will always help us.'

5 August 1988
'My dear children! Today my Son has sent me here to you and I am very happy to be with you — happy that you are here in such a large number. I would like the joy you have now to remain with you all day. Live this joy in prayer. I give you also love — love, live in love. Spread this love around you. I am your Mother and I love you. I would like you to help me and to work with me. Without you I can do nothing.'

8 August
'Dear children! In these days I invite you to pray more. Pray for the youth of the whole world. Pray for the renewal of your heart in those days, and pray to prepare yourselves for the feast.'

Then Ivan prayed with her one 'Our Father' and one 'Glory be to the Father'. 'Our Lady blessed us all, and then she left saying, "Go in peace, my children." '

15 August 1988
'Dear children! From this evening for you begins a new year — the year of youth. In this year pray for youth, speak with youth, because youth today are experiencing many difficulties. Help each other, everyone. I think of you in a special way, dear children, as youth today hold a very special place in the Church. Pray, dear children.'

Vicka's illness has been cured. She was asked early this year as on four previous occasions to forgo her apparitions for forty days. In the month of February Our Lady told her to write a letter to the chairman of the new episcopal commission, sending a sealed letter which he was to open when she would tell him to do so. On 22 September she gave him the instruction. He came to Medjugorje to open the letter. It contained the information that Vicka would be healed on 25 September, three days later. Thus it happened. Vicka had also sent a letter with similar contents to her Franciscan friend, the great Croatian poet, Fr Bubalo, her co-author of the book-long interview entitled, in English translation, *A Thousand Encounters with Our Lady in Medjugorje*. The nature of the illness was an inoperable tumour of the brain. The episode was made public by Fr Slavko Barbaric in a talk in Medjugorje on 2 November. Tapes of the talk are in circulation. Mention of Fr Bubalo's book recalls the fact that reading it gave the Italian sculptor, Carmelo Puzzolo, the idea of creating a set of Stations of the Cross in bronze, which now adorn Kricevaz. He made it fifteen, the last being of the Resurrection. I am reminded that we have in the statuary group at Knock, the white Carrara marble group, the work of a great Italian sculptor, Professor Ferri: his last work in fact.

Writers: The authoritative historian and theologian of Medjugorje, Fr René Laurentin, has now published eleven books on the subject. Among these, the series entitled *Dernières Nouvelles,* books of about one hundred pages giving an update of events up to the time of publication, now number seven issues. They constitute a precious factual record with theological comment. In chapter 4 of this book I have given the reasons why, at the present time, Fr Laurentin may be considered the greatest authority in the Church on apparitions of Our Lady. Last year in the Philippines the French theologian was encouraged by Cardinal Sin, Archbishop of Manila, to do a scientific study of all the reported apparitions of Our Lady at the present time. He has reported a number of these in *Chrétiens Magazine;* some he has been able to investigate personally, like the alleged phenomena in Damascus and in Korea, the apparitions in Kibeho in Rwanda and now, on his eighteenth visit, Medjugorje. His book, *Multiplications des Apparitions de la Vierge* (Fayard, Paris) has gone into a second edition in a month. An English translation is being prepared. Veritas Publications in Dublin have issued translations of his other recent works, *A Year of Grace With Mary* and *Scientific Studies on Medjugorje* (this in collaboration with Dr Henri Joyeux).

In *Dernières Nouvelles,* VII, June 1988, René Laurentin deals with a French Canadian, Louis Belanger, a writer who has received some publicity for his criticism of Medjugorje, and with Belanger's friend, Fr Ivo Sivric. I shall not go into detail about the work of Fr Sivric, a Croatian Franciscan living in the United States. The book, entitled *La face cachée de Medjugorje,* was based, like Belanger's publications, on the archives of Dr Zanic, Bishop of Mostar. He has been generous with help to those who take a negative view of the phenomena, in which I have no doubt that he acts as his conscience dictates.

But the written product is not impressive and has been respectfully demolished by Fr Laurentin and by Fr Sivric's brother in religion, Fr Rupcic, for years a student on the spot of all that happens in Medjugorje; his credentials are given earlier in this book. Whereas Belanger went only once to the scene of the events, Fr Sivric has been there three times. Fr Rupic gives an account of the family complications which are a sad background to the friar's study. He relies for his knowledge not on direct contact with the witnesses but on his own relatives, who have been in the five per cent of parishioners antipathetic to the apparitions. Much has been made of Fr Sivric's study of peasant culture in his native Croatia and this, we have been assured by one reviewer, is a determining factor in the visions.

We've had 'hallucination' as an explanation until serious scientists told the proponents of the theory to stop talking nonsense. We've had 'manipulation', but that was difficult to sustain with millions of people streaming in and out of the village, and thousands of us at one time or another present during the apparitions. So now it's the peasants!

Here a little history may serve. Practically every recognised Marian apparition has been granted to peasants: Guadalupe, the Miraculous Medal, La Salette, Lourdes, Knock, Fatima, Beauraing, Banneux. How right Oliver Goldsmith was: 'A bold peasantry, its country's pride, when once destroyed can never be supplied.' Who is the heroine depicted in picture or sculpture in every church in France, the one who inspired three dramatic masterpieces by Schiller, George Bernard Shaw and Jean Anouilh, and moved a great sculptor, Frémiet, to a miracle in bronze, her statue in the Rue de Rivoli? The peasant girl of Domrémy, Joan of Arc. Anyone who believes that these alert, happy, upright, devout children whom we have watched in ecstasy, were acting out some peasant syndrome, would believe anything.

Another protégé of Dr Zanic has been at it, one Michael Jones, editor of a review called *Fidelity*. I saw people waving advance publicity for the articles in this magazine, during the magnificent National Marian Congress organised by the Marytown Conventual Franciscans in Chicago, last August. Michael Jones, as I told him in a translantic discussion on Radio Éireann (Irish Radio), would have done well to keep away from this subject.

He made a most serious accusation against a man of irreproachable sanctity, Fr Tomislav Vlasic. What will we hear next? But, as Fr Rupcic concludes in his demolition job on Fr Sivric, these people serve the cause by showing that the case against Medjugorje does not stand up. Meanwhile Wayne Weible is past the 12 million mark!

Science: Let it have the last word. In autumn 1985 a group of ten qualified scientists, with René Laurentin as theological adviser, met in Italy to assess the evidence for the apparitions. Their judgement was positive. It was submitted to the Vatican. On 24 March this year an important group of doctors, convened by the Italian agency, ARPA, met at Milan to judge the mental health of the children, the visionaries. Verdict: totally normal.

AMBASSADOR KINGON'S LETTER
TO MARIJA PAVLOVIC

United States Representative
to the European Communities
14 December 1987

Ms Marija Pavlovic
Ms Kathleen Perisod
88266 Medugorje
Yugoslavia

Dear Marija and Kathleen:

I hope by this time you have received my letter to you of December 9.

I have spoken to our Ambassador to the Soviet Union, Jack Matlock. He says write the message in either English or your native tongue. He will then ascertain if the Ambassador to the Soviet Union from Yugoslavia is willing to deliver it. If the Yugoslavian Government is not, then Jack will attempt to get it to Secretary Gorbachev.

He says do not worry about the translation. Gorbachev's aides or we Americans can do it in Moscow.

What a wonderful thing if, indeed, the two leaders of the most powerful countries on earth would know of your prayers and the Lady's message.

Jackie and I will leave for the United States this coming Sunday and return somewhere around the middle or end of January. If your message is here by then, I will get it transmitted quickly to Ambassador Matlock.

Wishing you a wonderful Christmas holiday, a very happy new year and all prayers and blessings for the work you do.

Sincerely,
Alfred H. Kingon, Ambassador

MISSIONARY FOR MEDJUGORJE

If Medjugorje seems now to resemble some of the great stirrings of Christian renewal which have marked new eras in the life of the Church, like the Franciscan movement in medieval times, many people besides the visionaries have had a part to play. One of the best known is surely Fr Slavko Barbaric, the Croatian Franciscan, highly qualified academically in the mental sciences helpful to work in this apostolate, confident of the young people whom Our Lady has favoured, their spiritual guide on occasion, indefatigable in writing, travel, lecturing.

With Fr Tomislav Vlasic, Fr Slavko has produced the books mentioned in Appendix VI of this volume. He has also issued a booklet on fasting and has recently brought out a *Medjugorje Manual of Prayer* entitled *Pray with the Heart*. It is a series of counsels on important points of piety, of devotional formulas for the due occasions and spiritual needs, of reflections on traditional exercises of piety like the Rosary and the Stations of the Cross. It will prove helpful to pilgrims, to devotees of Our Lady of Medjugorje — as, incidentally, will Peter Rodgers' *Croat-English Prayer Book*.

Fr Slavko has conducted worldwide lecture tours on the facts and message of Medjugorje. He has visited several European countries, some, like the 'Isles of the North', several times; he has been received enthusiastically in well-known Marian centres like Banneux in Belgium; he has spoken to tens of thousands in Brazil, to equally large audiences in the Philippines, where he was received by President Corazon Aquino.

Fr Slavko is a missionary for Mary in the great tradition. He deserves our thanks and our prayers.

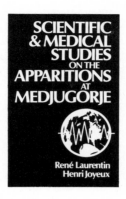

SCIENTIFIC AND MEDICAL STUDIES ON THE APPARITIONS AT MEDJUGORJE

RENÉ LAURENTIN / HENRI JOYEUX

The alleged apparitions of Our Lady in the Yugoslav village of Medjugorje have become the focus of worldwide attention in the Catholic Church. But what of the five young visionaries themselves? Apart from the obvious question of the authenticity of the apparitions what exactly are they experiencing? This study by world renowned mariologist, Fr René Laurentin, and scientist, Henri Joyeux, sets out to answer this question.

140 pp Paper £5·95

VIDEOS ON MEDJUGORJE

THE MADONNA OF MEDJUGORJE
A chronicle of one of the most compelling
stories of faith in our times.
A Westernhanger/BBC production.
Executive co-producer John Bird.
£14·95

MEDJUGORJE
A Message of Peace
This video will help the viewer to understand
the reported visions at Medjugorje.
£20

MEDJUGORJE -
The Miracles and the Message
Testimonies and discussions with people whose
lives have never been the same since their
'Medjugorje Experience'.
• **Briege McKenna** • **Michael O'Carroll** •
• **Heather Parsons** • **René Laurentin** •
• **Gay Russell** • **Wayne Weible** •
• **Vicka Ivankovic** •
A JPM Film Service Production
£35

AVAILABLE FROM ALL VERITAS BOOKSHOPS